Culture in Bits

The Monstrous Future of Theory

GARY HALL

continuum
LONDON • NEW YORK

CONTINUUM

The Tower Building, 11 York Road, London SE1 7NX

370 Lexington Avenue, New York, NY 10017-6503

www.continuumbooks.com

First published 2002

British Library Cataloguing-in-Publication Data

A catalogue record for this book is available from the British Library.

    ISBN 0-8264-5989-7 (hardback)

    ISBN 0-8264-5990-0 (paperback)

Library of Congress Cataloging-in-Publication Data

Hall, Gary, 1962–

    Culture in bits : the monstrous future of theory / Gary Hall.

      p. cm.

    Includes bibliographical references and index.

    ISBN 0-8264-5989-7 (hardback) — ISBN 0-8264-5990-0 (pbk.)

    1. Culture—Study and teaching. I. Title.

  HM623 .H35 2002

  306'.07—dc 21   2002022975

Typeset by CentraServe Ltd, Saffron Walden, Essex

Printed and bound in Great Britain by

Biddles Ltd, Guildford and King's Lynn

Contents

Bit (1) *n* cutting edge of a tool; interchangeable cutting point used by a carpenter in a brace or electric drill, by a miner in a rock drill, *etc.* . . . metal mouthpiece of a horse's bridle . . . *v/t* put the bit into the horse's mouth, accustom to the bit; (*fig*) curb, restrain.

Bit (2) *n* small piece or portion; a mouthful of food, morsel; a short time; . . . (*coll*) small part in film or play; (*sl*) role, attitude, course of action; (*computers*) unit of information; amount of information required to distinguish between two alternatives.

(The Penguin English Dictionary)

Preface

This book takes as one of its starting points the 'debate' between cultural studies and political economy over the future of cultural studies. To date, most of the emphasis in this debate has been on moving away from the theoretical approaches that came to dominate cultural studies in the 1980s: structuralism, semiotics, psychoanalysis, post-structuralism, deconstruction, etc. For many in the social sciences, and certain sections of media and communication studies in particular, cultural studies has become too 'textual', too focused on producing complicated Derridean or Lacanian readings of popular cultural images and texts which are far removed from the practical, political, material realities of power and oppression. What cultural studies needs now, it is claimed, is a good dose of social, economic and political analysis emphasizing the importance of the empirical over the theoretical, the material over the textual, the concrete over the abstract. Meanwhile, many of those associated *with* cultural studies have insisted that it should continue with the sort of theoretical investigations into the complex and often contradictory nature of consumption, representation, pleasure and subjectivity which were so characteristic of the field in the 1980s and throughout much of the 1990s. Acknowledging the force of those arguments which have condemned cultural studies for being little more than an apology for consumer capitalism, this approach is now however tempered by the idea that cultural studies practitioners should at the same time pay more attention to sociological questions. Yet in all the scholarly activity that has been provoked by this debate there have been few articles, and even fewer books, making a case for taking cultural studies' engagement with 'theory' further. Instead the emphasis, even from within cultural studies, has been on moving away from theory and 'back to reality' – or, at the very least, achieving some sort of *balance* between theory and political practice.

It is just such a case for the continuing importance of theory to cultural studies that I want to make with this book; not least because it seems to me that it is the reluctance, and in many cases refusal, to rigorously explore the consequences of theory for cultural studies that has, at least in part, led the study of culture to remain to all intents and purposes trapped in the 'cultural studies versus political economy' debate, unable to think of a way out. Certainly the conflict between cultural studies and political economy cannot be eluded simply by turning to the practices and methodologies of the social sciences. As Robert Young demonstrated in *Torn Halves*, to enter into this type of conflict by resisting one side in such a struggle with the other is to overlook the degree to which positions of this kind are 'implicated' in one another and are 'therefore not in any sense alternatives'. Nor is a dialectical response to the problem, whereby the two sides are somehow combined, likely to help. Although solutions of this sort have been put forward fairly regularly in recent years, they invariably remain blind to the way in which contemporary cultural criticism, by adopting such a dialectical form, runs the risk of merely repeating, re-enacting and reinforcing the 'radical logic of incompatibility between centrifugal and centripetal forces' which both Robert Young and Stuart Hall, among others, have identified as operating as the 'cultural and economic dynamic of late capitalist society'. It is this apparent impasse between practitioners of cultural studies and those who advocate a more social science orientated approach to the study of culture, however, that theory, and deconstruction in particular (as a theory which does not set such apparently antagonistic positions up in a relation of conflict with one another but shows how they can function in a productive, if irresolvable, tension), *can* help us think through, I believe. *Culture in Bits* thus argues for a rethinking of cultural studies' relation to deconstruction: a rethinking which avoids the simple binarism of recent attempts to translate between or even combine theory and practice; and which instead draws attention to some of the ambiguities that both constitute and disturb cultural studies, and open it up to forms of knowledge and inquiry (including deconstruction) that cultural studies can begin to appreciate only if it is prepared to radically reconceive its identity.

But if the dispute between cultural studies and political economy provides me with a starting point for opening another discourse on cultural studies and its future in *Culture in Bits*, and thus for conceiving cultural studies otherwise – indeed, for producing another cultural studies, a cultural studies which is quite different from that currently being put forward under the names of either 'cultural studies' or 'political economy', and which consequently may be, to some, unrecognizable *as 'cultural studies'* – it is only *one* such starting point. There are others, including those provided for me here by certain important accounts of the politics and the pedagogy of cultural studies and its institutionalization in the university, as well as cultural studies' relation to popular culture and new media technologies. For, as its name suggests, cultural studies is *more than one*. Cultural studies is not a self-identical, delimitable field – and hence is not reproducible or transmissible as such. Nor is cultural studies characterized by any one over-arching, totalizing, unifying idea. Cultural studies is not always and everywhere the same. And neither is this book.

Gary Hall
g.hall@mdx.ac.uk

Acknowledgements

It is going to be impossible for me to thank all of those who have assisted in some way with the writing of this book. Even if I could, merely including their names on a page of acknowledgements hardly seems sufficient. I would like to think I have already shown my appreciation to most of the people concerned in other, perhaps more meaningful, ways and that no one has had to wait until reading this to learn of my gratitude. However, with apologies to those I have left out, I want to take this opportunity to acknowledge a special debt to the following:

Rachel Bowlby, Geoffrey Bennington, Homi K. Bhabha, Peter Widdowson, Simon Morgan Wortham, Dave Boothroyd, Jan Campbell, Nicholas Royle, Timothy Clark, Joanna Zylinska and Mark Poster for their comments on various versions of the material included here. Ben Knights for his unstinting support throughout my time at the University of Teesside. The School of Law, Arts and Humanities at the University of Teesside for awarding me a sabbatical to write a significant portion of this book, and the Arts and Humanities Research Board for providing me with a Research Leave Scheme award which enabled me to complete it. My friends and colleagues at both the University of Teesside and Middlesex University – you know who you are. Ian Hall, not least because this book would literally not have been possible without him. Chris Gibbon, for scanning (and much more besides). Tristan Palmer, and all the team at Athlone/Continuum, for taking this project (and others) on in the first place, and for nurturing it with such patience and enthusiasm. And finally Dave Boothroyd and Simon Morgan Wortham, for sharing their friendship and ideas over a number of years now.

This one is for Asia.

Earlier versions of three of the chapters included here appeared as follows:

'"It's a thin line between love and hate": why cultural studies is so "naff"', *Authorizing Culture, Angelaki*, Vol. 2, No. 2, 1996 (reproduced here by permission of *Angelaki*); 'Beyond Marxism *and* Psychoanalysis' in Jan Campbell and Janet Harbord (eds), *Psycho-politics and Cultural Desires*, London and New York: Taylor and Francis, 1998; 'www.culturalstudies.ac.uk', *The Oxford Literary Review*, Vol. 21, 1999.

CHAPTER 1

Some Frequently Asked Questions

THE ONE ABOUT A 'DECONSTRUCTIVE CULTURAL STUDIES'

What you're providing with Culture in Bits *is a 'deconstructive cultural studies', is that right?*

I'm addressing certain issues in contemporary cultural studies from a cultural studies perspective which is sympathetic to deconstruction and deconstructive modes of thinking;[1] a cultural studies, in other words, which is thought through the work of Jacques Derrida as much as that of Raymond Williams, Stuart Hall or the 'Birmingham School'.[2]

But let's be as clear as possible about this right from the start: suggesting deconstruction can help us address some of the recent problems of cultural studies in a productive fashion is not at all the same as saying cultural studies and deconstruction should now be combined. To somehow reconceptualize cultural studies in the light of lessons learned from deconstruction would be to continue to operate with the sort of binary oppositions and dialectical logic (of both Western metaphysics and global capitalism) deconstruction is concerned to challenge. Nor is it my intention to break with the tradition of cultural studies as it has existed until now in order to found a new 'deconstructive cultural studies'. Any such attempt to 'break with' or 'critique' tradition would itself be quite traditional. As Samuel Weber remarks in a different context:

> Rather than waiting for the New, we would probably do better to re-examine the Old, under the suspicion that this theory – if we can even conceive of its possibility – is probably at work already, not as such or full-blown, but in bits and pieces. To recognize it, however, we may well have to adopt a perspective quite different . . . mindful, of course, of the fact that different is not the same as unrelated.[3]

And, to be sure, are there not a number of people in cultural studies who, even though they might not necessarily attach the label 'deconstruction' to their work, could nevertheless be regarded as having made use of deconstructive ideas and strategies, and even as having produced recognizable 'deconstructions'? It is certainly from someone who explicitly identifies herself with cultural studies, Angela McRobbie, that I have, at least in part, taken the idea of drawing on deconstruction to help address a number of issues to do with contemporary cultural studies.

That said, it *is* questionable just how much of theory and deconstruction cultural studies *has* explicitly incorporated. Sadie Plant is just one of those to have drawn attention to the way in which, when it comes to the 'so-called continental tradition of philosophy', cultural studies has adopted something of a pick'n'mix approach:

> Cultural studies has taken on board only those ideas it could recuperate and integrate within an already existing . . . political project . . . Elements of psychoanalytical theory, deconstruction and Foucauldian analysis have been adopted in the service of an idealist and humanist tradition, and any ideas which might have disturbed this picture have been left on the shelf. The consequence of this is that cultural studies has adopted watered down versions of the anti-humanism and post-dialectical thinking implicit in (some of) the work of Foucault, Lyotard, Irigaray and Deleuze and Guattari, all of whom, at their most interesting, are undermining the entire Western philosophical perspective which cultural studies continues to support.[4]

Cultural studies has thus tended to try to keep theory and deconstruction within certain limits; part of what I am attempting to do is draw attention to some of these limits. For as I said before, it seems to me that one of the things which has prevented cultural studies from productively reflecting on some of the problems which currently beset the field is this reluctance, and in some cases downright refusal, to consciously engage with certain aspects of theory.

THE ONE ABOUT DECONSTRUCTION AS CRITIQUE

So you're using deconstruction to critique cultural studies, then?

Deconstruction as I read it is, among other things, about showing how texts put forward irreconcilable positions. This includes positions that are different from, and in many cases opposed to, those they are generally portrayed, or portray themselves, as adopting. To ignore the different readings the cultural studies texts I'm dealing with here make possible, in favour of simply dismissing these texts as mistaken and wrong in an attempt to privilege deconstruction and the writings of Jacques Derrida, would therefore be somewhat 'logocentric' (if you'll forgive me for being a little 'naff' – naffness being something I will come back to) – which is of course something deconstruction helps us to understand. This is what I meant when I said that to reconceptualize cultural studies in the light of lessons learned from deconstruction would be to continue to operate with the sort of binary oppositions and dialectical logic deconstruction is concerned to challenge. '[D]econstruction, if there is any, is not a critique', to quote Derrida.[5] Neither is it an overseeing or meta-discourse – which is why I have refrained from attempting to provide an extensive explication of Derrida's thought in this book. (There are plenty of people who can do this kind of thing far better than I could hope to here.) I'm not coming from *outside* cultural studies to apply a body of theory to it, in this case supposedly deconstruction, which therefore needs to be explained. That would be to ignore the specificity of cultural studies. It is hard to see such an approach finding anything new in cultural studies that deconstruction does not already know, for instance. Deconstruction is rather the enactment of a certain problematizing reading, a reading which, rather than just imposing pre-established ideas and concepts, is open to the *difference* and alterity of the text. Which is why, contrary to the evidence provided by the above quotation from *Resistances*, I have tried to resist continually relying on the writings of Derrida for authorization. (Apart from this opening chapter, Derrida and deconstruction do not make an explicit appearance until halfway through Chapter 3, and even then it is thanks primarily, as I said before, to a suggestion from Angela McRobbie). While it would have been impossible for me to have read cultural studies in this problematizing and non-dogmatic fashion without Derrida's work, cultural studies in a sense doesn't need Derrida or deconstruction, or me for that matter, to come along and do this for it, on its behalf. Cultural studies, or at least certain aspects of it, can already do this for 'itself', as it were. If there is something called 'cultural studies', knowledge of what it might be is already displaced, deconstructed, as if by itself, without deconstruction since, as the chapters in this book attempt to show in various ways, cultural studies is 'in deconstruction' as the condition of its very possibility (and of course impossibility).

THE ONE ABOUT THEORY

This question takes a number of forms, but usually runs something as follows: *This is all well and good, but there's a reason for the current move away from theory in cultural studies. It isn't just a whim. People in cultural studies – and not just in cultural studies, but other fields, too – are turning away from theory, and deconstruction in particular, because it has been widely applied in ways which have ignored real politics in favour of a rather elitist theorizing. And in fact isn't this what you are doing in this book? Aren't you, too, substituting theory for practice?*

Of course, that I have felt the need to make this argument regarding the importance of theory suggests that the latter is possibly no longer as central to cultural studies as it once was. And to an extent this is true. There is certainly a lot of talk at the moment about the importance of politics to cultural studies, and about the importance of a *return* to politics in cultural studies. But I must admit I just don't see the situation in terms of the theoretical analysis of 'texts' on the one hand, and 'real', practical politics on the other.

Firstly, it is by no means certain that cultural studies *can* return to earlier forms of political engagement. It could even be argued that to attempt to do so is to ignore the very economic and political realities the move to politics is supposed to enable cultural studies to take into account. Charting the fate of the university in a world increasingly dominated by an economic and managerial logic of profit and loss, Bill Readings has shown how the 'human sciences can do what they like with culture, can do Cultural Studies, because culture no longer matters as an *idea* for the institution':[6]

> . . . since the nation-state is no longer the primary instance of the reproduction of global capitals, 'culture' – as the symbolic and political counterpart to the project of integration pursued by the nation-state – has lost its purchase . . . This shift has major implications for the University, which has historically been the primary institution of national culture in the modern nation-state. (12)

Perhaps most significantly, the 'notion of culture as the legitimating idea of the modern University has reached the end of its usefulness' (5) and has been replaced by the concept of 'excellence' which has the 'singular advantage of being meaningless, or to put it more precisely, non-referential' (22). This process of 'dereferentialization' means that we cannot return to what Readings calls the 'University of Culture': this institution is ruined and has lost its historical reason for being. Any attempt to dwell in those ruins with the aid of politics is simply to take 'recourse to romantic nostalgia' (169). Rather than returning to politics, then, the present political situation requires cultural studies to give up this 'religious attitude toward political action' and move 'beyond the work of mourning for a lost idea of culture that needs political renewal' (191).

Secondly, there is a danger (as my reference to Readings's work in this context is meant to suggest), that the emphasis currently being placed on a return to politics will result in cultural studies continuing to pay insufficient attention to the politico-institutional forces which help to shape and control its own operation and development. The kind of reflection on the instituting and institutional structures of academic discourse provided by Readings in *The University in Ruins* is something that is all too often overlooked by cultural studies. Instead, cultural studies has tended to emphasize the importance of forging links with social movements and forces belonging to the 'real world' of practical politics that lies 'outside' the university. Only by doing so, it is claimed, only by remaining beyond the institutionalizing and disciplining effects of the university, can cultural studies hope to achieve the sort of political impact on both society and the university it seeks. So much so that even on the relatively few occasions cultural studies *has* turned its attention toward the university, as in the 'radical pedagogy' of Henry A. Giroux or Tom Steele, this is again more often than not justified as an attempt to connect with 'real people'. This is why the analysis of the current 'crisis' in the idea of the university has been left predominantly to those such as Bill Readings, Samuel Weber, Peggy Kamuf, Robert Young, Simon Wortham and J. Hillis Miller, who are more closely associated with theory, and who have learnt the lesson that 'it is necessary to *think the institution*' from theory, and deconstruction specifically.[7] For the most part such self-reflection is regarded from a cultural studies point of view as being too naively elitist, too bound up with the very values of the university cultural studies is supposed to challenge. Yet could it not be argued that, of the two, it is the theoretical analysis in this scenario which is likely to prove the more 'politically' effective, at least to the extent that it will be more self-consciously aware of the politico-institutional factors which affect its operation and development, and therefore less prone to being blindly shaped and controlled by them?

Thirdly, to move away from theory because it is apparently *not political enough* is to subordinate everything to political ends. It is to imply things are only worth doing if it can be established *in advance* that they will have a practical, political outcome; an outcome which is itself decided *in advance*. Now it seems to me that there are a number of problems with ideas of this kind. Not only is the radically unpredictable nature of the future of both theory and politics overlooked (the way in which what seems initially to be the most 'theoretical' of issues may eventually turn out to have more practical and political effects than the most apparently 'political' of political actions and debates), there is also little or no interrogation of what politics actually is. Indeed (and as Chapter 4 shows), the last thing that is raised in all this talk about the importance of politics to cultural studies *is* the question of politics, for the simple reason that politics is here being placed in a transcendental position with respect to all other discourses. Politics is the one thing it is vital to understand, as it is that by which everything else is judged. But politics is at the same time the one thing that *cannot* be understood; for the one thing that cannot be judged by the transcendentally raised criteria of politics is politics itself.[8]

Rather than deciding the question of politics *in advance*, I want to keep this question *open* and *undecided*. Given that cultural studies' political commitment is for many one of its defining features, I realize that as a result what I am doing in this book may at times not look too much like cultural studies, at least as it is today commonly conceived and most easily recognized. As far as I'm concerned, however, this questioning of politics is 'perhaps' the most 'responsible', and political, thing for cultural studies to do, in Derrida's sense of the term responsibility, since there can be no responsibility, and hence no politics, without the experience of the undecidable; without, in this case, the constant (re)taking of the decision of what politics is:

> I will even venture to say that ethics, politics and responsibility, *if there are any*, will only ever have begun with the experience and experiment of the aporia. When the path is clear and given, when a certain knowledge opens up the way in advance, the decision is already made, it might as well be said there is none to make: irresponsibly, and in good conscience, one simply applies or implements a program. Perhaps, and this would be the objection, one never escapes the program. In that case, one must acknowledge this and stop talking with authority about moral or political responsibility. The condition of possibility of this thing called responsibility is a certain *experience and experiment of the possibility of the impossible: the testing of the aporia* from which one may invent the only *possible invention, the impossible invention.*[9]

What is more (and as we shall see), not only is it the most political thing for cultural studies to do, it turns out that this questioning of politics, and with it cultural studies, is an inextricable part of what it actually means to *do cultural studies.*

THE ONE ABOUT THE LANGUAGE

But isn't one of the problems with deconstruction to do with the language: that it's too elitist, specialized, rarefied, abstract; that it's not accessible to the majority of readers?

Look, I'm aware that I'm probably not going to win many popularity contests with this book. I've read far too many review articles in the academic press with titles like 'Timely Attack on Nonsense' and 'Leaden Theory in Boots of Concrete Jargon' to have any illusions about that.[10] Be that as it may, when it comes to deconstruction's current fashionability, or lack of it, 'this says nothing about the *"theoretical"* or philosophical issues raised by deconstruction', as Geoffrey Bennington has rightly observed. 'Deconstruction (or any other "theoretical" movement) does not depend on the number of people who believe in it or practise it or profess it'.[11]

But let's look at this charge a little closer. More often than not, complaints of this kind regarding the difficulty of the language associated with deconstruction have their basis in the idea that a cultural studies text should be accessible to a wider audience. It is an idea which itself rests on certain questionable assumptions. There are those, for instance, who believe cultural studies should be written in 'everyday' language so that it may be comprehensible and useful and therefore more likely to attract outside funding from those in the research councils, media industries and government, and who have often criticized cultural studies accordingly. Yet in an era in which the university is coming under increasing pressure to be more instrumentally and vocationally orientated is it really the role of cultural studies to simply go along with such forces? I'm concerned such reproaches may be indicative of what one former director of the Centre for Contemporary Cultural Studies at Birmingham, Richard Johnson, has identified as:

> . . . a general loss of nerve in intellectual practice in the academy, partly to do with the intense ideological commercialization of academic institutions and the slipping away of criteria other than 'what pays' [which] seems to me to fuel a desire to seek recognition from policy-makers, media and political professionals. . . .[12]

(From this point of view, many of the those who attack cultural studies for not being political enough are going along with the agenda set by market forces and government policy, and are thus themselves, one could say, *not being political enough*.)

There are also those – many of whom explicitly identify themselves with
cultural studies – who, adopting a variation on the traditional role of the
cultural critic as a public intellectual who hands down knowledge to the mass
of 'ordinary people' 'outside' the university, chastise theory and deconstruction
for being too difficult for these 'ordinary people' to grasp. But again a number
of questions occur. After all, is there not something elitist in this idea itself, in
that it is based on an originary and founding distinction between the intellectual and the so-called 'ordinary person'? Does this assumption not in effect
construct and maintain the very opposition it is trying to do away with by
means of the use of 'ordinary language'? (The 'legitimating instance', Bill
Readings has observed, 'is the passage outside the academy to the "ordinary
people", but at the same time this implies that the authors of academic essays
in Cultural Studies are "extraordinary people", vertical intellectuals'.)[13] Is the
notion that the so-called 'masses' cannot handle 'difficult' material not itself
somewhat elitist, not to say patronizing? To be sure, this idea appears to lack
an appreciation of the way in which there may be what Raymond Williams
called 'a positive deficiency' in the privileged knowledge of the educator or
intellectual themselves.[14]

Having said all that, I *have* tried to avoid merely mimicking the language of
deconstruction (if there is such a thing) in this book. To have done otherwise,
it seems to me, would have risked rendering my text too vulnerable to the kind
of easy dismissal with which those in cultural studies often greet deconstructive
texts and analyses. What is more, it would have signalled a lack of responsibility
on my part. It would have been to refuse to remain open to the specificity of
cultural studies by letting cultural studies speak for itself. Rather, cultural
studies would have been used much as a ventriloquist uses as a dummy, to
merely *speak* deconstruction. For these reasons I have preferred to remember
the words of Timothy Clark when, in drawing attention to both the 'sheer
difficulty' and, it has to be said, 'dullness' of much of the work done in
'Derrida studies' (and also the fact that requests for 'clarity', accessibility and
the use of more everyday language are not without motivations and interests
of their own), he suggests that 'to cultivate maximum accessibility can . . . give
one's writing a maximum openness or even vulnerability; hence it may become
one way in which a text of this sort can aim to be responsible'.[15]

THE ONE ABOUT TEXTUALITY

*Nevertheless, for all your talk of politics and the importance of analysing the
institution of the university, the whole discursive thrust of the book does seem to be*

motivated primarily by engagements with various texts rather than with empirical material.

A similar complaint was made by Geoff Mulgan (a member of the British Prime Minister's Policy Unit) in the November/December 1998 special issue of *Marxism Today*, when he criticized many left-wing academics and intellectuals for viewing the world 'at second-hand, through books, and through books about books'.[16] To see *Culture in Bits* in these terms, though, would be to hang on to precisely the sort of opposition between theory and practice, 'textuality' and the 'real', I'm trying to create problems for (an opposition which is admittedly quite prevalent within cultural studies, and which I'm afraid is often based on a rather poor reading of deconstruction – a reading which is of course not a reading at all if reading is understood, as it is for deconstruction, as a radical opening to the coming of the other). As I've already indicated, I'm just not comfortable with the idea that there are 'texts' on the one hand, and the 'real' world of politics and history and experience on the other; a 'real world' which we can apparently access only by sociological, empirical or positivist means.

Far from being a solely 'theoretical' gesture, is it not possible to see certain texts (and not just the writing but also perhaps the publishing, marketing, selling or reviewing of such texts) also as 'concrete' performative interventions into the 'real life' functioning of at least that set of political and institutional practices known as 'cultural studies'? And this regardless of whether such texts are overtly 'political' in content or not? This at any rate is what Richard Johnson, the above-mentioned former director of the Centre for Contemporary Cultural Studies at Birmingham, maintains when he writes that the 'academy is not just theory as opposed to practice; it is a site of practice itself'.[17] What matters about *Culture in Bits* from this perspective is not just its content but also its *performative* possibilities.

Furthermore, 'what we think of as *lived experience* involves textuality and reading no less than do books'.[18] It is therefore only through texts or, better, the analysis of textuality (including the deconstruction of the opposition between 'textuality' and the 'real'), that we can approach any sort of understanding of that part of textuality that is called the real world, lived experience, everyday life, etc. So, although I *could* have dealt with more 'empirical' subjects in this book, it is partly this turn toward the empirical that I have wanted to interrogate (rather than merely repeat). And I've focused on certain texts – including Meaghan Morris' 'Banality in Cultural Studies', Raymond Williams' 'The Future of Cultural Studies', Stuart Hall's 'Cultural Studies and its Theoretical Legacies' and Angela McRobbie's 'The Es and the Anti-Es' – in order to do so because for many of those in cultural studies this turn toward the empirical and the 'real' is authorized in and by these texts (among others, of course). If I want to argue that this move is problematic it is with these texts that I presumably need to be concerned. Merely providing another analysis of an empirical subject would not achieve this: I need to examine the ideas and texts that authorize this move. Nor have I forgotten what I said earlier about deconstruction being the enactment of a certain problematizing reading, one that is open to the alterity of the text. For it is also in these particular cultural studies texts that issues regarding the relation between textuality and politics, theory and practice, are in many ways thought about and dealt with most interestingly, it seems to me. Re-reading these essays by Morris, Williams, Hall and McRobbie thus enables me to think through some of these issues in a productive fashion.

THE ONE ABOUT THE SOCIAL SCIENCES

It's noticeable that most of the people you are dealing with here (Williams, Hall, Morris, McRobbie, etc.) are identified with cultural studies. Given your concern with the debate between cultural studies and political economy, why is there so little to do with anyone more closely associated with the social sciences?

My decision to concentrate on cultural studies in this book should not be taken as implying that those discourses associated more readily with the social sciences are incapable of providing a means of thinking through some of these issues (even if they *could* be diametrically opposed to cultural studies in this way, which is not the case). If some of cultural studies' accounts of theory, and theory's accounts of cultural studies, appear to me to be based on rather unknowing stereotypes, I want to avoid making the same mistake myself with regard to the social sciences by dismissing them as either homogenous or wrong. No doubt it would have been possible for me to have reinscribed the relation between politics and theory using the social sciences. But I would probably have had to work a lot harder to do so with the social sciences than I do with cultural studies, if for no other reason than because the relation between politics and theory is such an explicit feature of cultural studies. Indeed, in many of its most influential versions this is precisely what cultural studies is held to be: by definition, cultural studies is regarded as a politically committed questioning of culture/power relations which at the same time theoretically interrogates its own relation to politics and to power. Hence the subtitle of Routledge's major international cultural studies journal *Cultural Studies*: 'Theorizing Politics, Politicizing Theory'. It is therefore through cultural studies, rather than the social sciences, that I have chosen to approach the question of the relation between politics and theory, as cultural studies seems to provide me with a privileged point of access to this relation.

THE ONE ABOUT RECONCEPTUALIZING
CULTURAL STUDIES

OK, so your book is about reconceiving or reconceptualizing cultural studies. But what form will such a reconceptualized cultural studies take? What will it look like?

It's probably worth emphasizing, once again, that one form such a 'reconceptualized' cultural studies will *not* take is that of 'pure' theory (presuming such a thing were possible). By drawing on deconstruction to bring some of the fundamental premises of cultural studies into question, and in this way keep the question of cultural studies, including the 'question' *form* that this questioning takes, open and undecidable, it is not my intention to suggest cultural studies practitioners should no longer concern themselves with such things as politics, policy, lived experience or everyday life, and that they should *just do* 'theory' instead (that, rather than addressing issues of political power, oppression and injustice, they should embark on an endless deconstruction of the idea of cultural criticism as it occurs throughout the history of Western thought in general, and cultural studies in particular, or produce metaphysical theories of the subject/object relation instead of pursuing specific political goals). What it *is* to suggest is that to cease paying attention to theory *in favour* of so-called 'political practice' is for cultural studies to merely *do* unthought-out and uninteresting theory, as this idea of moving from theory to practice is itself a theoretical idea, the concept of 'political practice' being itself a classical, theoretical concept. Unless this is understood, and the complexity of the relation between theory and practice and what is meant by politics (and theory for that matter) is thought through accordingly, then the risk of adopting a politics or policy that is less than conscious of its own motivations and determinations remains.

It is the complexity of the theory/practice dichotomy that I have already suggested theory, and deconstruction in particular, can help us think through. In his essay 'The Conflict of the Faculties' Derrida emphasizes that:

what is hastily called deconstruction *as such* is never a technical set of discursive procedures, still less a new hermeneutic method operating on archives or utterances in the shelter of a given and stable institution; it is also, and at the least, the taking of a position, in the work itself, toward the politico-institutional structures that constitute and regulate our practice, our competences, and our performances. Precisely because deconstruction has never been concerned with the contents alone of meaning, it must not be separable from this politico-institutional problematic, and has to require a new questioning about responsibility, an inquiry that should no longer necessarily rely on codes inherited from politics or ethics. Which is why, though too political in the eyes of some, deconstruction can seem demobilizing in the eyes of those who recognize the political only with the help of prewar road signs. Deconstruction is limited neither to a methodological reform that would reassure the given organization, nor, inversely, to a parade of irresponsible or irresponsiblizing destruction, whose surest effect would be to leave everything as is, consolidating the most immobile forces of the university.[19]

Deconstruction, then, is both a 'theoretical' reversal and displacement of some of Western thought's major hierarchical oppositions *and* a grappling with specific political and institutional structures. This is an important point to make, as it offers a much-needed corrective to many of the misconceptions currently being propagated regarding theory and deconstruction, within cultural studies especially.[20] But as Derrida has also maintained on occasions too numerous to detail here, if deconstruction is not a set of theoretical or textual exercises that simply turns 'reality' into a book, neither is it limited to practices and procedures 'inherited from politics'. Deconstruction is both the taking of a position with regard to the political and at the same time a rethinking of the political: of what 'the political' is and of what it means to be 'political'.

So, to return to the question, one form such a 'reconceptualized' cultural studies could 'perhaps' take (because of course deconstruction's emphasis on singularity and the experience of the undecidable means it cannot be reduced to a programme or project, political or otherwise) involves the holding together of both of these irreducible approaches at the same time, while simultaneously challenging any simple differentiation between the two. As well as bringing some of the fundamental 'theoretical' premises of cultural studies into question – including (in the case of this book) ideas about capitalism, politics, resistance, the role of the intellectual, and so forth – such a reconceived or redefined cultural studies might also therefore wrestle, in both its content *and* its form, with specific political and institutional structures, including the 'politico-institutional structures that constitute and regulate our practice, our competences, and our performances' as cultural studies practitioners: structures which, as I said before, too often go overlooked in cultural studies' head-long rush to be 'political'.

THE ONE ABOUT WHY CULTURAL STUDIES?

Again, that's all very well, but it still doesn't explain the importance placed on cultural studies. If you're so interested in politics and the institution of the university, and deconstruction is already focusing on this, why the concern with cultural studies? Why not just produce a book on deconstruction?

Why cultural studies? Well, as Derrida reminds us, deconstruction is 'nothing by itself'.[21] Deconstruction is not 'a doctrine . . . a method . . . a set of rules or tools'. Deconstruction is only possible, can only be performed, and only takes place in relation to other discourses. And at the risk of repeating myself, cultural studies provides a privileged point of access when it comes to reflecting on the relation between theory and politics . . . although again it is only one: there are others, including those provided by both literature and philosophy. But cultural studies is *particularly* important when it comes to understanding the university because, as Bill Readings emphasized, cultural studies is the contemporary institution's way of thinking about itself. Whereas at one time the task of understanding the university was allotted, in the UK at least, to English literature, and elsewhere to philosophy, the uncovering of the colonialist and nationalistic origins of English literature has led to literary studies being increasingly replaced as a means of thinking the university by cultural studies.[22]

Now we have already seen Readings raise a number of issues regarding cultural studies' position and role in the contemporary university, especially as far as its politics is concerned. One way in which cultural studies can be pushed 'beyond the work of mourning for a lost idea of culture that needs political renewal', however, and so think the university without resorting to either nostalgia for a national culture or the discourse of consumerism and excellence, is by addressing the question of disciplinarity: by '[w]orking out . . . how thoughts stand besides other thoughts' (191). Again we need to proceed carefully. This is not a matter of cultural studies simply being, in Angela McRobbie's words, 'aware of the power which its competing discourses wield in its self-constitution'.[23] Structuralist and poststructuralist methods of analysis have 'travelled further and faster than their culturalist counterparts', McRobbie maintains, because these methods 'could easily be applied to texts independent of context'. More materialist concerns have consequently been pushed 'back towards sociology' (173). Yet (and this brings me a little closer to answering the previous question regarding what such a reconceptualized cultural studies might 'perhaps' look like) it is not enough for cultural studies to attempt to redress the balance by bringing sociology and social policy 'back in from the margins to expand the political potential of the field and to enter dialogue with those other strands [including poststructuralism and psychoanalysis] which appear to occupy the high ground' (183). And not just because by placing so much emphasis on politics, the empirical and the ethnographic, other aspects of cultural studies may be marginalized or excluded in turn. By switching attention back onto methods associated with the social sciences, does such an approach not in effect continue with cultural studies' interdisciplinarity project whereby some disciplines are used to draw attention to, and compensate for, the blind-spots of others? Of course, interdisciplinarity has at times been both necessary and extremely useful to the challenge cultural studies has offered to certain critical, cultural, institutional and academic orthodoxies. Nevertheless, and as I have tried to suggest both here and elsewhere, this approach is not without problems of its own:

- At the same time as challenging the idea of the university, interdisciplinarity also supports it (as Chapter 6 demonstrates). In particular, there can be detected in *inter*disciplinarity a desire to get back to the 'unity and synthesis' of knowledge that is seen as being the case before the academic division of labour and the trend toward specialization took place that is characteristic of the modern university; a desire moreover which lies at the very heart of the academic institution, as the word '*university*' suggests. Nor can interdisciplinarity be defended on the grounds that it provides a means of combating the *modern* university since, as Readings acknowledges, the 'increased flexibility' offered by interdisciplinary programmes and modes of study 'is often attractive to administrators as a way of overcoming entrenched practices of demarcation, ancient privileges and fiefdoms in the structure of universities' (39). Far from challenging disciplinary logics, cultural studies' commitment to interdisciplinarity now appears to collude 'with the larger strategies of corporatization/capitalization in the university (for example, downsizing, union breaking, etc.)'.[24]
- Interdisciplinarity rests on the idea that we already know the identity and relationship of the different disciplines that go to make up the repertoire of cultural studies. By simply repudiating, rather than investigating thoroughly, the notion of a discipline, cultural studies' interdisciplinary project has too often failed to distinguish itself from the prior concept to which it therefore remains terminally and terminologically rooted. (This is a point Simon Wortham and I have made elsewhere, but it is perhaps worth repeating in this context).[25]
- Little or no account tends to be taken of the extent to which many of the disciplines and discourses that go to make up cultural studies' interdisciplinary repertoire – cultural studies and political economy, for example,

or Marxism and psychoanalysis[26] – cannot be simply combined or articulated together but are in fact *incommensurable*.

- It is noticeable that whereas so-called 'legitimate' discourses and forms of knowledge, those that either fall within or can at least be ascribed to recognized disciplines – literary studies, sociology, social policy, politics, economics, philosophy, history, communication and media studies, etc. – have been privileged and included in cultural studies' interdisciplinary canon, those 'less legitimate' discourses and forms of knowledge – hypnosis, for example[27] – that have not been encapsulated by the 'established' disciplines have tended to be excluded or ignored.

Consequently, and surprising as it may seem to some, although cultural studies is important for me here, for all the above-mentioned reasons, the sort of cultural studies I am attempting to enact in this book does not simply take the form of an interdisciplinary study of culture. It is not trying to bring culture back to some wholeness and unity that has otherwise been lost as a result of the adherence on the part of the academic institution to capitalism's emphasis on differentiation and specialization. Rather, by interrogating the identity of disciplines and discourses such as politics and psychoanalysis it places in question the very idea of interdisciplinarity; and with it, cultural studies, for which interdisciplinarity has functioned as one of its dominant characteristics. Instead, attention is turned, not just back to obvious, already defined areas of study like economics, sociology, history, etc., or to 'newer' fields such as those associated with discourses around popular culture, representation and identity, but also to what Derrida at one point calls 'less visible, less direct, more paradoxical, more perverse' discourses[28] – discourses which cultural studies can begin to appreciate only if it is prepared to radically rethink its identity.

THE ONE ABOUT 'PARADOXICAL' DISCOURSES

Can you explain what you mean when you refer to 'less visible . . . more perverse' discourses and forms of knowledge?

Perhaps the easiest way of explaining this is by turning to the book's last chapter, which concentrates on one such 'less visible' discourse in particular, namely that associated with 'new media technologies' (CDs, VCRs, DVDs, cell phones, computers, printers, faxes, televisions, teleconferences, communications satellites, the World Wide Web, hyper-text, the e-book, etc., but specifically, in the case of Chapter 6, the Internet, e-mail and electronic publishing). What is so interesting about these technologies is not so much the extensions and improvements they offer to existing practices of scholarly research and publication; nor the way they expand the field of academic interest so that multi-media, virtual reality and cyberspace can now all take their place alongside the other areas of 'legitimate' research; but rather the challenge these technologies present to the academic community's very mode of legitimation. In *Archive Fever*, Jacques Derrida draws attention to the way in which new electronic media technologies are not only transforming the process of analysing, communicating, exchanging, classifying, stocking and conserving knowledge, they are transforming *the very content and nature* of knowledge. (The 'retrospective' example Derrida gives in *Archive Fever* concerns the consequences for psychoanalysis of e-mail. However, in a related passage in *The Post Card* he also refers to the effects of changes in the 'technological regime of telecommunications' on literature, philosophy and love letters.)[29] It follows that the effects, consequences, limits and possibilities posed by these technologies for research into cultural and theoretical questions cannot be explored simply by using the 'recognized', 'legitimate', disciplinary forms of knowledge. New media technologies change the very nature of such disciplines, according to Derrida, rendering them 'unrecognizable'. In order to appreciate the kinds of knowledge new technologies make possible, it is necessary for academic research to adopt new forms, forms which it may not recognize as 'legitimate'.

THE ONE ABOUT OTHER EXAMPLES

Is that associated with new media technologies the only example of such a 'paradoxical' discourse?

No, but it *is* perhaps one of the most easily recognized. *Culture in Bits* nevertheless describes a number of others including, as I said, hypnosis, and also the naffness which I regard as an inherent feature of cultural studies' relation to popular culture. (As Chapter 2 shows, naffness is what makes cultural studies' analysis of popular culture both possible and impossible. So, yes, this book *is* a bit 'naff'.) What is so interesting about the new electronic media technologies, however, is the challenge they offer to the accepted, conventional forms of culture and interpretation by placing the normal and the usual in a 'strange and disorientating new context', thus forcing us to see it again 'in a new way', as if for the first time, and so account for it and judge it anew.[30]

For instance, one of the questions I might be accused of leaving out of this book concerns the very nature of culture itself. What is culture for me here? In a way it would have been relatively easy to have provided an answer to this question (just as, according to Angela McRobbie, those working in cultural studies in the 1970s, and she includes herself in this, constructed 'something called the "culture" of, for example, working-class girls').[31] I could then perhaps have characterized the 'culture jamming' and parodying of corporate logos Naomi Klein details in *No Logo*,[32] or, say (and to pick up on the suggestion of one of the reviewers of my initial proposal for this book), the 'London dance scene of the early 90s' as a deconstruction of this form of culture, and thus have provided something of a 'Jacques Derrida remix' of these phenomena. But what I have tried to show in *Culture in Bits* is that to have done so would have been to have constructed this culture by 'virtually plucking it out of something much more amorphous and bestowing on it a shape and a reality which was as much my invention as it was a recognizable reality'.[33] What is more, the question of culture would not actually have been raised. This question would already have been decided *in advance*.

I'm *not* therefore claiming to know the true nature of culture here: what culture is and what it is not, what it is legitimate to ascribe to culture and what it is not. Nor am I attempting to construct a better model of cultural studies, one that is somehow more accurate, true, real. And I'm certainly *not* endeavouring to present deconstruction as a mode of thinking which can come along and save or cure cultural studies by making it more efficient or effective, so it can finally get at its proper object, whatever that may be. Thinking about culture for me requires another kind of thinking altogether, a thinking that strives to keep the question of culture open *as a question*. As I said before, there can be no responsibility to culture, and what's more no politics, no ethics and *no cultural studies*, without the experience of the undecidable; without the constant taking, in each singular situation and event, of the (founding) decision of what culture, and cultural studies, is.

THE ONE ABOUT THE FUTURE

Given your concern with texts which discuss the future of cultural studies it seems strange you don't provide a clear model of cultural studies' future?

If cultural studies is to have a future, this future cannot be predicted or predetermined. The 'condition on which the future remains to come is', as Derrida emphasizes, 'not only that it not be known, but that it not be *knowable as such*'.[34] Any model of cultural studies' future I could have provided would therefore not have said very much about cultural studies' future at all. It would have been merely a repetition of the past, an attempt at domesticating or closing down the 'monstrous' nature of cultural studies' future by making it more of the same.

THE ONE ABOUT HISTORY

You may not want to talk about cultural studies' future, but what of its past? Isn't history noticeable for its absence here? Why haven't you related all this to history more? And why is a history of cultural studies not provided in particular? Or, at the very least, a history of the debate over theory between cultural studies and political economy?

History is far from absent in this book. *Culture in Bits* contains numerous references to the history of capitalism, society, culture, the university, tech-nology, etc., as well as to the history of the formation and structure of cultural studies (including its origins in Adult Education), to put it all rather crudely. Nor could it be otherwise, even if I *had* wanted it to be. *Culture in Bits*, like all texts, bears the marks of its historical location – even if, like all texts, its meaning cannot be simply read off that location. However, a history of the kind that begins, say, 'The dispute over the future of cultural studies first took shape in . . .', and then proceeds to trace this dispute within the horizon of a much larger history of debates concerning cultural criticism, popular culture, consumerism, Marxism, ideology, 'false consciousness', 'New Times', the influence of Gramsci, the role of the intellectual, sexual politics, race, ethnicity, gender, subjectivity, 'political correctness', post-Marxism, the university of 'excellence', 'theory', and so on, would have risked presupposing too many of the ideas and concepts I have wanted to examine. Which is not to say such a history would have been without interest. A history of this kind is no doubt required and remains to be written. I'm just saying *this is not it*; that this is not what I have either wanted or tried to provide in *Culture in Bits*. And not *just* because there is a related problem with respect to the transcendental position-ing of *history* in cultural studies as has already been identified with regard to *politics*. A history of this kind would also *presuppose* that cultural studies is sufficiently self-contained and self-identical as to be able to have such a history – whereas the question of cultural studies, of what it is and what it means to *do cultural studies*, is one of those I have endeavoured to keep open here.

Culture in Bits* thus offers neither a comprehensive map of the cultural studies field nor a continuous history of the struggle over the future of cultural studies. While for reasons of economy I do at times refer to cultural studies in general, not least so that I may proceed more quickly to other questions, rather than attempting to enclose or exhaust cultural studies, the chapters which make up *Culture in Bits* take as their starting points merely some specific moments of more or less stable and coherent configuration. Consequently, although the chapters in this book were written at different times, in different places and in different institutional contexts, I have not attempted to bring them together to form a smooth, homogeneous whole. If they can nevertheless be read in terms of a number of interconnecting themes, ideas, concepts and narratives, as this opening chapter has hopefully made clear, I have deliberately chosen not to privilege ultimately any one such theme or idea. Which is why this opening chapter is not an introduction of the type that attempts to sum up, or close down, the contents of what follows. There are many points of conjunction and divergence, association and separation between the different pieces in this book, only *some* of which I have attempted to draw attention to. But *Culture in Bits* is not the mere working out of a pre-established historical or political or theoretical project or plan, and is consequently not solid and tight in its structure in that sense. That would have been an irresponsible, not to say rather *boring*, thing to do. When it comes to thinking and writing about culture, and about cultural studies, I prefer (for both 'theoretical' *and* 'political' reasons, one could say), to leave myself, and perhaps also my reader, open to the possibility of being surprised.

CHAPTER 2

'It's a Thin Line Between Love and Hate':
Why Cultural Studies is so 'Naff'

Naff . . . 1. Worthless, rubbishy, faulty . . . 2. Unfashionable;
socially awkward (*The Oxford Dictionary of Modern Slang*)[1]

CULTURAL STUDIES AND POPULAR CULTURE

Once upon a time cultural critics knew where they stood with regard to
popular culture. For those on the left, it was passive and distracting, the vehicle
for the transmission of those myths, values and traditions with which the
dominant class sought to infect other classes in order to ensure its hegemony.
For the conservative defenders of Culture with a capital 'C', it was barbaric
and banal, evidence of a process of Americanization and levelling down which
was increasingly coming to threaten the continuity of culture and tradition.
And that is how it was in the years *before cultural studies* . . . or so the story
goes. Then, very gradually (although looking back it seemed to happen almost
overnight – as if a group of academics and intellectuals got together at a party
somewhere and finally admitted to having been Barry White fans all along), a
different attitude began to take shape. Reacting in part against what they saw
as an elitist and pessimistic dismissal of popular culture, and in particular the
kind of thinking which presented consumption as a mindless and passive
activity, cultural critics began to focus on the meanings that could be extracted
from popular culture. The effect was dramatic. Consumers of popular culture
were suddenly freed from their mythical inscription as 'idiots' or 'cultural
dopes'.[2] Now they were discerning and skilful manipulators; and wonderful
stories were told of appropriation, transformation and subversion. So much so
that by today many versions of this 'theory' have been offered: from Dick
Hebdige's account of how youth subcultures can invest commodities with
'forbidden meanings';[3] through Erica Carter's description of the way in which
nylon stockings enabled one young woman to resist the 'dominant codes of

social taste';[4] to John Fiske's analysis of Madonna and her ability to show girls 'that the meanings of feminine sexuality *can be* in their control, *can be* made in their interests, and that their subjectivities are not necessarily totally determined by the dominant patriarchy'.[5]

This is not to suggest that all these contributions are the same. Within what has been called, or what calls itself, cultural studies, questions about popular culture – what is it, where is it located, who uses it, and how should it be regarded and represented – have been raised in a multiplicity of different ways, depending on whether it is understood in terms of ideology, hegemony, the politics of identity, representation, pleasure or consumption, and the extent to which an emphasis on class has been superseded by a preoccupation with one of the regularly invoked triumvirate of gender, race and sexuality.[6] Nevertheless, many analysts have detected the marks of a number of broad theoretical and political developments in such arguments.

Mica Nava charts two of these in an essay on 'Consumerism and its Contradictions' which is often referred to as having provided a superb summary of these developments.[7] The first is a more 'nuanced understanding of subjectivity'. This is particularly apparent in 'refutations of the notion that the media and advertising have the power to manipulate in a coherent and unfractured fashion'. For Nava, such refutations mark a significant change from the idea of 'mass man and woman as duped and passive recipients of conspiratorial messages designed to inhibit true consciousness' (207). Instead, she sees such 'theories of culture and subjectivity' as taking far more 'seriously notions of personal agency, discrimination and resistance, as well as (drawing on psychoanalysis) the contradictory and fragmented nature of fantasy and desire'. Feminists have thus argued that 'women can read glossy magazines critically and selectively yet not disavow more traditional feminine identities and pleasures' (207); while from a different perspective others have maintained that 'the desire for commodities is not in itself evidence of duping and indoctrination' (208). Change, from this point of view, must be sought in the personal as well as the public realm, and must be concerned with sex and gender as well as class.

The second development Nava identifies is thus 'played out variously in the arena of sexual politics' (208). Whereas consumerism had generally been held to reinforce the subordination of women, attention was now focused upon the 'contradictory way in which the relative status and power of women has paradoxically been enhanced by consumer society'. Consumption can accordingly be seen to have 'offered women new areas of authority and expertise, new sources of income, a new sense of consumer rights; and one of the consequences of these developments has been a heightened awareness of entitlement outside the sphere of consumption'. As a result, the 'buying of commodities and images can be understood', according to Nava, 'both as a source of power and pleasure for women . . . and simultaneously as an instrument which secures their subordination'. In addition, 'there has been a blurring of the conventional distinctions in the advertising address to men and women; constructions of masculinity and femininity are less fixed; shopping and self-adornment have become less gendered – less specifically female – activities' (208). A quick flick through many of the male fashion magazines that have been published in recent years thus finds men being 'represented in many of the erotic and frivolous ways that feminists have traditionally found so objectionable when deployed in representations of women'. For Nava this signals not only a change in practice:

> [B]ut also a destabilization of the positioning of men and women in fantasy. At the same time, women's magazines today like *Mizz* and *Seventeen*, *Cosmopolitan*, even *Vogue*, and television programmes like *Brookside*, have increasingly become vehicles for the dissemination of ideas and the popularization of issues (among both men and women) placed initially on the political agenda by feminism. (208)

It is these two aspects of cultural discourse in particular, then – an emphasis on subjectivity and sexual politics – that Nava identifies as marking a change in the study of contemporary culture. However, I would add at least one more commonly identified development to Nava's list. This concerns the collapsing of 'critical distance': that space which distinguishes the critic from the object under study. The grand narratives of emancipation and enlightenment which legitimated the idea of cultural criticism are now seen by many as having undergone a process of fragmentation and decline in the 'postmodern' world of the late twentieth century.[8] The traditional position 'outside' material society that the cultural critic customarily adopts is regarded as no longer being possible. Instead, local, limited and subjective forms of engagement have come to replace 'elitist' ideas of critical distance and intellectual mastery. No longer do critics strive to do away with the 'masses' and their culture from the 'outside'; the goal now is to join with the 'masses' in order to show how the signs that make up contemporary culture can be manipulated from 'within'.

Now for some these developments are highly desirable, helping as they do to overcome the gulf that divides intellectual theory from the practice of everyday life. In this version of the story cultural studies represents the fulfilment of the avant-garde desire to traverse 'the great divide' between high and mass culture.[9] But for others all this has produced a sense of disquiet about 'left populism': a feeling that this lack of a 'critical distance' has led to a naturalization of the meanings produced by capitalism, and to a celebration of consumption for its own sake. More than a few commentators have thus taken cultural studies to task for becoming less and less *critical*, complaining that those who have drawn attention to the pleasures of consumerism have failed to fully situate such activities in their larger social and historical context. From this point of view, cultural studies is seen as having taken too little account of the way in which popular culture is materially constructed by forces operating beyond the understanding and control of those who embrace it.[10]

And of course these commentators have a point. Optimistic and democratic though its thesis may be, there are a number of charges that can be raised against cultural studies. Among these is the claim that, as Nava acknowledges, it is all too easy for such positive theories of popular culture to take on the appearance of a rationalization of their theorists' desires; 'an accommodative response to the new generation; a way of keeping up; in sum, a cop-out' which is 'diversionary', evidence merely of a 'capitulation to the right' (209, 204). What makes these rebukes so hard to take is that they are rarely accompanied by any real consideration of the factors and issues that helped to determine the approaches they attack. All too often it is difficult to distinguish the positions of those who have censured cultural studies for what they regard as its failure to maintain a critical attitude toward popular culture from those of previous cultural critics. Complaints of this sort consequently remain susceptible to many of the reproaches that are levelled by cultural studies in the first place, returning, as they frequently appear to do, to a traditional conception of the cultural critic as the intellectual vanguard of civilization and guardian of society's mental and moral health.

But these are not the only accusations that have been directed at cultural studies. Even among those who are sympathetic to the challenge it offers to intellectual elitism, and who are reluctant to censure the positivity of its enabling thesis, there is still the feeling that there is something not quite right about cultural studies; that it is all a bit 'naff'.[11] To some extent this feeling ties in with concerns over the lack of a critical attitude displayed by cultural studies. Now, however, it is not so much the resulting collusion with consumerism that is at issue, but rather the way in which many cultural studies practitioners have simply celebrated popular culture for doing what was previously attributed only to the radical avant-garde.[12] As a result, their analyses seem to have more to do with their own political investments and wishes than with popular culture.

This failure to acknowledge the analyst's own role in the analysis is particularly apparent in cultural studies' introduction into the old intellectual/ popular opposition of the principle of pleasure. By introducing the question of pleasure – undoubtedly, as Duncan Webster says, something of a 'blind spot' in many Marxist and feminist analyses – cultural studies is able to raise the issue of fantasy and desire, and thus slide from an emphasis on production to an emphasis on consumption.[13] But what cultural studies neglects in doing so is its own blind spot: the way in which there is in any gift such as that which cultural studies offers the consumer always some return for the self.[14] Cultural studies informs us of 'the people's' pleasure in the popular, but what about cultural studies' own pleasure in 'the people'?

The sense that there is a will to power and knowledge at work in cultural criticism which leads many theorists to find their own goals and assumptions in the objects of their analyses is of course felt in places other than cultural studies. Although it is perhaps more sharply visible around material customarily excluded from 'intellectual' institutions and agendas, it is also detectable with regard to a good many studies of what might be regarded as more 'legitimate' objects of intellectual interest. (I am thinking here, in particular, of those that have striven to posit anyone from Aristotle, through Shakespeare, to Hegel and Weber as an early poststructuralist/deconstructionist).[15] This is not to say that such studies are wrong, nor that they are not interesting in themselves, just that they don't have anything very interesting to say about their chosen object – revealing, as they do, more about the particular affiliations and identifications of the critic.

If concerns over the relation of the critic to the object under study are one possible cause of the feelings of unease associated with cultural studies, another is its attempt to transgress the high/low boundary. For is there not also something a bit 'naff' about intellectuals discoursing knowledgeably about events in *Big Brother* or ideas of 'hipness' in rave culture? I'm not talking about naffness here in the same way in which, for some, it does not seem naff for intellectuals to discourse knowledgeably about Shakespeare or the Romantic poets. To be sure there seems to be a more 'natural' fit between the latter than the former. But this can be attributed, to a large extent, to the continuing influence of certain legitimizing disciplines and institutions which, perceiving the popular as a threat to the bastions of high culture, have deemed it more fitting and valuable for cultural critics to read Keats than to watch David Beckham or listen to Bob Dylan. Much the same also applies to the argument that a good deal of the naffness of cultural studies can be attributed to the fact that popular culture inhabits a realm of 'lived experience' it is impossible for intellectuals to grasp. It is not so much that intellectuals are out of touch with this realm; that they are not very good at consuming popular culture in the way that they supposedly *are* good at consuming Freud or Brecht. Popular culture is not simply a 'way of life' that is beyond intellectual comprehension. To abide by such distinctions would be to again adhere to the boundaries that separate 'proper' objects of cultural study from the supposedly improper, the very boundaries that cultural studies is in many ways trying to disrupt. Indeed, if cultural studies has achieved anything it is a certain challenging of this 'naturalness', and the rendering problematic of the boundaries which determine legitimate objects of cultural study. Still, it is not enough merely to suggest that an analysis of Rolf Harris is somehow necessarily more radical or political than that of Picasso. A large proportion of the naffness of cultural studies arises precisely as a result of the assumption that the crossing of this intellectual/popular boundary is in itself a subversive move: that it is enough to transgress the high/low hierarchies (to bring high culture into the realm of the low, or vice versa). Of course a move of this kind has at times been necessary, and has had an important effect on some intellectual institutions and on some academic disciplines. But what often gets overlooked in all this is how recalcitrant these problems are, and, in particular, the way in which the structures informing these hierarchies – and especially those which actually define the intellectual and the popular – invariably tend to remain the same.

HATE AND WAR: CULTURAL CRITIQUE VERSUS CULTURAL POPULISM

At this point the analysis of popular culture appears to take on something of a pattern: that of a contrast between a traditional intellectual position of critical difference and distance, and a denial of any such difference. And, indeed, cultural criticism is often set up very much in this way, as a struggle between two opposing forces: 'cultural critique and critical distance versus a populist celebration of the popular', as Duncan Webster puts it (85). What is more, it is a struggle neither side seems able to win. What one side sees as being capable of bringing about a victory (or, if nothing else, as at least providing a preliminary outline of the parameters of the question), the other regards simply as a product of the same old problem, one that is all the more dangerous for being held up as some sort of solution. Cultural criticism has consequently become trapped in a conflict in which the study of popular culture is restricted to a choice between what appear to be two equally unacceptable positions, with each side charging the other with adhering to the very system of rules and values they should be questioning. For the more 'traditional' critics, what cultural studies needs is a supply of the sort of weaponry only they can deliver. From this perspective, cultural studies is not nearly objective, critical or political enough. Meanwhile many of those who identify themselves with cultural studies have argued in turn that, far from offering some sort of solution, such weapons are in fact part of the problem. As far as the latter are concerned, the only thing cultural studies would be making if it were to join forces with a mode of analysis already weakened by elitist, masculine norms, would be the sort of strategic mistake that has already cost cultural criticism too dear. Yet for others again this is precisely the mistake cultural studies *has* made. For all its well-intentioned efforts to avoid the elitism and pessimism of previous critiques, cultural studies is thus still met with what Webster characterizes as a 'cringe of embarrassment' (84).

It is this impossible impasse, these irreconcilable either/ors, I want to look at here. My concern in doing so is not so much with promoting the enabling qualities, or otherwise, of one side or the other. It is not my intention to join in the struggle by leading cultural studies, say, to a glorious victory over the forces of 'cultural critique and critical distance'. What interests me is rather the assumption that in a certain way dictates the relation between these two approaches to popular culture. The way in which cultural criticism is set up suggests that for a certain opinion today something called 'cultural studies' can be identified, and can be set up in a relation of bitter rivalry with something which can be perceived as a very different body of work – '*kulturkritik*', as Francis Mulhern calls it, or 'cultural critique', to continue with Webster's terminology.[16] It is this commonplace assumption I want to examine. Not to reject it. It is necessary to analyse such an assumption (which is why I have given an account of it), and to ask, can cultural criticism really take no other form than an opposition between the two: cultural and political optimism and pessimism? Is there not rather something wrong with this question itself? In particular, is there not something wrong with the way in which the relation between these two approaches is expressed predominantly in hostile terms? Without doubt these theories exist in a state of mutual conflict with each other. But the relation between these two modes of cultural criticism isn't *just* a matter of conflict and competition. It isn't simply – as Dick Hebdige would have it in his variation on the theme – a 'war of the worlds' between two 'apparently separate semantic planets'.[17]

Before moving on to discuss some of the features of this relation in detail, it is perhaps worth taking the time to raise a few points regarding its general structure. One reason why the relation between these two approaches to popular culture cannot be positioned solely in terms of a conflict, for instance, is that this relation is also one of mutual dependency and support. Witness the way in which what is sometimes called cultural critique attempts to establish itself as objective and critical by distancing itself from that which it sees as unobjective and uncritical: namely, the sort of subjective, celebratory approach it associates with cultural studies. And the identity of cultural studies is likewise closely bound up with this more traditional attitude to cultural criticism. It, too, is able to construct the difference and the identity of its reading only by referring to the latter as a deluded other. This is often evident from cultural studies' accounts of its own conception: the idea that cultural studies was produced, at least in part, as a response to elitist condemnations of popular culture; that its emphasis on subjectivity, sexual politics, and working 'with' the popular represents an intellectual and political break, a sea change. In each case, cultural critique and cultural studies alike, the gesture is basically the same. For both, the other assumes the role of a supplement with regard to its analysis.[18] It is part of the main body of work as it were, yet an extra, an addition: something which it cannot do without in order to complete itself, but which it nevertheless at the same time attempts to situate as external and separate. Consequently, their relation cannot be positioned *just* in terms of a conflict between two distinct discourses. While each represents an enemy to be struggled against, they also constitute the means by which the other is able to establish and define its identity in the first place.

Furthermore, this relation is not one of pure antagonism. Each side does not merely contrast itself to the other (at least, not in terms of an inside/ outside dichotomy); each also contains the other to a certain extent, explaining it and accounting for it. Hence the way in which many of those critics who advocate, or who are said to have advocated, a stance of cultural critique and critical distance do not just oppose their position to that of cultural studies; they also attempt to *explain* cultural studies: historically, socially, economically, politically. In doing so they endeavour to enclose cultural studies within the confines of their own theory, surpassing it by inscribing it within their own body of thought. Similarly, cultural studies, for all its emphasis on non-totalization, has often tended to position itself not just as one theory among many; in many of its more dominant versions at least, it has struggled to establish itself as a new intellectual paradigm in its own right. As such it has striven to understand and explain all other theories, thereby incorporating them within itself. This may be one reason why cultural studies' own analysis of postmodernism frequently remains so contiguous to concepts of social totality; why the collapse of critical distance tends to be regarded, not just as an epistemological question, but as a historical and material process. For it, too, has to construct a theoretical narrative that is 'grand' enough to explain and account for the change from 'critical distance' to 'populist celebration', thereby encompassing traditional criticism within itself, and so establishing cultural studies as a body of work in its own right.[19] This is something that both of these approaches are in fact trying to do. Both are trying to account for the other in order to encompass it within their own field of knowledge, and thereby establish their own field as the *one and only field*.[20] This no doubt explains why this struggle creates such a dilemma for cultural criticism. For it is only by fully explaining and accounting for, and hence absorbing, the other that each side can establish itself as a distinct and unified field of knowledge. If neither side is able to do this, if neither side is able ultimately to win this struggle, and in this way establish itself as the one and only interpretative paradigm, the very identity of each approach is threatened. Cultural criticism is consequently left in a state of confusion and impasse as a result of having to choose between what appear to be two equally incomplete and unsatisfactory positions.

A third reason why their respective identities cannot be positioned as diametrical opposites, one which is closely related to the previous two, is that each side also contains, and is made up of, many elements it otherwise describes as belonging to the other. Take, once again, those critics who are said to advocate a stance of critical distance. They habitually condemn what they see as the populist, celebratory approach of cultural studies for being too closely connected to the popular, and so for not being *critical enough*. Yet these critics are themselves dependent on a certain degree of connection with the popular. For one thing, the boundary that divides the intellectual from popular culture is not just one of separation; it is also one of joining. Even this attitude of critical distance still implies some form of relationship and connection with the other. Nor could it be otherwise. Not unless, that is, the critic is willing to give up her or his identity. For it is only by being opposed to the popular that the cultural critic can establish and define her or himself as different and as one who is 'supposed to know'.[21] As well as being one of opposition and contrast, their relation is also one of interdependency and support. For another, the relation between the critic and popular culture is not that of a simple inside/outside dichotomy. While on the one hand the critic needs to be sufficiently distant from the popular so as to be able to contemplate and explain it, on the other the critic needs to be close enough to the popular to be able to 'know' and understand it. It is thus impossible for the cultural critic to remain completely 'outside' popular culture. An appropriate understanding of popular culture requires that it be grasped totally, that is from the outside, like an object. But, at the same time, it must also be grasped like an object which contains inside itself the subjective knowledge (conscious or unconscious) that the critic would have of it if the critic were that object (if, for example, the critic were living as part of the consuming masses instead of observing them from afar).[22]

All of which raises a number of questions for those who see the more traditional forms of cultural criticism as having a purely external and hostile view of popular culture. Take Adorno and Horkheimer's analysis of 'The Culture Industry'.[23] As Mica Nava notes in a follow-up to her earlier analysis of consumerism, this essay is usually read as a 'relentless invective' against 'the nature and quality of the capitalist culture industry'. The 'products of the culture industry, like cinema, radio and magazines', are here seen as being 'distinguished from "art"' and 'condemned repeatedly for their uniformity,

falseness, vileness, barbaric meaninglessness and much more'.[24] Yet Adorno
and Horkheimer's attitude is not one of complete rejection. They do not
simply dislike capitalist culture. To know as much about it as they do they
must be interested in it to some extent. (Their references in this essay range
from Donald Duck and Betty Boop, through Bette Davis and Victor Mature,
to the Lone Ranger, the Marx Brothers, Benny Goodman and Chesterfield
cigarettes, and this is proper names alone.) In fact, as Umberto Eco demonstrates, just as convincing a case can be built for interpreting such anxiety
around the products of the culture industry as:

> the barely disguised manifestation of a frustrated passion, a love betrayed,
> or rather, the neurotic display of a repressed sensuality, similar to that of
> the moralist who, in the very act of denouncing the obscenity of an image,
> pauses at such length and with such voluptuousness to contemplate the
> loathsome object of his contempt that his true nature – that of carnal, lustful
> animal – is betrayed.[25]

Certainly, Adorno and Horkheimer cannot be completely 'outside' the culture
industry; they must also be 'inside' to some extent, too. Otherwise how are
they able to understand it? Without some form of connection to the capitalist
culture industry, it would be impossible for even the most objective and hostile
critic to know anything about it. Adorno and Horkheimer must be connected
to the culture industry in some way.

As in cultural studies, the gap between the intellectual and popular culture
thus becomes blurred. Indeed, from this point of view the so-called 'populist'
approach of cultural studies looks like it is capable of providing a far more
accurate representation of cultural criticism, since the blurring of the gap
between subject and object that is so apparent here is precisely the means by
which so much cultural critique also seems to work (it, too, is a form of
projection and identification, albeit one motivated by negative, as opposed to
positive, feelings).[26] However, the approach to culture of cultural studies itself
contains many of the problematic features it otherwise associates with the
more traditional forms of criticism. Cultural studies sees cultural critique as
trying to maintain a critical distance or gap between the subject and object,
and criticizes it accordingly: as old-fashioned, reactionary, elitist, etc. Yet this
is precisely what 'celebratory' cultural studies critics do themselves. They, too,
maintain a gap between the subject and object just as much as the supposedly
reactionary, traditional critic. This is just one reason why it is possible to
situate those responsible for the emergence of 'cultural populism' – Orwell,
Hoggart, Williams, etc. – on the 'traditional' side of the argument.[27] The two
are intimately and inextricably linked.[28]

At this point I want to shift focus somewhat by moving from the analysis of the general structure of this relation to take a closer look at the way in which one cannot identify what is today known as cultural studies without continuing to observe ideas, expressions and lines of inquiry which come from that which it in many ways wishes to set itself against: the elitist and pessimistic attitudes of cultural critique. I want to concentrate on this element of the struggle between cultural critique and cultural populism, as opposed to the others I have just enumerated (to cover them all in anything like sufficient detail would take too long), for two reasons. Firstly, because the way in which cultural studies retains many of the features of critical distance is not always immediately apparent: hence the more usual interpretations of cultural studies just given. And, secondly, because it seems to me that it may be this aspect of cultural studies which leads to contemporary cultural criticism being set up in this way: as a 'war' between two opposing world views. Since part of my aim is to place a question mark against this kind of mapping of the present conflicts in cultural theory, I want to take my initial cue from one of the ever-increasing number of books and essays which have mapped it in this way: in terms of a debate between two conflicting bodies of knowledge. Of these, Duncan Webster's account of 'The Future of Cultural Studies', first published in 1990, seems worthy of particular attention, as this is one of the places in which the 'impasse' between these two approaches has been most forcefully expressed. For the most part, however, Webster provides merely a broad critical survey of the history of cultural argumentation. I will therefore focus instead on one of the works Webster himself refers to as having captured this impasse 'quite brilliantly'. This is Meaghan Morris's 'Banality in Cultural Studies', first published in 1988. It is to this essay that I will now turn in order to take a detailed look at this aspect of the 'optimism/pessimism' debate, after a brief discussion, by way of introduction, of one of Morris's earlier texts.

'WE ARE NOT YOU'

In an essay which explores some of the problems that are raised by a study she is doing of the management of change in certain sites of 'cultural production' – 'shopping centres, cars, highways, "homes" and motels'[29] – Meaghan Morris describes the task that confronts her as involving two strategies. These she associates with the sociology of consumerism and cultural studies respectively. Whereas the first is 'outside' in the role of ethnographer, the second is 'inside' as the supposed celebrant of popular culture. Attempting to pursue the latter mode of analysis further, Morris refers to Iain Chambers' argument in his 1986 book *Popular Culture*,[30] that to 'appreciate the democratic "potential" of the way that people live through . . . culture – appropriating and transforming everyday life – we must first pursue the "wide-eyed presentation of actualities" that Adorno disapproved of in some of Benjamin's work on Baudelaire' (196). Adorno objected that Benjamin's study was '"located at the crossroads of magic and positivism. That spot is bewitched"'. Now for Adorno '"theory can break this spell"'. Morris, however, rejects both Adorno's 'faith in theory as the exorcist' and the 'strategy of wide-eyed presentation'. For her neither is 'adequate to dealing with the problems posed by feminism in the analysis of "everyday life"'. But although Morris is able to claim that 'it is today fairly easy to reject' what she describes as 'the rationalist and gynophobic prejudice implied by Adorno's scenario (theory breaking the witch's spell)' (196), she does not find it quite so easy to come up with reasons for rejecting the 'wide-eyed' pose which characterizes cultural studies. This she reserves for a later essay, 'Banality in Cultural Studies'.

Morris's intention in 'Banality in Cultural Studies' is not to contest cultural studies' 'enabling theses' (summarized, for Morris, by Mica Nava's 'excellent' article).[31] What interests her is the 'sheer proliferation' of restatements of these theses; and the 'emergence in some of them of a *restrictive definition* of the ideal knowing subject of cultural studies' (20). She identifies two dominant trends. The first she characterizes as an ethnographic approach. Here the popular occupies a double position in the analysis: both as a popular subject which is 'supposed to know' in its own right; and as an object which the critic, despite being located outside this culture by the very *'process of interrogation and analysis'*, is able to claim to understand. At first sight this seems to offer an improvement on the traditional approach to popular culture. In John Fiske's 1987 essay 'British Cultural Studies and Television', for example, Morris finds that, far from being 'cultural dupes', consumers are depicted as actually negotiating their own readings and as being able to actively shape their own culture. But this is of course also 'the function of cultural studies itself' (20). And it is precisely this sort of 'recognition', this awareness of its own possible investments in the analysis, of the 'double play of transference', that Morris sees as missing from the majority of populist arguments. 'What takes its place is firstly a citing of popular voices (the informants), an act of translation and commentary, and then a play of *identification* between the knowing subject of cultural studies', and the popular subject itself. As a result, the popular functions, in the end, not just as the cultural critic's object of study (the 'native informants'), but also as 'the textually delegated, allegorical emblem of the critic's own activity'. It is 'both a source of authority for a text and a figure of its own critical activity' (20). From this perspective, the ethnographic approach to culture is both 'circular' and 'narcissistic'. The critic does not so much criticize popular culture; the popular acts rather as a screen onto which the critic's own ideal of what cultural criticism should be is narcissistically projected.

The second trend Morris identifies is that which tries to break down the barriers between these two realms (the intellectual and the popular) by means of what, borrowing a term from Kuan-Hsing Chen, I want to define as a 'cut'n'mix' approach.[32] Referring to the 'figure that Andreas Huyssen, Tania Modleski, and Patrice Petro have described in various contexts as "mass culture as woman"' (22), Morris draws attention to the way in which, in pop epistemology, contemplation is generally assumed to be the property of male intellectual audiences. To this end she cites Patrice Petro, in particular, as having pointed out that the 'contemplation/distraction opposition is historically implicated in the construction of the "female spectator" as site, and target, of a theorization of modernity by male intellectuals'.[33] There is thus a clear boundary separating the place of the intellectual from that of the popular. Taking as her example Iain Chambers' *Popular Culture*, Morris illustrates how, in an attempt to cross over and eliminate this boundary – either to bring popular culture into the intellectual sphere, or to make high culture somehow more accessible to the masses – the populist critic refuses to approach 'mass culture' from the point of view of the masculine, contemplative gaze of official culture. The argument here is that when applied to the 'tactile, transitory, expendable, visceral world of the popular, contemplation' is a vain and presumptuous mistake. It is Walter Benjamin's principle of 'distracted reception'[34] that 'really characterizes the subject of "popular epistemology"' (22). This is seen to have a number of consequences for the heavily smitten populist. Not least among these is the fact that the critic can imitate popular culture only by borrowing from Benjamin the strategy of 'writing through quotations' and 'refusing to "explain . . . references fully"'.[35] To explain this subject would merely be to attempt to pull it back under the auspices of the contemplative gaze, and so reaffirm the 'authority of the "academic mind"' (22).

So, in an effort to cross the boundary separating the intellectual from the popular, the 'knowing subject of popular epistemology no longer contemplates "mass culture"' as feminine/woman, but instead lovingly takes on the supposed characteristics of 'mass culture' in the 'writing of his own text'. There thus emerges the idea of a 'hero of knowledge' operating in the guise of what Morris calls 'the *white male theorist* as bimbo' (or should that be 'himbo'?) (22).[36] The problem with this type of manoeuvre, Morris argues, is not so much the intellectual 'slumming' – the 'cross-dressing' as Elaine Showalter has characterized it.[37] Nor is it the continued anti-feminism and cultural elitism of the concept of distraction. The problem is rather that in anti-academic writing of this sort, although the border separating the contemplators from the contemplated may be crossed – the popular now inhabiting the space of the intellectual, literally, in being incorporated into the critic's text – the identity of that which is incorporated remains the same.

At this point cultural studies does indeed appear to be a bit 'naff'. Cultural studies tries to challenge convention by 'mixing and matching' genres: high and low, intellectual and popular, academic and everyday. But, as Morris shows, doing so involves adhering to the very categories it is supposedly attempting to bring into question. As a result, what is enacted stylistically continues to be an idea of the popular precisely as 'feminine'/'bimbo': '[d]istracted, scanning the surface, and short on attention-span' (22). Not only is this fairly naff, as far as cultural studies is concerned it is also contradictory: criticism of this sort merely enacts a return, in this case at the 'level of *enunciative* practice', to the thesis of 'cultural dopism' that cultural studies – 'going right back to the early work of Stuart Hall, not to mention Raymond Williams' – originally sought to contest. What is more, it is this return to 'cultural dopism in the *practice* of writing' that, according to Morris, has led cultural studies to produce 'over and over again the same article which never goes beyond recycling and restating its own basic premises'. For '[i]f a cultural dopism is being enunciatively performed . . . in a discourse that tries to contest it, then the argument in fact *cannot* move on' (22). Cultural studies can nevertheless 'necessitate and enable more repetition' by projecting 'elsewhere a mis-understanding or discouraging Other figure' (usually feminism or the Frankfurt School) which needs to be constantly reminded of consumerism's complexities. 'To discredit such voices', Morris writes, is 'one of the immediate political functions of the current boom in cultural studies' (23).

Morris's essay can thus be placed alongside Webster's and a number of other more recent books and articles, all of which question the actual achievements of this 'audience' research. Morris expresses particular frustration at what she sees as the apparent choice in cultural criticism between 'cheerleaders and prophets of doom'. She is 'equally uneasy about fatalistic theory on the one hand' (by which she means accounts of the impending apocalypse, *à la* Baudrillard), but also about 'cheerily "making the best of things" in the name of a new politics of culture on the other' (24). The trouble with cultural studies, she argues, is that it is not discriminating enough, regardless of whether it attempts to understand popular culture (Fiske), or mimic it (Chambers); while simply accusing those who are 'trying to develop a critique of popular culture of succumbing to "elitism" or pessimism' she sees as producing a depleted critical vocabulary (25).

Morris's attempt in 'Banality in Cultural Studies' to describe a 'more positive approach to the politics of theorizing popular culture' (24) deserves long and careful analysis.[38] But for the time being I'm more concerned with what her analysis has to say about cultural studies and, in particular, the impasse between optimists and pessimists. The first thing I want to do in this respect is reiterate my earlier point: that the approach Morris associates with cultural studies, and 'British' (or Anglo-Australian) cultural studies especially, cannot simply be opposed to that of so-called cultural critique, since it contains many of the features it otherwise ascribes to the latter. And, indeed, although Webster is quite right to frame the debate in these terms, and to see Morris as having captured 'quite brilliantly' some of the 'problems of recent cultural studies',[39] there is a greater degree of congruence between these two approaches in Morris's account than either she, or Webster, seem to cater for. Morris may well see cultural studies as 'actively [striving] to achieve "banality"' (15), but she is unable to portray it as such without also continuing to recognize in it many of the attributes she otherwise associates with that which she opposes to cultural studies: the elitist and pessimistic attitudes of cultural critique.

This is particularly apparent with regard to the issue of 'critical distance'. In her earlier essay on 'Shopping Centres' Morris positioned cultural studies in terms of a contrast with cultural critique. Whereas the latter (in the guise of the sociology of consumerism) is 'outside' in the role of ethnographer, the former is 'inside' as the supposed celebrant of popular culture. When she comes to examine cultural studies more closely in 'Banality in Cultural Studies', however, both of the trends Morris identifies – ethnography and populist mimicry – are revealed as retaining an attitude of critical distance. In populist mimicry, the popular is brought into the sphere of the intellectual in being incorporated into the writing of the critic's actual text. In ethnography the trajectory of this journey is reversed. The benevolent cultural critic decides to journey down among 'the people' in order to get a closer look. But once again, at the same time as the gap that separates the intellectual from the popular is crossed, so that the critic can either study it (ethnography), or imitate it (mimicry), it is also effectively reinforced. Although the intellectual and the popular may now occupy the same place (as when Margaret Drabble decides to travel by bus, or Stuart Hall rides through Brixton in the back of a taxi;[40] or, alternatively, when the cultural critic decides to write her or his text in a popular style, or when *Star Trek* and *The Sex Pistols* are taught on university courses), and may even share the same critical activity (as in Morris's account of Fiske), their respective identities remain very much intact. What Morris says about ethnography applies just as well to mimicry. For both, although as an 'understanding' and 'encouraging' subject the critic may share some aspects of that culture, the very process of investigation and analysis locates them 'outside' it (20).

As well as demonstrating some of the contrasts between these two approaches, then, Morris's essay also has the effect of pointing to what is perhaps the most significant reason why they cannot simply be opposed. For while the celebratory cultural critic may love and identify with the popular, and the more pessimistic, traditional critic hate and reject it, for both the popular is maintained in a position of being precisely 'other'. No matter how close the critic may want to get to it, no matter how much the critic may identify with it or love it, popular culture is always separated from the critic by signs that say 'WE ARE NOT YOU'.[41] The optimist's love for popular culture can thus be seen to share the same place as the pessimist's hatred: the popular occupies the same position in both their analyses (the optimist merely giving what is to all effects and purposes the same object a different – more positive and loving – inflection). Although the attitude may be different, what is to be analysed, along with the terms of that analysis, remains much the same. Cultural studies, like cultural critique, still holds to the idea of the popular as a readily identifiable and definable 'space' within both society and the system of the analysis; a space that is decidedly 'non-intellectual'.

AT THE CROSSROADS OF MAGIC AND POSITIVISM

At the same time as supposedly crossing the gap that separates the intellectual from popular culture in order to study and comprehend that culture, then, the populist, like the more traditional critic, works to sustain and reinforce this boundary. For both, the intellectual and the popular continue to be viewed in oppositional terms – and this despite each side's positing of an original difference between them. Consequently, there seems to be little to choose in this respect between cultural studies' celebratory approach to popular culture and the more pessimistic attitude of, say, Leavis or the Frankfurt School.[42] At the very least the line between them appears blurred and hard to distinguish.

But the maintenance of this boundary on cultural studies' part does not mean that the issue of the critic's relation to popular culture is settled. Far from it. For (and as we saw earlier with regard to the stance of cultural critique) this boundary is one of joining as well as separation. Even the most rigid of boundaries still implies a relationship to the other. Just as it is impossible for the celebratory critic to remain completely inside popular culture, so, too, is it impossible to remain completely outside it. The problem in the end centres upon the precise nature of this relation: the gap between them seems to be both sustained and overcome by cultural criticism at the same time. The relation between the intellectual and popular culture, the critic and the object (and by implication cultural studies and cultural critique), is thus a paradoxical and contradictory one. It is a question neither of crossing, nor of not crossing, the gap that exists between them. Rather, criticism crosses in the form of a non-crossing. Cultural studies is both 'inside' and 'outside' at once. Once again ambivalence rules.

Interestingly, Morris herself acknowledges the ambivalence of this relation with her quotation of Adorno via Chambers. She uses this to draw attention to the 'wide-eyed' and celebratory stance she associates with cultural studies, as well as to provide a description of 'shopping centre mystique'. But what this quotation also points to is the ambivalence of this stance – the way in which the celebratory cultural critic is in a sense 'bewitched' – through its locating of the critic's position precisely at 'the crossroads of magic and positivism'.[43] I want to say more about the ambivalence of this position – the way in which the cultural critic is located 'magically', both 'inside' and 'outside' at once – in a moment. But for now I'll restrict myself merely to drawing attention, once again, to the similarity between this position and that of the traditional cultural critic; and in particular, to the way in which this recalls that ambivalence already identified in the attitude of critical distance: the way in which the more pessimistic critic both hates and loves at the same time, too.

This in turn brings to mind a second moment from Morris's earlier essay on 'Shopping Centres' where Morris writes that both of these poses, 'inside' and 'outside', 'seem to amount to much the same thing'.[44] It is a brief comment, made in parenthesis, and one which, significantly, is never followed up (either by Morris, or by Webster, who also mentions it). Nevertheless, this appears to pose questions for the kind of mapping Webster constructs using Morris's work, and which a number of commentators have also recently supplied: the historical/political/economic/social narrative which is used to explain the conflict with cultural critique, and to account for much of the recent enthusiasm for cultural studies. Contemporary cultural criticism cannot be set up in terms of an opposition between the two: cultural optimism and pessimism, inside and outside, 'critical distance and objectivity versus a populist celebration of the popular'. Theirs is a far more ambiguous and paradoxical relation.

There is much still to be said about the relation between these two bodies of work: particularly about the way the ambiguous and paradoxical nature of this relation makes it difficult to identify what a 'body of work' such as cultural studies, or cultural critique (or even Morris's own writings, for that matter) might be: what it stands for, what it represents, where its limits are, and what form its relations take to those who object to it or oppose it; but also about the possibility that this ambiguity may provide a way of reading not only Morris differently, but cultural criticism as well. Again, this is something I'll come back to. What I'm most interested in for the time being is the light this may shed on the current predicament of cultural criticism, and on why these two approaches are seen as being opposed in the first place. For it seems to me that it is the very maintenance of this gap between the intellectual and the popular, as opposed to cultural studies' supposed eradication of it, that causes many of the problems Morris describes. Indeed, if the popular is seen as an 'other' like this, then perhaps the only alternatives that can be offered are those of seeing it as either different (popular, distracted, feminine, dopey)[45] or the same (intellectual, academic, contemplative, subversive, resistant).

Having said that, there is a third option: that of seeing popular culture as an absolute 'other' that is *beyond* analysis. At first sight, this looks like it is capable of dislodging the cultural critic from the central and privileged position of the one who is 'supposed to know', by contending that the critic cannot comprehend what the 'other' is doing or thinking: that popular culture is unrepresentable as it operates according to completely different laws from the intellectual. But to argue that popular culture is absolutely different from the intellectual, that it inhabits an arena of 'lived experience' it is impossible for intellectuals to grasp, changes very little. All these supposedly unrepresentable thoughts and actions are still referred to as belonging to an identifiable subject; and this is still a representation of that subject, no matter how unknowable or unrepresentable it is deemed to be.[46] Although the cultural critic's position may be dislodged, it is not therefore dislodged very far. In fact by continuing to treat the popular – even though its fragmentation and difference may be acknowledged – as a distinct and separate subject in its own right, a move of this sort merely reaffirms the centrality and privilege of the critic's position.

The problem, then, is not so much how the critic describes popular culture, but that the intellectual and popular culture are seen in opposing terms in the first place. From this perspective, it is not surprising that cultural criticism should be constantly articulated in terms of conflictual or competitive relations between the strong and the weak, masculine and feminine, active and passive, contemplator and contemplated – this difference is valorized within the very system of inquiry itself. If the popular is positioned from the very beginning as an 'other' like this, then the critic *can* only describe it in simplistic, contrasting and oppositional terms.

This places the optimism/pessimism impasse in a very different light. The problem of the relation between these two approaches can now be seen to be embedded in the *process* of cultural criticism itself. It is the contradictions (between the object of study as 'other' and the object as the same) that produce the analysis, not the other way around. Or, to put it another way, it is not so much criticism which produces the impasse, as the impasse which produces criticism. Cultural criticism is attempting to 'know' that which, by the very nature of the critical process, it is also required to distance itself from, to establish as different, 'other'. The problems Morris and others identify in

cultural studies are consequently the result, not of its indiscriminate attach-
ment to the other (although this of course is part of it), but of the process of
cultural criticism itself. They, along with the oppositions between intellectual
and popular, contemplator and contemplated, cannot be removed from the
analysis; they are part of what makes the analysis possible. Accordingly, any
decision as to what the popular is, is made *in advance*. In other words, the
decision as to what constitutes the popular is made *before* it is actually studied.
One could even go so far as to say that cultural critics are only interested in
that space which is defined as popular culture because it is already constituted
as *non-intellectual*: what they, as cultural critics, supposedly *are not*. Which
implies that it is not studied at all, since the question of what popular culture
is, where it is to be found, what its limits are, is never actually raised.[47]

There is of course a risk here of portaying popular culture as entirely
fictional: of presenting cultural critics as being concerned solely with a mythical
object; and thus of seeing those places associated with the 'intellectual' –
universities, libraries, museums, bookshops and lecture halls – as the only
places in which popular culture *can* actually be found. And certainly there
appears to be little room for the popular itself in the analysis. In studying
popular culture, not only does the critic produce an analysis of the 'other';
what the critic also and inseparably produces is the 'otherness' itself. Popular
culture is produced in, and by, the act of studying it. However, in spite of the
impression one sometimes gets that if Madonna didn't exist cultural critics
would have had to invent her, the introduction of the question of the critic's
own involvement in the investigation (from where it has never really been
missing) does not mean that the 'truth' of the analysis is now reduced to the
status of fantasy. This would merely be to replace one truth with another.
Moreover, such a suggestion would continue to carry with it the implication
that there is something 'real' behind the fantasy: that there is something – the
'people', the 'popular' – which acts as a screen onto which intellectual fantasies
are projected. In short, it would continue to function in terms of an intellectual/
popular, fantasy/reality opposition. But if the cultural critic is not a magician
who conjures up the popular, '*Hey Presto*', before the reader's very eyes, neither
is there an 'original' or 'real' popular culture which can be distinguished from
the critic's representation or fantasy. Truth/fiction, reality/fantasy, positivism/
magic: none of these concepts seem to translate this relation. Once again,
ambivalence reigns. There is an essential and irreducible ambiguity in the
intellectual's relation to popular culture. The popular is not just an 'inner
reality' projected by the critic; but neither is it an 'outer reality' belonging to
the world of things.

It is not hard to see the difficulty this creates for cultural criticism. If the
investment of the critic can no longer be kept out of the analysis, it becomes

difficult to distinguish between the critical examination of popular culture and the mere projection of the critic's desire: between truth and fiction, reality and fantasy, knowledge and non-knowledge. How, for example, is it possible to determine whether the analysis of popular culture is correct, if that culture is itself, at least in part, the product of the critic's own involvement in the analysis? Far from being a particular effect or quality that should and could be eliminated from the study of popular culture, naffness now appears to be an irreducible element of that study. Naffness inhabits the analysis of popular culture as the condition of both its possibility and impossibility.

But it is not just a matter of the difficulty this creates for the critic's relation to popular culture. There is also in this situation a model of criticism which at once radically questions and displaces traditional notions of this relation. As a result, there is now the additional difficulty over the very distinction of the intellectual from popular culture, the critic from the object of inquiry. This question is crucial for cultural criticism: what is at stake is its very identity. Yet it is an issue that is rarely raised, since doing so involves putting this identity in question. It is, in effect, to risk cultural criticism becoming something other than itself, something different, something that cultural criticism might regard as almost unrecognizable as 'cultural criticism'.

Nevertheless, it seems to me that it is the reluctance, or refusal, to take this risk and rethink the identity of cultural criticism that explains the difficulty many critics (Morris included) have experienced in theorizing a way out of the optimistic/pessimistic impasse. To argue whether we should regard popular culture either optimistically or pessimistically is to miss the point. We are not dealing here with a choice between two separate and distinct social spheres: the one intellectual, critical, contemplative, subversive, resistant, the other popular, distracted, feminine, dopey. Nor can this issue be resolved by an analysis that attempts to dislocate the poles of this relationship merely by means of some combination of the two: ethnographic objectivity and distance with wide-eyed immersion in 'feeling'. It is something of this sort Webster suggests. He talks of rejecting current positions in favour of a project which maintains 'criticism while respatializing "distance"' (96). So, too, in her essay on 'Shopping Centres', does Morris. She speaks of a feminist analysis achieving a position of ambivalence between 'staring hard at the realities of the contemporary world we all inhabit', and a 'discontent with the "everyday" and with wide-eyed definitions of the everyday as "the way things are"' that allows the 'possibility of rejecting what we see and refusing to take it as given' (197). But very little is likely to be changed by an analysis which attempts to achieve a third position of ambivalence between the two: optimism and pessimism, critical distance and populist celebration. Indeed, there is a distinct danger that a move of this sort will merely repeat the mistakes of the 'cut'n'mix' approach to cultural studies. For although the two elements (in Morris's terms 'astonishment' and critical 'assessment') may be combined, their respective identities, with all their attendant characteristics and problems, tend to be left very much intact. And this danger is only increased by the way in which, although these two approaches to popular culture may themselves be articulated together, the actual distinction between the intellectual and the popular is left unquestioned. It is not the gap between the intellectual and the popular that is at issue here, but how to cross this gap. The place the popular occupies in the system of the analysis remains the same.

Nor does it seem likely that these difficulties can be eluded by adopting a more 'critical' or discriminatory approach to popular culture. On the contrary, an analysis which attempts to respond more 'critically' to popular culture, in an effort to escape some of the problems in contemporary cultural criticism, seems destined only to uncritically repeat them. For the very process that is looked to in an attempt to avoid making these 'mistakes' is precisely that which is responsible for bringing them about. To recast Morris's words, this cultural difference is being enunciatively performed (and valorized) in a discourse that tries to contest it. The argument cannot move on. The last thing cultural criticism can understand, it seems, is cultural criticism itself.

CHAPTER 3

'Something Else Besides':
The Third Way of Angela McRobbie

My vision for the 21st century is of a popular politics reconciling themes which in the past have wrongly been regarded as antagonistic. (Tony Blair)[1]

I: THE THIRD WAY

POSSIBILITIES

What is the future of cultural studies – supposing for the moment we know the meaning of the words 'future' and, still further, 'cultural studies', which is by no means certain? Current opinion seems to hesitate between at least three possibilities.

1st possibility: For many of those in the social sciences, and certain strands of media and communication studies in particular, cultural studies has been led up something of a blind alley in recent years by its celebration of popular culture and the power of the consumer. It has become too 'textual', too theoretical, too focused on producing complicated Derridean or Lacanian readings of popular cultural images and texts far removed from the practical, political, material realities of power and oppression. As a result cultural studies has moved too far away from its social, political and material roots. It has become too concerned with ideas of identity and difference, subjectivity and pleasure, with not enough attention being paid to political and economic changes in national and global media systems, or the way in which inequalities in the distribution of wealth and employment opportunities have resulted in significant sections of the population being unable to partake in the pleasures of consumption. What cultural studies therefore needs now is a strong dose of the sort of political reality that can only be provided by a turn to the practices and methodologies of sociology and the social sciences, with their emphasis on economics and production and on more empirical modes of inquiry.

2nd possibility: For a good many of those *within* cultural studies, however, it remains to be seen exactly how (re)introducing sociology into the mainstream of cultural studies (from which I'm not sure it was ever really absent)[2] is going to avoid the problems of essentialism, reductionism (whether economic or class based) and reflectionism (in terms of the base/superstructure model) cultural studies identified in social science orientated approaches in the first place. All too often there appears to be lurking behind these attacks on cultural studies a desire to return from a world riven by differences of gender and sexuality, race and ethnicity to a simpler model of domination in which all such differences are subsumed into the higher category of class, where people are seen as passively manipulated 'cultural dopes', and where production, 'narrowly understood as the practice of manufacturing and abstractly under-stood as the mode of production, is . . . assumed to be the real bottom line'.[3] From this perspective, for cultural studies to turn toward the practices of the social sciences would be very much a retrograde step.

As an account of the recent and ongoing struggle over the future of cultural studies this is all too crude and too quick. But having begun by sketching the parameters of this 'debate' it is not my intention to provide a complete history of the different attacks that have been made on cultural studies over the last ten years or so;[4] nor of the various defences that have been offered by those working in the field.[5] These arguments have already been well-rehearsed and widely discussed elsewhere. Besides, not only is setting the issue up in this way – as a conflict between two opposing sides – 'boring', it is also unhelpful.[6] There is too great a danger of positioning these two 'sides' in terms of a series of simple, homologous oppositions between 'cultural studies' and 'political economy', theory and politics, 'textuality' and materiality, culture and society, ideas and action, whereas neither 'side' in this relation is a self-identical homogeneous entity. These bodies of knowledge differ within themselves as well as between themselves; and if it is important to pay attention to, and even participate in, this debate (or better, these debates), it is just as important not to conflate what are largely heterogeneous and unequal discourses, styles and discursive contexts.

Granted, the very names 'cultural studies' and 'political economy' could be said to induce, encourage or give rise to such a confusion, not least by implying that there are two more or less unified bodies of work that can go under these names. But for the sake of economy let's continue, for the time being at least, with the terminology of Lawrence Grossberg's dispute with Nicholas Garn-ham, and proceed to my main reason for not wanting to participate directly in this debate.[7] This is quite simply that to enter into the conflict by resisting one side in such a dialectical struggle with the other would be to remain blind to the degree to which approaches of this kind are 'implicated' in one another and are 'therefore not in any sense alternatives'.[8] Indeed, following the groundbreaking work of Robert Young, I would even go so far as to argue that this kind of antagonism 'in which incommensurable arguments from two or more sides' are opposed, their conflict representing the 'founding division by which the field has been both been developed and contested . . . repeats the ambivalence of an incompatible dialectic that operates today within the forces that determine the material culture that frames them'.[9]

Young makes this point in *Torn Halves*, a collection of essays in which he traces the dialectical form of such conflicts as they occur across a range of recent controversies in literary and cultural theory (although, interestingly, he does not concentrate specifically on cultural studies). Yet as the above quotation indicates, this tension is not something that lies merely at the heart of most recent academic work on literature and culture; this dialectical structure is also the 'secret doubled logic' (5) which governs capitalism itself:

> Far from ever collapsing from contradiction, it becomes increasingly clear that capitalism works most effectively through its contradictions . . . open up 'emerging markets' (the banks' and brokers' term for much of the former Third World) for investment, extol the virtues of the introduction of free-market economies throughout the world. But as soon as an economy or currency threatens to collapse, forget *laissez-faire* and arrange for interven-tion: call in the IMF and World Bank to prop it up with loans, the conditions for which allow the West to dictate its own terms for political freedoms or repression, according to investors' requirements. The free market only works properly by being carefully controlled. The same contra-dictory structure works at the interface of ideology and economics: formerly it was most glaringly evident in irreconcilable moralities of the home and the market-place. Today it is equally visible in the way in which the demand for human rights, free speech and democratic institutions is directed at totalitarian governments as a matter of humanistic Western virtue, the minimum values necessary for a civilized society; yet, the introduction of human rights, political choice, and freedom also functions as the stealthy vanguard, the necessary requisite at the level of freedom, to produce the identificatory needs of consumer capitalism, destroying social forms of identity and creating a demand that enables outside politico-economic control through the introduction of a free-market economy, the opening up

of new markets to corporate Western capitalism, the importation of Western consumer goods, and the parallel exploitation of new sources of cheap labour. (4)

Not only would attempting to chart the history of this debate by outlining the practices or methodologies of one side in relation to the other be to take little account of the way in which, although they may *appear* to be dialectically opposed, both sides in this dispute are in fact equally important to the continuation of cultural criticism in its present form, as is the antagonism between them, such an approach would also run the risk of overlooking the extent to which contemporary cultural criticism, by adopting such a dialectical form, repeats and reinforces the 'radical logic of incompatibility between centrifugal and centripetal forces, simultaneously forcing cultures and peoples together as it pulls others apart, [which] operates as the cultural and economic dynamic of late capitalist society' itself (8). In fact it is the failure to realize this, I want to suggest, that *has* led cultural studies to remain to all intents and purposes trapped in the impasse with political economy, unable to think a way out.

3rd possibility: Nowhere is this more apparent than in the main defence of the field that has been put forward in the last few years, and which represents the third of the three possible futures I began by alluding to. The argument here is that cultural studies is indeed *not* a homogeneous body of work, and that a lot of cultural studies does not automatically associate the popular with pleasure and political resistance. On the contrary cultural studies, in Grossberg's words, 'often recognizes that pleasure can be manipulated by or at least articulated to forms of power and existing structures of inequality'.[10] Despite the way in which it is often portrayed Angela McRobbie thus insists that cultural studies has not 'abandoned all commitment to understanding relations of power and powerlessness, dominance and subordination as they are expressed in culture'.[11] Instead, many of the criticisms emanating from the direction of political economy are regarded as being based on partial and selective readings – usually, as David Morley has said, of 'John Fiske's popularization of certain aspects of de Certeau's work'.[12] These function according to a procedure Morley encapsulates rather nicely whereby:

> having identified some particular case in which consumer/audience 'activity' is uncritically celebrated by an author with cultural studies allegiances, they then retrospectively declare that this is the kind of (bad) thing to which cultural studies, in general, was bound to lead, and that therefore (conveniently reversing the terms of the argument) we can now see that the whole

cultural studies enterprise was, from the start, misconceived – as it has (in fact) led to whatever example of bad practice they have identified.[13]

Among other things such critiques are perceived as having failed to take into account both the extent to which such points have already been raised within cultural studies,[14] and the important work that is already being done within the field on questions of economics and production.

From this point of view cultural studies should continue with the kind of theoretical investigations into the complex and often contradictory nature of consumption, representation, pleasure and subjectivity which were so characteristic of the field in the 1980s and throughout much of the 1990s. Responding to the force of those arguments which have condemned cultural studies for being little more than an apology for consumer capitalism, however, this approach is now tempered by the insistence that cultural studies practitioners must at the same time pay more attention to sociological questions. Still, a number of issues remain. Not least is that which concerns how such questions are to be articulated into analyses of culture, and particularly cultural studies, with its use of poststructuralism and psychoanalysis, and emphasis on difference, subjectivity and pleasure. For it is not just carelessness on cultural studies' part that has led so-called 'concrete' sociological and empirical modes of inquiry to be (relatively) underprivileged in recent years. As we have already seen, cultural studies' interrogation of the authority and legitimacy of academic scholarship and research and its questioning of notions of critical distance and cultural value has meant such work is often regarded as being too essentialist, reductionist and reflectionist. Integrating social science approaches with their emphasis on economics and production into cultural studies' theoretically inflected analysis is thus not quite the simple task it is often presented as being in such arguments. Indeed (and to take just one example), for Ernesto Laclau a theory of subjectivity cannot be added to Marxism (and therefore by extension political economy, for which Marxism, as we shall see, continues to play a fundamental if somewhat under-articulated role), as 'the latter has been constituted, by and large, as a negation . . . of subjectivity'.[15] How, then, is such a combination of Marxism and psychoanalysis, politics and theory, political economy and cultural studies, as it were, to be achieved within cultural studies?

For all the heated – and, yes, at times rather ill-tempered – discussion that has taken place in recent years over the value and future of cultural studies, insufficient time and effort has been given over in this context to considering this question. No doubt there are a number of reasons for this, including the way in which, as Morley and others suggest, those on the political economy side of the fence *have* often been too partial and selective in their readings of cultural studies, and *have* tended to concentrate primarily on those instances which *do* appear to emphasize the power of the consumer to the exclusion of the social and the economic. But all the blame cannot be laid at the door of the political economists. That continuing with this debate is regarded by many of those associated with cultural studies as a 'boring' thing to do is also a factor. From the latter standpoint, cultural studies is perceived as having spent far too much time deliberating over what it is or should be, and not enough getting on with the job in hand, 'combining clear-headed political analysis with an understanding of the importance of cultural forms', as Mc-Robbie puts it, which is the *real* business of cultural studies apparently.[16] Even when those in cultural studies *have* turned their attention to the problem of its relation to economics and production, a lot of energy seems to have been taken up with countering the charges of the political economists and others – to the extent that one of the main functions of this 'defence' appears to be to act as a means of deflecting criticism elsewhere. (It's as though the priority of many cultural studies practitioners is to say to their critics: 'We take your point, but really your complaints are misdirected. It's not us you want. You're talking about someone else' – this someone else again being almost invariably poor John Fiske.) As a consequence, although a number of writers have highlighted certain contemporary work in cultural studies as a way of fending off the various attacks issuing from sections of media studies and the social sciences, not enough emphasis has been placed on exploring the difficult question of exactly how the turn toward sociology and economics in cultural studies is going to work; or even if it is going to work at all.

But regardless of the particular reasons for the lack of attention to this question, it remains the case that without thinking carefully about the 'real business of cultural studies', and in particular about the nature of the relation between cultural studies and political economy, attempts to leave this debate behind by simply *getting on with* cultural studies invariably get caught up in repeating, often without realizing it, the very structure of conflict and antag-onism (with all its attendant problems) that the attempt to 'get on with it' is supposed to be providing a means of moving beyond. And lest I be accused of partiality and selectivity myself, let me try to illustrate what I mean by turning away from vaguely identified bad objects to concentrate on one of the specific places within cultural studies where the argument for getting 'on with the job' by focusing on questions of production and the economic is perceived as having been developed most consistently and effectively in recent years. In his dispute over the future of cultural studies with Nicholas Garnham, Lawrence Grossberg identifies Angela McRobbie, Meaghan Morris, John Clarke, Judith Williamson and himself as people within cultural studies who have criticized it for getting 'caught up in a rather celebratory mode of populism',[17] and Dorothy Hobson, Angela McRobbie, Sean Nixon and Jody Berland as cultural studies practitioners who are now working on questions of production. Only one person's name appears on both of these lists, however. It is therefore to Angela McRobbie's work that I will now turn in order to take a closer look at this 'third way' in cultural studies.

'A NEW KIND OF MATERIALISM'

In a series of essays published over the course of the mid to late 1990s and recently collected in her book *In the Culture Society*, McRobbie makes a strong case for the importance of sociological methods and approaches to cultural studies.[18] 'Social intervention drawing on a cultural studies framework would be easier if even some of the theoretical work carried out in the 1980s had been backed up by more substantial concrete research', she argues in 'All the World's A Stage, Screen or Magazine':[19]

> We need to be able to do more than analyse the texts, we need data, graphs, ethnographies, facts and figures. It is unfortunate that debates on these kinds of questions have been so bifurcated along the lines of those on the side of political economy against those on the side of meaning and consumption (Garnham, 1995; Grossberg, 1995). There are in fact many points of intervention and analysis which neither of these approaches has as yet fully explored. (341)

McRobbie does not mean by this that 'those raves from the grave', what she calls 'the three Es: empiricism, ethnography and the category of experience' are merely raised from the dead: the impact of psychoanalytic and post-structuralist theory has been too great for that. Instead, by reconceptualizing the three Es 'in the light of the "anti-Es" (anti-essentialism, post-structuralism, psychoanalysis)' (338), McRobbie hopes that at least one strand of cultural studies will be able to position itself in the policy field, something she sees as missing from cultural studies as it currently stands.

The latter situation has arisen because too often in the past cultural studies critics have associated issues of cultural policy with being incorporated into contemporary capitalism's culture of lottery and corporate sponsorship. They have therefore preferred to focus instead on those forms of culture they hold as being marginal to, or outside of, the arena of state subsidy and industry sponsorship. Because the emphasis in such work has been on the end result, the finished product, and in particular the way in which it is consumed, little attention has been paid to the 'precise practices of cultural production' and the 'micro-economics' that make such culture possible. It is to these micro-processes that cultural studies now needs to start paying attention, McRobbie contends, if it is to understand the 'precise scale of the transition to a market economy' brought about in recent years (336).

But if McRobbie is critical of the previous practices of cultural studies she is equally critical of those of cultural policy. The latter she regards as having 'been concerned with either supporting culture as a kind of amateur or indigenous activity, or else with providing culture, or access to it'. The vision of society's social structure which lies beneath the first is now well past its sell by date. 'Where substantial numbers of people produce their own cultural forms using, for example, camcorders, with skill and expertise, and where broadcast TV like *Video Nation* or *Video Diaries* taps into the home video market, it is inappropriate to cast ordinary people in a purely recipient category or amateur role' (338), she argues. There are also problems with the second as the market often seems to be better than the public sector at providing both access to culture and culture itself:

> It is easier for a busy mother to buy a paperback on the way home from work than to get to the library after work, borrow a number of books and then remember to return them on time. Likewise it is easier and less exhausting to wait for a good film to come out on video at the local Blockbusters store than it is to get and pay for a babysitter, go out to the cinema and then arrange for the babysitter to get home safely. (338)

Taken together these changes mean that the attention of cultural studies needs to be directed not just toward the consumption of culture, but to culture as a 'substantial sector of the economy, a sizeable mode of production, and also a field of employment, increasingly of self-employment' (338).

In pushing for cultural studies to pay more attention to practices of cultural production, McRobbie is careful to distinguish her argument from that of earlier critics such as Frith and Savage, who in their infamous 1992 essay 'Pearls and Swine' attacked much of the cultural studies work produced in the 1980s for its over-emphasis on consumption. For Frith and Savage, the media, and with it the sort of style journalism that developed in the Thatcher years, are almost exclusively the bastions of the new right, and they condemn cultural studies – which they regard as the 'spawning ground' for much of this new right style journalism and media output – accordingly, for having abandoned the rigorous critique of capitalist culture in favour of a 'cheerful populism' and a 'new found respect for sales figures'.[20] This sort of approach McRobbie regards as now being obsolete:

Media workers are no longer exclusively Oxbridge elites nor are they necessarily supporters of the new right. Indeed, it would even be difficult to cast them as shining examples of 'enterprise culture'. What we should be talking about instead is a sprawling sector of micro-economics of culture which now traverses the boundaries of social class, ethnicity and gender. Many young working-class people now become self-employed in the cultural field (as 'stylists', make-up artists, or by setting up club nights, or making dance tracks at home in their bedrooms) as an escape from the inevitability of unemployment, or in preference to an unrewarding job in the service sector. In some cases, a desire for and commitment to producing culture in the form of music coincides with a criminal career, as the life histories of so many talented rap artists show. (339)

In an article on 'new sexualities in girls' and women's magazines' originally published in the same year as 'All the World's a Stage . . .', 1996, McRobbie thus finds that 'the language of consumption and production, most often deployed in cultural studies work, is too broad, too general, and for this reason unable to generate a more rigorous account of the complex and multilayered relation between the production of meaning . . . and the diverse ways in which these meanings are consumed by readers'.[21] What is required, she maintains, is a more specific and focused approach of the kind she identifies in the writings of Sean Nixon, Paul du Gay and Keith Negus, cultural studies scholars who 'have recently insisted not only on a return to more detailed study of the culture industries, but also to a more nuanced and less monolithic approach' (179). McRobbie advocates that the 'idea that production and consumption can be neatly understood as mechanical and parallel activities' be abandoned. Instead, she sees Nixon's research in particular as pointing to the importance of analysing the 'multiple and uneven practices' which make up cultural production (179).

It is important for McRobbie, then, that policy-orientated work is brought back into the fold of a cultural studies which has not devoted enough time to questions of economics and production, and which has instead concentrated on the 'meaning, significance and consumption of [cultural] forms once they are already in circulation'.[22] And certainly the 'new kind of materialism' McRobbie outlines in these articles appears to bring with it a number of benefits and advantages for cultural studies.[23] Not only is this 'new materialism' much more concerned with specificities and complexities, thus avoiding many of the sweeping generalizations of the more 'monolithic' approaches to culture associated with the social sciences; it also usefully draws attention to the way in which, as Meaghan Morris has insisted, production and consumption are much more complicated and less stable concepts than a lot of cultural analysis otherwise seems to allow.[24] As McRobbie observes in another essay from 1996 in which she reflects on the recent history of cultural studies and its concern with consumption and the power of the consumer:

> Morris argues for a greater consideration to be given to the re-integration of the economics of culture than a reworked version of the old base-superstructure model allows . . . What Morris is suggesting here is that the whole idea of production and consumption being stable and somehow fixed processes needs to be revised.[25]

Nevertheless, for all her emphasis on particularities and specificities and the way in which production and consumption are, in Morris' phraseology, now somewhat 'anachronistic terms', it is questionable to what extent McRobbie actually provides a means of overcoming the bifurcation between cultural studies and political economy, theory and concrete sociological research she regards as creating so many difficulties for the study of culture.

To be sure, McRobbie acknowledges many of the problems that have been raised for empiricism, ethnography and the category of experience (the 'three Es') by post-structuralism and psychoanalysis (McRobbie's 'anti-Es'), includ-ing the 'exposing of these sites of "truth" and "knowledge" as artificially coherent narrative fictions';[26] and she limits the scale and scope of 'the three Es' accordingly. What she does *not* provide in these essays is an account of how empiricism, ethnography and experience can be 'reconceptualized' by 'the anti-Es' so that the 'gap' between economic and 'textual' analyses *can* be 'bridged', and these conflicting approaches to culture *can* be thought together as part of what she obviously regards as a more informed and useful cultural studies, one which *will* be able to engage effectively with issues of policy. Instead, her focus is predominantly on the exclusion of sociological questions from cultural studies. Cultural studies needs to do more empirical research and to reinstate ethnography 'despite and in response to Clifford's testimony to its poetic character' (338), she argues. And again, '[d]espite all the problems of dealing with "personal accounts" as evidence, testimony or simply data, it still seems worthwhile to me to ask how these cultural workers experience this form of economic activity' (339). '[E]ven if these facts and figures are "fictions"', as she puts it in a slightly later essay, 'they are useful fictions and the extent to which current talk about consumer cultures is ungrounded by sustained historical or sociological research seriously weakens the case of those who suggest the political mobilization that can be done around consumption'.[27] Rather than reconceptualizing the three Es in the light of the anti-Es, then, the 'real issue' for McRobbie is that 'a good deal of . . . consumerist studies remain sociologically ungrounded' (38). Consequently, while she is critical of those approaches which try to privilege one side in this tense relationship to the exclusion of the other, and while she is able to talk quite clearly about why it is important that at least one strand of cultural studies is able to locate itself in the fields of political economy and social policy,[28] and why there should be a 'dialogue' between 'materialists' and 'culturalists',[29] at no point in any of these essays does she address the *real* real issue, which is how is this going to be achieved? How are questions of sociology and economics to be articulated into analyses of culture and the study of production 're-integrated' (41) with the study of consumption? What exactly is the nature of the relation between these conflicting modes of thought here?

(IR)RECONCILING THE IRRECONCILABLE

Nor is McRobbie any more successful in this respect in her more recent work. I am thinking of two essays in particular: her 'Afterword: In Defence of Cultural Studies',[30] which was written especially for inclusion in *In the Culture Society* and with which she closes that section of the book given over specifically to the discussion of contemporary debates in cultural studies; and an article on 'Feminism and the Third Way' which appeared in the journal *Feminist Review* in 2000, a year after the publication of *In the Culture Society*.[31] In the first of these McRobbie takes a number of cultural studies' latest critics, including Ferguson and Golding (whose work is itself, for McRobbie, a culmination of that earlier stage of critique set in motion by Frith and Savage's essay), Miller and Philo, Garnham and Mulhern to task for not dealing directly with what she sees as the issue underlying all these conflicts: 'the pivotal position occupied by Marxism (and to a lesser extent feminism)' (100). Placing the debate over cultural studies in the wider context of a general 'crisis' in Marxism, McRobbie draws attention to the way in which, although these critics condemn cultural studies writing on subjectivity and difference and feminist work on pleasure for moving away from Marxism and a concern for fundamental social structures (and the inequalities therein), they themselves do not provide an indication of how their own mode of analysis (whatever it is since, as McRobbie observes, the 'Marxism' of these critics invariably 'remains completely undiscussed' (100)) can address the broadening out of cultural and political theory, from an initial concern primarily with class and economics, to take in questions of gender and sexuality, race and ethnicity. With respect to race and ethnicity, for example, McRobbie makes it clear how:

Neither [Ferguson and Golding], Miller and Philo or Mulhern demonstrate in their various essays any willingness to engage with the new arguments around race and ethnicity and the enormous impact they have had in shaping the cultural studies field . . . Instead there is a suggestion that by focusing on notions of difference, by introducing aspects of psychoanalysis, and by being over-concerned with texts, representations and meaning, writers like [Said and Gilroy] have given up all interest in where the roots of racial oppression really lie, which according to Garnham is in the international labour market. (99)

McRobbie thus places a question mark against Garnham's proposed solution to the problem of cultural studies' relation to political economy, which involves bringing about some sort of 'reconciliation' between them.[32] Clearly, such a reconciliation is only possible for Garnham on the grounds that differences of race and ethnicity are subordinated to the higher category of class and economics (Garnham conflates the latter two, as Grossberg notes).[33] But if Ferguson and Golding, Miller and Philo, Mulhern and Garnham offer no 'engagement with what is at stake in retaining a commitment to Marxism in the late 1990s' (100), a similar complaint can be levelled at McRobbie. Although she criticizes Ferguson and Golding *et al.* for marginalizing issues of gender and sexuality, race and ethnicity, she herself neglects to show how these 'new arguments' can be conjoined with a continuing commitment, if not to Marxism necessarily (although, as we shall see, given her conclusion this is still an issue), then certainly to an emphasis on economics and production.

The nearest McRobbie gets to this in her 'Afterword' is in her conclusion. Here she provides an account of a response by Judith Butler to repudiations of identity politics in the US – attacks McRobbie sees as synonymous with those directed at cultural studies in the UK.[34] For many on the left in America identity politics is perceived as a 'retreat from real, materialist politics in favour of something more individualist and life style-related'. For McRobbie, however, such attacks are a means of 'resisting the current uncertainty about political priorities' (105). She does not make this point in a spirit of chastisement: her focus is on the 'disunity among the academic left and the need to urgently re-establish shared political and intellectual priorities'. But how can this be done, she asks, if 'no such clear set of priorities can be arrived at'? McRobbie endeavours to answer this question by drawing on Butler's analysis of the way in which the 'proliferation in recent years of social movements for whom material and symbolic injustices are interwoven do not add up to some hierarchy of the oppressed' (105). The task in the 'post-Marxist era is to recognize the diffusion of different political movements (which means alliances rather than faith in eventual unity) and to conceptualize these movements so as to broaden the span of radical democracy'. In particular, Butler condemns the 'bifurcation of sexuality into a separate [cultural] sphere' inherent in these arguments on account of its jettisoning of 'sexuality from the sphere of fundamental political structure', a manoeuvre she regards as enabling the 'energy, dynamism and theoretical challenge of queer politics and scholarship' to be contained (105).

Transferring Butler's analysis into the context of the conflict over the value and future of cultural studies, McRobbie draws attention to the way Miller and Philo, as well as Ferguson and Golding, have, in their 'bid for power' and desire to be 'listened to by the new Labour government . . . as experts and spokespersons for media studies' (106), attempted to 'define the territory and police the boundaries of both media and cultural studies' by means of a 'caricaturing, demeaning and domestication of difference'. Accordingly, McRobbie argues against this marginalization of culture and difference from cultural and media studies. However, while I wouldn't disagree with McRobbie on this point, this still doesn't explain: firstly, how these 'new arguments' around gender and sexuality, race and ethnicity, even if they are no longer excluded, are to operate in an 'alliance' with the continuing commitment to some form of Marxism (as opposed to post-Marxism) of Ferguson and Golding *et al.*; and, secondly, how economics and production are to be articulated into analyses of culture? Once again cultural criticism appears to be caught in a tension between continually trying to think both together while ultimately being unable to do so: between, on the one hand, attempting to combine cultural studies and political economy in a totalizing unity in which one category, *class*, subsumes all others, thus negating their differences (the solution proposed by the 'political economists'); and, on the other, refusing any such overarching unity in favour of a diffuse, detotalized alliance of different political and social movements in which the category of class is positioned as being just one among a number of often conflicting others (McRobbie's approach in this essay). The problem with the former is that cultural studies and political economy are not united: instead, as McRobbie shows, cultural studies' emphasis on difference and diversity is subsumed into political economy's stress on the primacy of class and labour inequalities. The problem with the latter is that cultural studies and political economy are not allied: because by refusing the primacy of class and economics in favour of difference and diversity, the Marxism of political economy becomes in effect a post-Marxism and is thus removed from the relation; but also because no account is given of what it is that actually holds cultural studies and political economy together in such a scenario. And without an answer to this question it is hard to see how they are going to operate in an alliance as opposed to continuing in their current state of conflict and 'divorce'.

Despite being one of the places which is repeatedly cited by those wishing to defend cultural studies from the charges of the social scientists as a prime

example of cultural studies getting 'on with the job' by focusing on questions
of production and the economic (it is to McRobbie's work that Lawrence
Grossberg also advises us to look for a consideration of the place of economics
within cultural studies in his introduction to *Bringing it all Back Home*),[35]
McRobbie's attempt to escape the impasse between cultural studies and
political economy by bringing methods and approaches associated with sociology and the social sciences to bear on cultural studies actually remains trapped
in the very logic of late capitalism it is trying to find a means of analysing.
Indeed, far from enabling cultural critics to provide a more detailed and all-
encompassing critique of capitalism, the sort of dialectical approach of which
McRobbie's work is often held as being emblematic[36] repeats the 'radical logic
of incompatibility between centrifugal and centripetal forces . . . [which]
operates as the cultural and economic dynamic of late capitalist society' – and
in doing so 're-enacts and reinforces it'.[37]

McRobbie's article on feminism and the 'Third Way' politics of the current
Labour government in the UK only serves to bring this link between the logic
of late capitalism and her 'new materialism' into further relief. As the ideologi-
cal rationale for New Labour, McRobbie sees the 'Third Way' as the government's means of resolving 'the tensions around women and social policy'.
Endeavouring to combine aspects of left social democracy with right neoliberalism, the Labour government 'wants to see women as a social group
move more fully into employment . . . At the same time it wants to see through
further transformations of the welfare state, along the lines set in motion by
Mrs Thatcher'.[38] McRobbie thus presents the Third Way as an attempt to
combine two opposing, and indeed, contradictory positions, as the 'former
principle is [clearly] made more difficult by the latter policy' which 'inevitably
. . . involves further cuts in spending' on the likes of child care provision and
subsidies for education and training (97). But is this not analogous to what
McRobbie herself is attempting with regard to cultural studies? Granted:

> . . . the Third Way in practice appears to mean pursuing the politics of
> triangulation which has been a hallmark of the Clinton administration in
> the US. Right and left are 'appeased' on the basis of the implementation of
> both right and left policies. The role of the Third Way is therefore to give
> distinctive shape and character to New Labour's policies, and to 'brand'
> them as different from old Labour. (106)

Yet can't McRobbie be said to be pursuing a similar politics with her so-called
'new materialism'? Aren't both sides here, too, ' "appeased" on the basis of the
implementation of both . . . policies', that of cultural studies and political
economy? Just as New Labour is attempting to find a middle way between 'the

excesses of free market economics and the so-called rigidity of state-led social democracy' (101), isn't McRobbie likewise trying to 'reconcile the irreconcilable' (100), Marxism and psychoanalysis, politics and theory, political economy and cultural studies, in an attempt to produce a 'third way' in cultural studies? Certainly, it seems possible to describe the role of McRobbie's 'new materialism' in similar terms: as being 'to give distinctive shape and character' to cultural studies' 'new' policies, and to 'brand' them as different from the cultural studies of old (i.e. that stereotypically associated with Fiske) (106).

II: 'SOMETHING ELSE BESIDES'

It is tempting to conclude at this point with a few remarks regarding the consequences of all this for cultural studies; and especially the idea that the difficulties encountered in the dispute with political economy can be overcome by the (re)introduction into cultural studies of elements of sociology and the social sciences. On this evidence, neither cultural studies, nor political economy, nor some dialectical combination of the two, appears capable of providing a means of escaping the current impasse in cultural criticism. Instead, all three (including what I have characterized as the 'third way' in cultural studies, represented here chiefly by McRobbie's 'new materialism') remain trapped in contemporary capitalism's irreconcilable dynamic. But if cultural studies, for McRobbie, cannot be conflated into an 'undifferentiated and uncritical monolith', neither can her own recent writing.[39] To be sure, the latter, given the importance that has generally been attached to it, provides a strategically useful means of illustrating the manner in which the 'third way' approach to the future of cultural studies merely repeats the cultural and economic dynamic of late capitalism. However, it is still possible to catch a glimpse of a very different future for cultural studies in her work. And, ironically, according to McRobbie it is with 'theory' – in the shape of what she refers to as the anti-Es: 'anti-essentialism, post-structuralism and psychoanalysis' – that this possibility seems to lie.

I say *ironically* because to date most of the emphasis in this debate, even within cultural studies, has been on moving away from 'theory' and 'back to reality'[40] and what McRobbie calls the 'three Es': the empirical, the ethnographic and the experiential – albeit in McRobbie's case the three Es after they have been 'reconceptualized' by the anti-Es. The problem of course is that, as we have seen, such is her preoccupation with the 'sociologically ungrounded' nature of much recent cultural studies that as far as the majority of McRobbie's work is concerned the three Es are not reconceptualized with any degree of rigour. As a consequence her version of cultural studies remains trapped in the tension between cultural studies and political economy the return to 'reality' sets up and which her reconceptualization of the three Es is positioned as a means of resolving. And yet thus far I have left out of my analysis any consideration of that text in which McRobbie can perhaps be said to go furthest toward reconceptualizing the three Es. This is her 1997 essay on 'The Es and the anti-Es', which is also included in *In the Culture Society* but which was, interestingly enough, first published as her contribution to Ferguson and Golding's *Cultural Studies in Question*.[41] By turning our attention to this essay, it is possible to see that although in the end many of the same problems remain, by drawing on theory, and deconstruction in particular, McRobbie is nevertheless able to provide an indication of at least one way in which we might begin to think through the impasse between cultural studies and political economy.

MORE 'NEW QUESTIONS FOR FEMINISM AND CULTURAL STUDIES'

McRobbie describes her intention in 'The Es and the anti-Es' as being twofold: to address the possible consequences of recent poststructuralist and post-colonialist writing – particularly the 'deconstructive exercises' of Judith Butler and Gayatri Spivak – for what she loosely terms 'feminist cultural studies'; and to explore the possibility of using this work to 'inject some renewed intellectual energy into those areas which cultural studies has, over the last few years, neglected', by which McRobbie means sociological questions, particularly those which have a bearing on matters of policy (170). By tracing the recent history of feminist debates over culture she is able to illustrate how the latter has tended to get stuck in a series of rigid binary oppositions between 'those for whom the category of "woman" represents an unproblematic and fixed set of meanings which are understood and shared by all who count themselves as female (the essentialists)' and those 'who see the category of "woman" as continually contested' (the anti-essentialists) (173). From this starting point McRobbie proceeds to show how the deconstructive feminism of Butler and Spivak provides a rigorous rethinking of feminist cultural studies which 'forces feminism to confront its own, often invisible boundaries and limits' (175). At the same time as she points to Spivak's 'strategic use of essentialism' – 'which grants feminism the authority to speak on behalf of a "global sisterhood"' (176) – McRobbie also draws on Butler's notion of 'the category of woman [as] fluid' in order to assert that 'there can be no natural female body'.[42] Gender here is instead 'unstable', 'a performance enacted on a daily basis' (177). In this way McRobbie is able to demonstrate how deconstruction, as a theory which does not set such apparently antagonistic positions up in a relation of conflict with one another but shows how they can function in a productive, if irresolvable, tension, is able to help us think through the rationalist logic of contradiction between totalization and detotalization, at least as it is played out in the sphere of 'feminist cultural studies'. It does so by holding both essentialism and anti-essentialism together at the same time in a productive economy, an economy in which their irreconcilable differences are neither subsumed into some all encompassing collective unity based on some notion of there being 'a truth of womanhood', nor left in the sort of debilitating 'disunity' which for many is likely 'to follow from the disaggregation of the category of women' (185).

I should perhaps just make clear that in drawing attention to this aspect of McRobbie's thought I'm not suggesting that the deconstructive critic's relation to the logic of capitalism is one of privilege: that it is only deconstructive writers and their followers who can really appreciate the ambivalent logic of late capitalism. That would take us back to a form of nostalgia for the lost position of the idealist intellectual.[43] Instead, as Robert Young has shown, the very 'scission within culture, between cultural forms, allows not a transcendental point for the critic but a differential reversible fulcrum from which critique can be constructed':

Just as it is not the choice between different forms of culture, high or low, in themselves but their estranged division that represents the critical potential for cultural criticism, so too is it not totalization or detotalization in itself that holds radical potential, but the opening of an incompatible division between the two. It is in the split itself, the hinge between these two dissonant movements that the cultural critic needs to be located.[44]

And while it is certainly the case that, by 'suggesting that any position can "articulate itself only in and through an ambivalent relation to an other that it can neither fully assimilate nor totally exclude"',[45] deconstruction (along with psychoanalysis, and indeed Marxism)[46] can help us to identify and exploit this scission between totalization and detotalization, essentialism and anti-essentialism, deconstruction as Derrida himself reminds us is 'nothing by itself'.[47] Deconstruction is only able to do so by means of its reading of, and engagement with, other discourses.

Nor, by the same token, should any of this be taken as implying that cultural studies has up until now been somehow unaffected by that body of work known as 'deconstruction', and that it is only with McRobbie that it has been made use of within cultural studies. There are a number of people in cultural studies who, even though they might not necessarily attach the label 'deconstruction' to their work, can nonetheless be described as having employed certain 'deconstructive' ideas and strategies – and even as having produced recognizable 'deconstructions'. The work of Stuart Hall, Paul Gilroy, Henry A. Giroux, Dick Hebdige, John Frow, bell hooks, Meaghan Morris and Henry Louis Gates all comes to mind. McRobbie is certainly quite right to describe the work of Hebdige in *Subculture: The Meaning of Style*, and before that, of Hall and Jefferson in *Resistance Through Rituals*, as not being a million miles away from 'Butler's notion of sexual re-signification', for example (182). Nevertheless, cultural studies *has* tended to take on board only those aspects of deconstructive theory it can incorporate into its already existing political project; those elements which might force cultural studies to fundamentally reconceive the terms of its own theory all too often remaining excluded. And, indeed, for all her use of deconstruction to draw attention to the 'often invisible boundaries and limits' of feminism, it is noticeable that McRobbie endeavours to keep deconstruction within specific boundaries and limits. At the same time as she acknowledges the usefulness of the deconstructive theory of Butler and Spivak in helping to liberate feminism from the 'earlier fantasies of freedom, unity and universal sisterhood' of 'more activist forms of feminism' (178), McRobbie thus criticizes Derrida and other 'deconstructionists' for producing texts written in an highly impenetrable and intimidating manner. 'To the sociologist or cultural studies feminist concerned with making ideas accessible to a wider audience, this can seem like a real abrogation of political responsibility', she writes (185). (The last section of McRobbie's book is given over to putting forward her ideas in a way she believes is more accessible to students.) In particular, McRobbie accuses those in the anti-Es of exclusivity, and of not paying enough attention to the processes whereby their ideas might be translated and so have a 'broader political impact':

> More attention might therefore be paid to the practical mechanisms through which, for example, Homi Bhabha's or Dick Hebdige's writing is taken up and used in Isaac Julien's films, or for that matter how [Judith] Butler's ideas find their way into discussions, debates and interviews in the gay and lesbian press. This at least would demonstrate that high theory can have relevance to cultural and political practice. (186)

Rather than drawing on what theory and deconstruction has to say about politics and responsibility,[48] then, in order to re-examine, and dare I say it 'reconceptualize', the relation between theory and political practice, the 'Es' and the 'anti-Es', McRobbie merely endeavours to place deconstruction at the *service* of politics by bringing it into dialogue with other stands within cultural studies (i.e. the three Es) so that it may be of more practical political value when intervening 'in cultural and social policy issues'. Witness her desire to extract from 'a sustained and rigorous poststructuralism' some 'note of political hope and some prospect of human agency' (182). McRobbie consequently remains trapped in the incompatible dialectical tension between theory and politics, cultural studies and political economy. And yet her turn to theory in this essay does seem to offer a glimpse of at least one way in which the impasse between cultural studies and political economy might be thought through. And in this respect McRobbie's idea of examining the consequences of recent poststructuralist and postcolonialist writing for cultural studies is far more radical than she seems to realize or allow. For if we follow the logic of McRobbie's suggestion we quickly find that the sort of reconceptualizing of the three Es McRobbie looks toward in 'The Es and the anti-Es' goes much further than her attempt to simply 'connect or culturally translate between theory and practice' (182) by showing how 'poststructuralism can be made use of more productively' (170).

CULTURAL STUDIES
(ANGELA McROBBIE/JACQUES DERRIDA MIX)

For the sake of economy let's focus on just the first of McRobbie's examples: the writing of Homi Bhabha. Isaac Julien has of course spoken interestingly of Bhabha's (and indeed Hebdige's) influence on the Sankofa film and video workshop.[49] But even the briefest examination of Bhabha's work is enough to place a question mark against the notion that his ideas need to be 'translated' in some way so that they can have a 'broader political impact' (186), and that this process should be highlighted so the relevance of 'high theory' to cultural and practical practice can be demonstrated. Take the following passage from an essay, first published in 1988, in which Bhabha very much confirms his own 'commitment to theory'. Here Bhabha states that his concern is with:

the process of 'intervening ideologically', as Stuart Hall describes the role of 'imagining' or representation in the practice of politics in his response to the British election of 1987. For Hall, the notion of hegemony implies a politics of *identification* of the imaginary. This occupies a discursive space which is not exclusively delimited by the history of either the right or the left. It exists somehow in-between these political polarities, and also between the familiar divisions of theory and political practice. This approach, as I read it, introduces us to an exciting, neglected moment, or movement, in the 'recognition' of the relation of politics to theory; and confounds the traditional distinct between them.[50]

Given this interest in a politics which 'exists . . . between the familiar divisions of theory and political practice' and which 'confounds the traditional distinction between them', any attempt to put Bhabha's theory into the service of an already decided upon political position or project would appear to have somewhat missed the point. As Bhabha himself puts it a little later in the same essay:

> A critical discourse does not yield a *new* political object, or aim, or knowledge, which is simply a mimetic reflection of an *a priori* political principle or theoretical commitment. We should not demand of it a pure teleology of analysis whereby the prior principle is simply augmented, its rationality smoothly developed, its identity as socialist or materialist (as opposed to neo-imperialist or humanist) consistently confirmed in each oppositional stage of the argument. Such identikit political idealism may be the gesture of great individual fervour, but it lacks the deeper, if dangerous, sense of what is entailed by the *passage* of history in theoretical discourse. The language of critique is effective not because it keeps forever separate the terms of the master and the slave, the mercantilist and the Marxist, but to the extent to which it overcomes the given grounds of opposition and opens up a space of translation: a place of hybridity, figuratively speaking, where the construction of a political object that is new, *neither the one nor the other*, properly alienates our political expectations, and changes, as it must, the very forms of our recognition of the moment of politics . . .
>   . . . In such a discursive temporality, the event of theory becomes the *negotiation* of contradictory and antagonistic instances that open up hybrid sites and objectives of struggle, and destroy those negative polarities between knowledge and its objects, and between theory and practical-political reason. (25)

Nor can Bhabha's writing be said to stay in its theoretical sphere, capable of acting only as, say, a 'critique, as a warning device, a cautionary practice' (unless, that is, someone like McRobbie comes along to translate it and demonstrate its hitherto hard to recognize relevance to cultural and political practice presumably).[51] Rather, it constitutes an attempt to rearticulate or translate the elements that lie on either side of the theory/practice, ideas/politics oppositions so that, in the case of a group of women involved in the miners strike in Britain of 1984–5, for example, they are '*neither the One* (unitary working class) *nor the Other* (the politics of gender), *but something else besides*, which contests the terms and territories of both' (28). As Bhabha himself puts it with respect to his own work, 'it is precisely that popular binarism between theory and politics, whose foundational basis is a view of knowledge as totalizing generality and everyday life as experience, subjectivity or false consciousness, that I have tried to erase' (30).

Analyses similar to this could, I believe, be developed with regard to the writings of Dick Hebdige and Judith Butler. (Having said that, it is of course worth emphasizing the importance of not generalizing here: just as cultural studies is not a unified field, neither is what McRobbie terms 'high theory'. Although McRobbie makes a number of slides between what she calls 'anti-essentialism', poststructuralism, postcolonialism, deconstruction and psycho-analysis, these 'theories' – even presuming 'anti-essentialism' and 'post-structuralism' *are* identifiable and recognizable modes of thought – are very different from each other. Likewise, the three thinkers McRobbie refers to, Bhabha, Hebdige and Butler, are in no sense identical: there are many points of similarity and difference between them. And all this is complicated still further by the way in which, as Judith Butler notes, the line between cultural studies and cultural theory is itself blurred and problematic. So much so that it becomes hard to tell whether her 'own work or the work of Homi Bhabha, Gayatri Chakravorty Spivak or Slavoj Žižek, belongs to cultural studies or critical theory'.)[52] But for the time being at least analyses of the thought of Hebdige and Butler seem unnecessary, as we can already see theory presenting a challenge to the second part of McRobbie's twofold intention in 'The Es and the anti-Es': that which involves using 'this work to inject some renewed intellectual energy' into cultural studies so that the latter might have a (more) practical, political effect. We cannot 'return to the "three Es", the empirical, the ethnographic and the experiential', on the basis of insight gained from 'theory' – an aim which underpins McRobbie's essay and in many ways her whole project in *In the Culture Society*. We cannot do so because it is the dialectical impulse behind this attempt to look toward a 'more applied feminist cultural studies', by using theory to refresh cultural studies and in this way enact a 'reconciliation of sorts between the poststructuralists and those who consider themselves on the side of studying concrete material reality' (170), that theory challenges. As McRobbie's essay demonstrates with regards to issues of gender and sexuality, it is this sort of binary opposition between essentialism and anti-essentialism that theory, and deconstruction in particular, provides us with a means of uncoupling; the difference being that deconstruc-tion does not attempt to stop at uncoupling the 'binary partners of male and female' to make available a 'range of less rigid sexual possibilities' (177), but is also concerned with other oppositions which require rearticulation and reconceptualization (such as that between theory and practice, Marxism and post-Marxism and state-led social democracy and free-market economics – as well as of course that between cultural studies and political economy themselves).

There is thus little point in looking 'outside "theory"', as McRobbie attempts to do, in order to ask some 'practical questions about the world we live in' (170). Theory does not have an 'outside' in any simple sense. In fact it is this very idea of there being an 'outside' to theory (and of course the text) that much of 'poststructuralist' thought endeavours to complicate and bring into question. Nor can the 'deconstructive exercises of these writers' be 'usefully applied' (175) and used 'more productively' in the manner McRobbie suggests (170). Leaving aside for the moment the difficult question of exactly what it means to be 'productive' in such circumstances (there is at the very least a danger of going along with government rhetoric about utility and usefulness),[53] Jacques Derrida has insisted on numerous occasions that decon-struction is not a theory or program that can be simply 'applied' to a given text or object:

> . . . it cannot be applied because deconstruction is not a doctrine; it's not a method, nor is it a set of rules or tools; it cannot be separated from performatives, from signatures, from a given language. So, if you want to 'do deconstruction' – 'you know, the kind of thing Derrida does' – then you have to perform something new, in your own language, in your own singular situation, with your own signature, to invent the impossible and to break with the application, in the technical, neutral sense of the word.[54]

But if '[d]econstruction cannot be applied', neither can it 'not be applied'. Derrida readily acknowledges that if, 'on the one hand, there is no "applied deconstruction" . . . on the other, there is nothing else' precisely because 'deconstruction doesn't consist in a set of theorems, axioms, tools, rules, techniques, methods':

> If deconstruction, then, is nothing by itself, the only thing it can do is apply, to be applied, to something else, not only in more than one language, but also with something else. There is no deconstruction, deconstruction has no specific object, it can refer to, apply to, for example, the Irish problem, the Kabbalah, the problem of nationality, law, architecture, philosophy, amongst other things. It can only apply. (218)

(Which is why, if this chapter is not simply an application of deconstruction, it is not simply *not* an application of deconstruction either.)

If dealing with this 'aporia' is 'what deconstruction is about', according to Derrida, dealing with this aporia is not always what McRobbie is about (218). Although she demonstrates how deconstruction can be used to help explore some of the current problems in cultural studies, McRobbie herself is willing to do this only within certain limits. What is required, on her own account, is a rigorous reconceptualizing of cultural studies which, rather than continually replaying the irreconcilablity of theory and practical politics, cultural studies and political economy, both explicitly recognizes the ambivalent nature of this incompatible dialectic, and provides a means of thinking through their difficult relation by holding both together at the same time in a productive tension, a tension in which their differences are neither subsumed into an all encompassing unity nor left in some debilitating 'disunity'. McRobbie, however, is concerned primarily with issues around feminism, gender and sexuality. She thus in effect represses her own insight into how deconstruction might be helpful when it comes to considering some of the other issues troubling contemporary cultural studies. While she takes enough deconstruction on board to 'uncouple' the male/female and heterosexual/homosexual binaries, she does not take it quite so far as to allow it to fundamentally redefine her overall project in this essay, which in effect sets theory and deconstruction up in an oppositional relation with political practice. In fact, rather than exploiting deconstruction's analysis of this ambivalent relation to produce a theory of cultural studies and political economy's incommensurability (as she does in relation to notions of gender identity, for example), McRobbie avoids the more awkward questions raised by any attempt to reconceptualize the three Es (and by extension cultural studies) in the light of deconstruction by relying, as a way of dealing with the issue, on the very dialectics of cultural criticism deconstruction brings into question.

The result is that McRobbie once again gets caught up in simply reproducing the structure of incompatibility deconstruction, on her own account, theorizes. Her proposed 'solution' to the 'debate' over the value and future of cultural studies in this essay – the 'strategic' use of both of these positions together: the Es and the anti-Es, cultural studies and political economy, theory and political practice (evident in her title – 'The Es and the anti-E's', and in her suggestion that feminist cultural critics can 'perform as empiricists in the public domain when that is appropriate . . . The particular authority of the empirical mode . . . can both be used where appropriate and deconstructed elsewhere for its narratives of truth, its representation of results' (183)) – may thus initially appear as something of an improvement on seeing the two sides as opposed and as mutually exclusive. Yet, and as we have already seen to be the case with regard to McRobbie's later work on identity politics, without an adequate and consciously developed theory of their incommensurable relation it is hard to see how these two positions, rather than just separating out again into their 'original' state of conflict and 'divorce', can actually forge an alliance. (Which is not to say theory and politics, cultural studies and political economy cannot be thought together, although it does mean that they cannot be synthesized; just to point out that their relation is an incommensurable one; and that any attempt to think them together needs to recognize and explicitly thematize this incommensurability before it can do so productively.) McRobbie thus remains trapped in an irreconcilable dialectical logic between totalization and detotalization, between constantly trying to bring these two sides together while at the same time being ultimately unable to do so – a dialectical logic which is also, of course, as Robert Young makes clear, that of late capitalist society – with the result that many of the main difficulties and dilemmas currently facing cultural studies (such as the precise nature of the relation between theory and political practice, subject and object, psyche and the social, agency and structure) remain effectively unaddressed.

Still, what is so interesting about McRobbie's work (and why I have chosen to focus on her writings) is that, at the same time as she remains caught within an interminable dialectical tension between theory and politics, cultural studies and political economy, she is also able to provide us with at least a glimpse of another (but not dialectical, or at any rate not simply dialectical) possible future for cultural studies: one which offers an opportunity to take a chance, to take the risk, of asking certain radical questions regarding cultural studies, of what it is and what it might become; and thus of conceiving cultural studies otherwise, of re-thinking, re-inscribing cultural studies. Indeed, of producing another cultural studies, a cultural studies which is 'neither, the one nor the other', theory nor politics, cultural studies nor political economy, 'textuality' nor 'lived experience', culture nor society, *but something else besides*'.

CHAPTER 4

The (Monstrous) Future of Cultural Studies

> ... the future is necessarily monstrous ... A future that
> would not be monstrous would not be a future; it would be a
> predictable, calculable, and programmable tomorrow.
> (Jacques Derrida)[1]

ONE MORE TIME: THE POLITICS OF CULTURAL STUDIES

'What differentiates cultural studies from, say, philology, biographical criticism, the sociology of art, or American studies?', asks Janice Radway in 'A
Dialogue on Institutionalizing Cultural Studies'. 'For me', it is 'the self-
consciously interested, committed, wholly political nature of cultural studies
[that] marks it off from its predecessors', she continues. 'Indeed, it is cultural
studies' self-construction *as political practice* that I find most exciting'.[2] Meanwhile, in their introduction to *Cultural Studies* Cary Nelson *et al.* go so far as to
suggest that, even though there are many competing ideas as to what it means
to *be* political and to act politically, the one thing on which almost everyone
working in cultural studies appears to agree is that it is, at bottom, a politically
committed body of knowledge. '[I]n virtually all traditions of cultural studies,
its practitioners see cultural studies, not simply as a chronicle of cultural
change but as an intervention in it, and see themselves not simply as scholars
providing an account but as politically engaged participants.'[3] Yet despite this
(or perhaps precisely because of it), one question that is all too rarely addressed
when it comes to thinking about contemporary cultural studies is that which
concerns politics.

At first sight this may seem a strange thing to say. After all (and to take just
one of many possible examples), aren't we witnessing an attempt at the
moment to take cultural studies forward by returning it to a version of the
politics that is seen as lying at its roots? Despite differences in their respective
conceptualizations of politics and what it is exactly that represents acceptable

political affiliation, don't the various parties in the ongoing struggle over the future of cultural studies pride themselves on their political commitment?[4] Isn't this debate in fact precisely a debate over politics? And in a way all this is true. And yet . . .

And yet the very question that is *not* raised in all this is *the question of politics*. Nor *can* it be, for the simple reason that the various participants in this dispute tend to place politics in a transcendental position with respect to other discourses. Politics here is the one thing it is vital to understand, as politics is that by which everything else is judged. But as Geoffrey Bennington has made clear in an analysis of a set-up he identifies as being repeated across a whole range of 'Left criticism', historicism especially, politics is at the same time the one thing that *cannot* be understood; for the one thing that cannot be judged by the transcendentally raised criteria of politics is politics itself. Consequently, the last question these 'political' discourses *can* raise is *the question of politics*.[5]

'Theory', of course, could have helped with this – not least by drawing attention to the general structure of this debate whereby that question it is most important to raise, politics, is precisely that which is excluded from the analysis – if it were not for the fact that it is not theory that is seen as being of primary importance here: it is politics. So not only is the question of politics missing from the terms of the discussion, theory, too, tends to be censored for not being sufficiently political – for not being politics, in effect – only for this repressed to return by virtue of the fact that this argument regarding theory's supposed lack of politics is itself a theoretical argument. (The very discourses that are advocating a return to politics as a way of moving forward in cultural studies are thus recuperated by that which they are attempting to leave behind – theory; only, because of their reluctance to pay attention to theory, this now happens in a somewhat blind and unconscious fashion.) The result is what Bennington describes as an 'interminable self-confident and self-righteous political-cum-cultural-studies-speak' which lacks the necessary 'theoretical sophistication' and self-awareness to even understand its own political and cultural situation, let alone set about changing it (106).

Now, as I said, 'theory' could have helped with all this. But if the question of cultural studies' politics is missing from current discussions over the future of cultural studies, it is hardly any less absent from the majority of recent 'theoretical' responses to cultural studies. To be sure, this general structure, whereby politics is unknowingly treated as a pre-given transcendental category, is one that a number of theorists have identified in cultural studies. Analyses of this kind are especially prevalent among those associated with deconstruction (as the above references to Bennington's work might be taken to suggest). Once cultural studies has been suitably chastised for its sloppy thinking, however, the usual response on the part of such theorists is to turn off *The*

Late Show (or *The Art Zone*, or *Late Review*, or *Newsnight Review*, or whatever its latest incarnation happens to be called) and go and do something more interesting instead – which, in the case of those associated with deconstruction, usually means retreating back into the frontier zone between philosophy and literature from whence they came.[6] And to a certain extent these theorists have a point. When it comes to the question of politics I'm afraid cultural studies *has* been guilty of a certain amount of complacency and lack of rigour. Still, is there not a danger of fixing cultural studies into a rather totalizing and homogenous stereotype? Without doubt literature and philosophy are capable of providing extremely productive ways of thinking about politics. But do such 'deconstructive' approaches to cultural studies not overlook, or ignore, some of the specific and particular ways in which cultural studies may also provide a way of thinking through the problem of the relation between politics and theory? Moreover, no matter how theoretically sophisticated they may be, is there not also a risk of such readings of the openness and ambiguities of literature or philosophy – even the literary or philosophical discourses that lie at the heart of cultural studies – merely confirming the distorted (mis)conceptions many people in cultural studies already have of deconstruction, not least that it is of only limited relevance to their (overtly politically committed) work? In order to displace cultural studies' mistaken perception of deconstruction as a primarily 'theoretical' or 'textual' discourse, is an analysis somewhat 'closer to home' not also needed; one that is perhaps a little harder for cultural studies practitioners to dismiss?

It is just such a 'deconstructive' encounter with cultural studies that I want to stage in this chapter. And I want to start by turning to one of the places in the cultural studies canon where the tension between politics and theory has been most clearly articulated. This is Stuart Hall's much cited 1992 essay 'Cultural Studies and its Theoretical Legacies'.[7] Here, in his own attempt to address the question of cultural studies' future (the 1990 conference in Chicago where Hall first presented this paper was titled 'Cultural Studies Now and in the Future'), Hall reflects on 'certain theoretical moments in cultural studies', going right back to cultural studies' roots as traced by Raymond Williams in 'The Future of Cultural Studies', in order thereby to 'take some bearings on the general question of the politics of theory' (277). Conscious that I cannot provide an exhaustive account of this extraordinarily rich and rightly celebrated text, and aware that a lot of work remains to be done on the many issues it raises, I want to offer what is merely a selective, partial and preliminary contribution to any such future analysis by picking out two moments from 'Cultural Studies and its Theoretical Legacies' as being of particular interest when it comes to the question of the politics of cultural studies. These can be crudely categorized as having to do with the beginning and the end of Hall's essay. And it is with the end that I want to begin, as this is where Hall makes cultural studies most explicitly the object of his own demand for politics.

THE POLITICS OF 'THE POLITICS OF CULTURAL STUDIES'

Hall endeavours to bring 'Cultural Studies and its Theoretical Legacies' to a close by addressing the problem of the institutionalization of British and American cultural studies, and by saying 'something about how the field of cultural studies has to be defined' (285). In doing so, he focuses on what he sees as the astonishing theoretical fluency of American cultural studies, something he regards as going hand in hand with the profound danger of institutionalization:

> Some time ago, looking at what one can only call the deconstructive deluge (as opposed to the deconstructive turn) which had overtaken American literary studies, in its formalist mode, I tried to distinguish the extremely important theoretical and intellectual work which it had made possible in cultural studies from a mere repetition, a sort of mimicry or deconstructive ventriloquism which sometimes passes as a serious intellectual exercise. My fear at that moment was that if cultural studies gained an equivalent institutionalization in the American context, it would, in rather the same way, formalize out of existence the critical questions of power, history and politics. Paradoxically, what I mean by theoretical fluency is exactly the reverse. There is no moment now, in American cultural studies, where we are *not* able, extensively and without end, to theorize power – politics, race, class, and gender, subjugation, domination, exclusion, marginality, Otherness, etc. There is hardly anything in cultural studies which isn't so theorized. And yet, there is this nagging doubt that this overwhelming textualization of cultural studies' own discourses somehow constitutes power and politics as exclusively matters of language and textuality itself. (286)

Although by no means 'anti-theory' (281), Hall thus laments what he perceives as a loss of political commitment on cultural studies' part, and he advocates the return of the project of cultural studies from what he terms in an earlier part of the essay 'the clean air of meaning and textuality and theory to the something nasty down below' – by which he means the '"worldliness"' of cultural studies, its '"political" aspect' (278). This has led Jon Stratton and

Ien Ang to interpret Hall as displaying feelings of regret in this essay regarding the 'Americanization' of cultural studies: 'regret over the loss of a "Birmingham moment" when cultural studies was still a marginalized practice and arguably a more genuinely "political" one as well, when doing cultural studies was not primarily concerned with academic professionalism but connected with and energized by the metaphor of the organic intellectual'.[8] For Stratton and Ang, there 'is a sense in which the Birmingham moment is constructed in this narrative, if not as the origin, then at least as representing a purer, more authentic, more unco-opted mode of cultural studies' (373). But it is not so much the narrative Hall constructs regarding cultural studies' political origins that interests me. Nor is it the myth of marginalization and fear of institutionalization Tony Bennett has identified as accompanying this narrative: the idea that cultural studies was initially 'an autonomous cultural, political and educational project', formed 'outside the institutions and practices of higher education', and that it later became something else upon being institutionally co-opted.[9] Bennett argues forcefully that cultural studies should stop subscribing to this romantic idea that it can be 'somehow outside of or marginal to institutions' (3) – a myth he sees as rendering cultural studies practitioners blind to their own positions in such institutions – and instead take account of how, right from the start, the 'dynamics of higher education have played a key role in shaping the intellectual agendas of cultural studies' (2), in a more 'thoroughly self-conscious and strategic fashion' (3). I will discuss some of the possible consequences for cultural studies of such a self-conscious appreciation of its institutional origins shortly. For the moment I'm more interested in another feature of Hall's argument: his adherence to a certain juxtaposition between politics and theory.

This is particularly evident in the final paragraph of 'Cultural Studies and its Theoretical Legacies' where Hall, in offering some guidelines for cultural studies work in the future, emphasizes the importance of 'organic intellectual political work':

> I come back to the critical distinction between intellectual work and academic work: they overlap, they abut with one another, they feed off one another, the one provides you with the means to do the other. But they are not the same thing. I come back to the difficulty of instituting a genuine cultural and critical practice, which is intended to produce some kind of organic intellectual political work, which does not try to inscribe itself in the overarching metanarrative of achieved knowledges, within the institutions. I come back to theory and politics, the politics of theory. Not theory as the will to truth, but theory as a set of contested, localized, conjunctural knowledges, which have to be debated in a dialogical way. But also as a

practice which always thinks about its intervention in a world in which it would make some difference, in which it would have some effect. Finally, a practice which understands the need for intellectual modesty. I do think there is all the difference in the world between understanding the politics of intellectual work and substituting intellectual work for politics. (286)

Hall is not alone in setting up the relation between theory and politics in this way. This kind of response to what Hall calls 'critical theory' (285) is by now familiar. It is likely to be recognized by anyone who has attended a conference on cultural studies or critical or cultural theory in the last fifteen to twenty years. It is the sort of response which usually begins with a 'Yes, but . . .', before proceeding to add any one of a number of seemingly interchangeable scenarios: 'Yes, but . . . how does that work out in practice?'; 'Yes, but . . . how is that going to affect ordinary kids on the street?'; 'Yes, but . . . what about Northern Ireland?', etc., etc. In each case the argument is the standard one in which theory on its own is seen as not being enough, and in some cases as actually taking away from the 'real' job in hand, which is that of practical, political analysis and intervention. Intellectuals here need to do more than just sit around in their studies and libraries, reading books and writing papers; they need to be capable of having a practical effect on the economic, political and social realities of the 'real world' 'outside'.[10] For all its common currency, however, it is Hall's version of this argument that I want to concentrate on specifically; not least because, as Fredric Jameson contends in his review of *Cultural Studies*, the now canonical book of the Chicago conference in which 'Cultural Studies and its Theoretical Legacies' first appeared (and from the introduction to which my earlier quotation from Cary Nelson *et al.* was also taken), it is this aspect of Hall's essay which perhaps most accurately sums up cultural studies, in many of its more dominant versions at least. 'The desire called Cultural Studies is best approached politically and socially, as the project to constitute a "historic block"', insists Jameson, 'rather than theoretically, as the floor plan for a new discipline'.[11] This desire has one of its clearest and most open expressions, according to Jameson, in Hall's view of cultural studies as a project shaped by the attempt to 'align intellectuals with an emerging historical movement'.[12] From this perspective the essential political aim of cultural studies is to form a layer of intellectuals who, through the 'forging of a heterogeneous set of "interest groups" into some larger political and social movement', would operate as organic intellectuals of the type described by Gramsci.[13] And this is so even when, as Hall acknowledges was the case at the Birmingham Centre, cultural studies is uncertain as to where such a historical movement is to be located: 'we couldn't tell then, and can hardly tell now',

Hall writes, 'where that emerging historical movement was to be found. We were organic intellectuals without any organic point of reference'.[14]

Yet, regardless of the privileged place it occupies within cultural studies, isn't rather a lot taken for granted by this idea that theory is not enough, and that as well as keeping one at the 'forefront of intellectual theoretical work' (281), theory should also be able to connect with or even help to bring about the kind of goals that are associated with politics? In particular, is the argument that it is possible to object to theory's 'textualization' of cultural studies' discourses on the grounds that insufficient attention is paid to politics, not itself guilty of: (1) paying insufficient attention to politics, not least by assuming that the identity of politics, what politics is, what it means to be political, is already more or less known (at least to the extent that it is possible to say that the supposed 'textualization' of cultural studies by theory is *not political*, or *not political enough*);[15] and (2) paying insufficient attention to the 'textuality' of theory? Without doubt there has been a certain amount of both 'deconstructive mimicry' and 'theoretical fluency' around in recent years – and not just in America, or in cultural studies. But, in arguing that although 'questions of power and the political have to be and are always lodged within representations' (286), textuality 'at the same time . . . is never enough' (284), is Hall not in danger of sustaining precisely the kind of mistaken critique of theory, and deconstruction especially, that holds it to account for overemphasizing language and meaning and textuality at the expense of the 'world'?[16] If some of those who are interested in deconstruction have, as Rodolphe Gasché argued some time ago now, produced a version of Derridean deconstruction that is merely a 'newer form of new criticism'[17] or, as Hall puts it elsewhere, 'old-style practical criticism, close textual reading of a good old Leavisian kind, but with some fancy Sausserian or poststructuralist terms and a bit of identity and subject position thrown in',[18] then many opponents of deconstruction have focused on these versions in order to criticize deconstruction generally for being a primarily formal, textual, literary mode of subversion. But as Geoffrey Bennington, among others, has pointed out, as far as deconstruction and Derrida are concerned:

'Text' is not quite an extension of a familiar concept, but a displacement or reinscription of it. Text in general is any system of marks, traces, referrals, (don't say reference, have a little more sense than that) . . . Deconstruction does not have a place for language over here, and a world over there to which it refers . . . There is no essential difference between language and the world, the one as subject, the other as object. There are traces . . . Of course text does not mean discourse. Perception is not a discourse, it is a

text. Discourse is a text. (But nobody thinks you can separate deconstruction from language. Nor from the world. Text is not a mediation between
language and world, but the *milieu* in which any such distinction might be
drawn.)[19]

Making this clear has been the subject of a number of Derrida's written works.
Perhaps the most appropriate to cite in this particular context is his response
to Anne McClintock and Rob Nixon's misunderstanding of 'textuality' in
relation to a short piece of Derrida's on the *apartheid* regime in South Africa.
Given the frequency with which this aspect of deconstruction has been
misunderstood, it is worth quoting Derrida at length:

> an hour's reading, beginning on any page of any one of the texts I have
> published over the last twenty years, should suffice for you to realize that
> *text*, as I use the word, is not the book. No more than writing or trace, it
> is not limited to the *paper* which you cover with your graphism. It is
> precisely for strategic reasons . . . that I found it necessary to recast the
> concept of text by generalizing it almost without limit, in any case without
> present or perceptible limit, without any limit that *is*. That is why there is
> nothing '*beyond* the text'. That's why South Africa and *apartheid* are, like
> you and me, part of this general text, which is not to say that it can be
> read the way one reads a book. That's why the text is always a field of
> forces: heterogeneous, differential, open and so on. That's why deconstruc-
> tive readings and writings are concerned not only with library books, with
> discourses, with conceptual and semantic contents. They are not simply
> analyses of discourse . . . They are also effective or active (as one says)
> interventions, in particular political and institutional interventions that
> transform contexts without limiting themselves to theoretical or constative
> utterances even though they must also produce such utterances. That's
> why I do not go '*beyond* the text,' in this *new* sense of the word text, by
> fighting and calling for a fight against *apartheid*, for example. I say 'for
> example' because it also happens that I become involved with institutional
> and academic politics or get myself imprisoned in Czechoslovakia for giv-
> ing seminars prohibited by the authorities. Too bad if this strikes you as
> strange or intolerable behaviour on the part of someone whom you, like
> others, would like to believe remains enclosed in some 'prison-house of
> language'. Not only, then, do I not go 'beyond the text', in this new sense
> of the word text (no more than anyone else can go beyond it, not even the
> most easy-to-recognize activists), but the strategic reevaluation of the con-
> cept of text allows me to bring together in a more consistent fashion, in
> the most consistent fashion possible, theoretico-philosphical necessities

with the 'practical,' political, and other necessities of what is called deconstruction.[20]

Now I mention all this, not so much because I think a little more care should perhaps have been taken with the analysis of politics and theory in 'Cultural Studies and its Theoretical Legacies'. In many respects the above commentary on Hall's essay is unnecessary (although in others it obviously is not, which is why I have provided it here). After all, Derrida's thoughts on 'textuality' (including his deconstruction of the opposition of politics *to* language and meaning and textuality) have been available for some time now to those who are interested, even in translation. They are certainly well known enough, one would have thought, to require little restatement from me (a variation of this dispute between 'politics' and 'theory' having already been played out some years ago now in the sphere of literary criticism).[21] What is more, is it not at least partly due to Stuart Hall that a lot of this theoretical work is by now so familiar? Did his openness, from a relatively early stage of his intellectual career, to Marxist European theory, particularly that of Gramsci and Althusser, not play an important role in helping to pave the way for the wider acceptance of 'theory' generally, in the UK at least (Hall taught a course on Cultural Theory on the CCCS MA programme at Birmingham in the 1970s, for example)?[22] In the light of this the more interesting question surely is 'Why?'. Why, in the face of all the evidence to the contrary, in Derrida's work and elsewhere, does Hall continue to portray theory and deconstruction in this way with his comments on the institutionalization of cultural studies in the United States and its 'theoretical fluency'? On approaching the issue from this direction it soon becomes clear that there may be some rather 'understandable' motivations behind the apparent reluctance to pay more attention to theory and deconstruction in this essay, given that the identity of cultural studies is for Hall here closely bound up with its ' "political" aspect' (278).[23] For if this *is* the case, if its politically committed nature is a fundamental part of what cultural studies *is*, then to risk opening the possibility of rethinking this ' "political" aspect' would presumably be to risk opening the possibility of fundamentally rethinking cultural studies. One answer to my 'Why?' question, then, may be that theory is presented like this in 'Cultural Studies and its Theoretical Legacies' because it is only by doing so, only by using the question of politics as an accusation or form of correction (via the application and enforcement of the pre-established norms of what politics is and what it means to be political), and thus as a means of closing down and limiting the space for thinking differently about politics and the political that is opened by theory, by deconstruction and by Derrida, that the identity of cultural studies *as cultural studies* can be maintained.

CULTURAL STUDIES AND THE POLITICS
OF DECONSTRUCTION

Again, Hall is not alone in this. Despite frequent calls for cultural studies to move forward by means of a *return* to its politically committed roots, the politics at these roots – much less the politics of this actual *return* to politics – is rarely examined. Contemporary cultural studies, for the most part, tends to take the concept of politics for granted (one reason being, as I say, that it may no longer be possible to recognize cultural studies *as cultural studies* if the question of its politics is opened up). Nevertheless, for all that it may represent a challenge to cultural studies, the general reluctance or refusal on the part of many of those in the field to engage seriously with deconstruction's thinking on the question of the political seems something of an opportunity missed, especially since, although it is 'not a political position and cannot even be said to offer a politics as such', deconstruction *does* provide 'a way of thinking through certain conceptual problems in politics and knowledge, including the relation of politics and knowledge'.[24]

Interestingly, this is something that at least one cultural studies commentator on Hall's essay *has* acknowledged, albeit inadvertently, and in parenthesis. In an essay entitled 'Post-Marxism and Cultural Studies' which is positioned as a 'post-script' to Grossberg *et al.*'s book of the 1990 Chicago conference, Angela McRobbie insists that the debate 'about the future of Marxism within cultural studies has not yet taken place'.[25] Any potential space it may have occupied has been taken over by that around modernity and postmodernity, with its questioning of any attempt to prioritize 'economic relations and economic determinations over cultural and political relations by positioning these latter in a mechanical and reflectionist role' (719). This is why McRobbie sees Stuart Hall's contribution to this conference, 'Cultural Studies and its Theoretical Legacies', as being so important: because it begins to open up a dialogue between cultural studies and Marxist European theory. Hall's work notwithstanding, McRobbie laments the general loss of Marxism within cultural studies, and the sense of political urgency that goes with it; and she sees deconstruction as having played a major role in this. Although McRobbie refers quite favourably to those instances of deconstruction she regards as having maintained a link with politics in its most easily recognized sense (she mentions the work of Gayatri Spivak and Homi Bhabha, the latter himself, ironically, the author of an essay on 'The Commitment to Theory'),[26] she sees it as too often leading to purely formal or textual excursions where there is no talk of policy, lived experience or everyday life. 'Intellectually, deconstruction is dazzling', she writes. 'Politically, it is enabling. But in the name of deconstruction there can also be produced a series of tasteful and elegant forays into the field of culture, dipping into it in the absence of the need to be constrained by materialism (*a requirement or obligation which itself would be subject to deconstruction*), or held to account by a political agenda.' (720, my emphasis)

Yet is this not partly the point? As recent disputes over the future of cultural studies demonstrate only too clearly,[27] to be constrained by the need to be 'political' is not necessarily to be particularly political at all, since the last thing such 'political' discourses can understand is politics. Discourses of this kind can in fact only take place once the idea of politics has been settled *in advance*; the question of politics is that which must be answered *before* they can begin. This is why in many of his published texts and interviews Derrida repeatedly refuses to elaborate a political theory or a deconstructive politics. Speaking in response to a question on the subject of politics at the University of Sussex in 1997, Derrida makes it clear that:

> I don't think that even now I am answering the demand for politics, that is to propose something which could fit into what one calls in our tradition, politics. What I am trying to do now, especially in the books *Spectres of Marx* or in the *Politics of Friendship*, is to try to understand or to re-think, I'm not the only one doing that of course, but to try with others to re-think what the political is, what is involved precisely in the dissemination of the political field. So, I'm not proposing a new political content within the old frame but trying to re-define, or to think differently, what is involved in the political as such, and for the very same reason I don't propose a political theory . . .
>
> So it's not a political theory – part of what I'm trying to say in these texts is not part of a theory that would be included in the field known as politology or political theory, and it's not a deconstructive politics either. I don't think there is such a thing as deconstructive politics, if by the name 'politics' we mean a programme, an agenda, or even the name of a regime.[28]

Instead of simply succumbing to the demand for politics, deconstruction attempts to think through the 'requirement or obligation' to be 'constrained by materialism' or, indeed, to be 'political' or 'held to account by a political agenda'. While not in itself a politics, this is very different to an avoidance of politics. Indeed, far from having a depoliticizing effect, this questioning of the political is the very condition of the possibility of politics:

> If the whole political project would be the reassuring object or the logical or theoretical consequence of assured knowledge (euphoric, without paradox,

without aporia, free of contradiction, without undecidabilities to decide), that would be a machine that runs without us, without responsibility, without decision, at bottom without ethics, nor law, nor politics. There is no decision nor responsibility without the test of aporia or undecidability ... There is no 'politics', no law, no ethics without the responsibility of a decision which, to be just, cannot content itself with applying existing norms or rules but must take the absolute risk, in every singular instant, of justifying itself again, alone, as if for the first time, even if it is inscribed in a tradition.[29]

The whole thrust of Hall's concern about theory in 'Cultural Studies and Its Theoretical Legacies' now appears to be reversed. Ironically enough, the very thing that is venerated for being more 'political' – politics – is perhaps the least radical or political thing to do; while that which is criticized for not being political enough – deconstructive theory, which Hall sees as having corrupted cultural studies in America – turns out to be possibly the most political of all. Yet to make this point that the concept of politics cultural studies has inherited is not necessarily commensurate with its political ambitions is not to simply reject or renounce cultural studies in favour of theory and deconstruction. Nor is it to break with the tradition of cultural studies as it has existed until now in order to found a new, say, 'deconstructive cultural studies'. As Johan Fornäs acknowledges in a speech originally given as a keynote address to the second international 'Crossroads in Cultural Studies' conference, in which he debated the future of cultural studies with Lawrence Grossberg, such an attempt to break with or critique tradition would itself be quite traditional: 'the philosopher Paul Ricoeur once emphasized: "Critique is also a tradition. I would even say that it plunges into the most impressive tradition, that of liberating acts, of the Exodus and the Resurrection"'.[30] To make this point is rather to appeal to a latent aspect of cultural studies which, if not exactly forgotten, has been somewhat downplayed and marginalized in all this; but which, interestingly enough (given the way in which the pendulum of critical and cultural fashion seems to be swinging away from theory at the moment and back toward, if not political economy, then at the very least cultural studies' politically committed 'origins') can nevertheless be found at the very 'pre-theoretical', politically committed 'origins' of cultural studies it is today argued we should return to as an antidote to theory and its supposed lack of politics. We can see this simply by following Hall back to the 'roots' of cultural studies as traced by Raymond Williams in *his* essay on 'The Future of Cultural Studies'.

CULTURAL STUDIES TO COME

Two essays are probably appealed to more than any others by those in cultural studies wishing to stress the importance of politics as traditionally conceived. One is Hall's 'Cultural Studies and its Theoretical Legacies'; the other is Raymond Williams' 'The Future of Cultural Studies'.[31] Williams' essay is generally held to authorize a return to an emphasis on politics within cultural studies in at least two ways. Firstly, and most obviously, in its stress on a point Williams regards as lying 'at the heart of Cultural Studies': that 'you cannot understand an intellectual or artistic project without also understanding its formation . . . its context or its background . . . or, in older terms . . . [its] society' (151–2) – something cultural studies is perceived as having too often forgotten in recent years as a result of its enthusiasm for all things textual. Secondly, through the importance Williams attaches to pedagogy.

Given the way in which the opportunities presented by pedagogy as a site of theoretical and practical engagement have, with one or two notable exceptions, been consistently ignored by cultural studies academics over the last twenty years or so, this last point may come as something of a surprise.[32] However, cultural studies' increasingly visible presence at the centre of a 'new' 'mass' higher educational system, a system which is being driven more and more by an economic and managerial logic,[33] has led many critics to conclude that its claims to be able to intervene politically in the world 'outside' the institution of university are now at best romantically naïve, and at worst hopelessly outdated. Cultural studies practitioners are consequently seen as being faced with a choice. Either they accept that, as Cary Nelson has maintained, 'political action and cultural studies are not interchangeable', and that cultural studies is just 'a set of writing [textual] practices', a 'discursive, analytic, interpretative tradition',[34] with little direct, practical connection to the 'real' world of politics and materiality; or they develop ways of grounding cultural studies that take more account of the specific institutional contexts within which it currently operates.[35] In the last few years there has thus been a slow but steadily increasing number of calls for cultural studies to pay more attention to the possibilities of connecting the development of radical cultural theories with radical cultural practice that Williams describes pedagogy as having offered in 'The Future of Cultural Studies', in the belief that this may provide cultural studies with at least one way of having a direct, practical, political impact.[36] And yet, while there is certainly a link between cultural theory and the politics that lies at cultural studies' roots in this text, this is only part of the story. For on close inspection what Williams' essay reveals, precisely through its attention to the 'kind of formation it was from which the project of

Cultural Studies developed' and its occurrence in specific institutional and pedagogic contexts, is that there exists at cultural studies' roots, not just a commitment to politics, but also, and at the same time, a degree of radical questioning which contains the possibility of radically questioning cultural studies' commitment to politics.

This little remarked upon *double* aspect of Williams' text is most readily apparent from his location of the initial emergence of cultural studies, not in the usual texts, but in an area which was, until relatively recently, frequently excluded and marginalized from histories of the field. Cultural studies is often presented as having begun as an adjunct to a university department of English literature.[37] But 'it can hardly be stressed too strongly', Williams writes, 'that Cultural Studies in the sense we now understand it' first 'occurred in Adult Education: in the WEA [Workers Education Authority], in the extramural Extension classes':

> We all know the accounts which will line up and date *The Uses of Literacy*, *The Making of the English Working Class*, *Culture and Society*, and so on. But, as a matter of fact, already in the late forties, and with notable precedents in army education during the war, and with some precedents – though they were mainly in economics and foreign affairs – even in the thirties, Cultural Studies was extremely active in adult education. It only got into print and gained some kind of general intellectual recognition with these later books. (154)

This hitherto neglected aspect of cultural studies' history has recently become the focus of a certain amount of attention, largely, as I say, because it is seen as a way of decentering the history and origins of cultural studies away from 'theory' and 'textuality' and back toward a more direct concern with social movements and the concrete, practical, political world of everyday materiality. Here, too, there is a tendency to construct the history of cultural studies in terms of the sort of narrative of institutionalization Tony Bennett has drawn attention to, the marginal place occupied by adult education being held as having 'given cultural studies a unique access to forms of intellectual wholeness which, in turn, have provided it with a privileged insight into the social totality'.[38] This place is something cultural studies is regarded as having since lost with its move toward the centre of the education system. Again, however, it is not so much the ability of adult education, or lack of it, to 'connect with the industrial or political sectors of the working classes' that interests me here. (For Bennett, for example, the extra-mural departments are 'more accurately described as the centre's outposts than as its margins' (47) and 'function more as a vehicle for transmitting the dominant culture to the remoter parts of the social body than as a crucible for the development of a tradition of radical cultural critique' (48)). Nor, for the time being at least, is it Williams' emphasis on the importance that is clearly attached to paper in cultural studies: his account of how the history of cultural studies has been traced primarily through written paper *texts*, with the result that 'many people who were active in that field at that time who didn't publish' have been marginalized or excluded from such histories.[39] What concerns me for the moment is the way in which Williams' return to adult education in this text is motivated, not so much by a wish to critique 'current academic practices of cultural studies as having strayed too far from their radical and grounded origins' and 'return them to a more direct concern with political economy and social movements',[40] but by a desire to call attention to a dimension of experimental and self-reflexive questioning he associates specifically with adult education. It is an aspect of 'The Future of Cultural Studies' clearly evident in the emphasis Williams places on one form of adult education in particular: the WEA.

The stress which has been placed on the marginality of extra-mural teaching has meant that, even on the relatively few occasions cultural studies practitioners *have* turned their attention to the place of adult education in the history of cultural studies, the significance of the WEA has often been overlooked, or at best underestimated. Yet the specific nature of WEA teaching is crucial to any understanding of Williams' account of the beginnings of cultural studies, as the WEA was far more than a vehicle for transmitting what eventually came to be known as cultural studies to those who had a direct and grounded connection to 'real life'. The importance of the WEA, Williams suggests, resided not so much with its politics as with the nature of WEA classes themselves. These were characterized by the fact that they had no fixed syllabus or assessment. WEA tutors decided the courses with their students, and this 'crucial process of interchange and encounter between the people offering the intellectual disciplines and those using them' (157) enabled WEA teaching to be highly experimental and self-reflexive. 'There isn't any rule about how to do it', Williams maintains in 'An Open Letter to WEA Tutors' written in 1961. 'Working with the WEA is . . . a matter of constant experiment in teaching, and the WEA is one of the very few institutions in which this is possible, because of its freedom from external requirements'.[41]

The full significance of Williams' tracing of cultural studies' roots to the specific institutional setting and educational circumstances of the WEA in 'The Future of Cultural Studies' can perhaps be grasped best by turning briefly to one of his most substantial accounts of WEA teaching: his 'Adult Education and Social Change' of 1983.[42] Here, having begun by linking teaching to politics by acknowledging that the 'deepest impulse' of adult education at this time 'was the desire to make learning part of the process of social change itself'

(257), Williams stresses that the radicality of the WEA lay in the way in which it contributed to social change, rather than simply reflecting it. Importantly (especially as far as the argument of those who wish to portray pedagogy as a means of putting the politics back into cultural studies is concerned), the WEA did so, according to Williams, not so much by attempting to forge direct links with the working class seen as an historical movement, as by changing 'the idea of learning itself' (260).[43] In particular, the WEA raised fundamental questions for the idea of education based on social conscience: on the belief that education should be a form of 'missionary' (259) work which involved bringing knowledge to those members of society seen as being less-privileged. This idea, which Williams identifies as being particularly prevalent in earlier forms of adult education, in the nineteenth century especially (and which I would argue is still inherent, albeit in modified form, in certain traditional notions of the role of the 'left-wing' intellectual today),[44] involved: first, identifying a section of society, 'mostly poor people', as lacking a 'humanizing' knowledge; and second, attempting to remedy that deficit by taking such a 'humanizing' knowledge and imposing it onto that 'class seen as in deficit, or to certain stranded exceptional individuals' in that class, from above. What such a conception of education lacked, however, was an appreciation of the fact that 'there was a positive deficiency in the centres of learning themselves'. Missing from this idea of education was an understanding of what it is that authorizes the privileged knowledge of the educator. What is it exactly that legitimates the 'heartland of learning's' claim to know 'what learning is', what a subject is, what evidence is? For Williams, such a lack of awareness 'that the real deficit is on both sides of the account' (259) has serious consequences for the democratic political ambitions of anyone involved in a system of learning of this kind. Far from overcoming inequalities of knowledge and learning, such a 'refining and humanizing' could in fact become, in Williams' words, 'anti-educational', in the sense that it would 'soften the terms of the discussion' by excluding 'controversial current material' while supporting other subjects 'precisely because they moved people away from those areas which would put the status and nature of official learning in question' (259).

This model of education Williams castigates as merely 'delivering some kind of boiled down pap which would indicate some already decided course of action' (263/4); and he contrasts it sharply with what went on in the WEA. There, ideas of what constituted learning, knowledge, evidence, etc., were not decided in advance and then simply imposed onto people from above. '[E]ven people who agreed that the point of Adult Education was the building of an adequate social consciousness didn't, in that sense, want messages', he writes. 'I mean they didn't want the conclusions of arguments: they wanted to reach their own conclusions' (262). At the roots of cultural studies in the WEA there thus lies, for Williams, a radical interrogation of the 'heartland of learning' which refuses to content itself with applying a pre-given knowledge or implementing a programme or project already decided in advance. The 'whole problem was not whether the message would be accepted or rejected or modified but – and I don't mean this satirically – what the message should be' (262). And, significantly, this included the radical interrogation of precisely those areas of 'official learning' defined as economics and politics:

There was a time as an adult tutor when you felt a second class citizen if you were not teaching Economics or Politics, because that had been the first interpretation of what the business of creating social consciousness was. I know in my own case . . . the first four Tutorial Classes I had were all in International Relations and in some curious way in the next year that had all become classes in Literature. The process by which this happened has never been satisfactorily explained. Yet I didn't get what might be called approval about this. And after all you can still see the case. Suppose you say now, 'What do we most need to be conscious about, since we are starting a class this winter?' You might easily ask if there is anything worth discussing this winter but the problems of nuclear disarmament and the problems of the British and world economy – I am not running any of these issues down – I am just saying the old assumption was that there and there only, and in those ways, was consciousness formed. And this was the curious change that happened in this post-war period, of which some of the political results are now taking some of the people who never noticed this shift by surprise. If I can again give one example, when I was teaching classes and writing about newspapers and advertising in the fifties one of my political friends said 'Well, I suppose it's amusing enough but what does it all have to do with politics?' But if you look back from the eighties, having seen what newspapers have to do with politics, you can recall the really virgin innocence of people who thought themselves hard, mature, political analysts. (262–3)

Now as Tom Steele noted in his history of the part played by adult education in the emergence of cultural studies:

The chemistry of this change is not hard to appreciate. The prime resource for the study of International Relations was newspapers. In class discussion, students were encouraged to read and compare the international coverage of a variety of newspapers . . . It is hard not to imagine Williams moving the discussion from the actual politics of International Relations to the construction of the news items from which 'the facts' were drawn. Thus the world became text and the methods of practical criticism were adopted appropriately.[45]

But it is not so much this shift from politics to culture I want to draw attention to, even if it is this that paved the way for the development of what we now know as cultural studies. It is the way this shift is made possible only by virtue of the fact that at least some of those working in adult education at this time, and specifically the institutional context of the WEA, were *not* constrained by the need to be 'political', and that the question of politics was *not* regarded as being already more or less decided.

Williams' tracing of the roots of cultural studies to the WEA thus has profound significance for an understanding of what cultural studies *is* and what it means to '*do cultural studies*'. As he puts it in 'The Future of Cultural Studies', what happened in the WEA was that academics took out from their institutions university disciplines such as 'English' or 'Philosophy' or 'Politics', and the students in adult education classes wanted to know what these disciplines were:

> This exchange didn't collapse into some simple populism: that these were all silly intellectual questions. Yet these new students insisted (1) that the relation of this to their own situation and experience had to be discussed, and (2) that there were areas in which the discipline itself might be unsatisfactory, and therefore they retained as a crucial principle the right to decide their own syllabus . . . These people were, after all, in a practical position to say, 'well, if you tell me that question goes outside your discipline, then bring me someone whose discipline *will* cover it, or bloody well get outside of the discipline and answer it yourself.' It was from this entirely rebellious and untidy situation that the extraordinarily complicated and often muddled convergences of what became Cultural Studies occurred; precisely because people wouldn't accept those boundaries. (156–7)

More than any syllabus or set of defensible disciplines or political project, it is this challenge to 'official learning' that represents what it is to *do cultural studies*, according to Williams. And, significantly, he extends this spirit of rebellion to take in not just the traditional academic disciplines, but cultural studies 'itself'. If cultural studies could decide what it is, 'define' itself as a 'defensible' discipline, 'justify its importance, demonstrate its rigour', then the meaning claimed for cultural studies would include anything but the meaning of cultural studies. Such pressures are 'precisely the opposite of those of the original project', he insists (158). It would be to confuse cultural studies with an 'institutionalized' codification of programmes and syllabi, with a pre-established final, fixed and limiting (political) agenda or set of norms and rules: whereas cultural studies is by definition always being judged and decided upon, the decision as to what cultural studies is is constantly being (re)evaluated and (re)taken, its identity continually being challenged and changed. This is what cultural studies is. And for Williams 'we should remind ourselves of that unpredictability', of cultural studies' openness to the future and to what is to come, 'as a condition likely to apply also to any projections we might ourselves make' (151).[46]

'. . . A THEORETICAL POINT . . .'

Clearly, then, enacting a return to its roots is not going to be enough to enable cultural studies to retain its identity as a politically committed body of thought. By following the advice of those critics who advocate a reengagement with politics in cultural studies and paying attention to the 'kind of formation it was from which the project of Cultural Studies developed' and, in particular, to cultural studies' initial occurrence in the specific institutional, educational and pedagogic context of the WEA, it becomes apparent that at the 'origins' of cultural studies there lies, not just a commitment to politics, but also, and at the same time, a degree of radical and experimental questioning which includes the possibility of opening the question of cultural studies' own politics.[47] And not just its politics. The challenge to pre-given, pre-decided knowledge Williams locates at cultural studies' roots contains both *the possibility and the promise* of questioning his own 'projections' regarding the future of cultural studies:[48] his desire for a democratic mutuality of exchange (something he idealizes in the adult education extra-mural class); his privileging of speech over writing (apparent in the emphasis he places on the importance of face-to-face interaction between tutor and class in adult education, over and above the reading of written texts);[49] and his humanism (witness his stress on people discussing cultural studies in relation to their own, lived, 'real-life' experience) – all of which *have* indeed been brought into question by changes in the formation and project of cultural studies. In an article on 'the usefulness of cultural studies', for instance, Martin Ryle has indicated how the 'coherent project' that formed at the origins of cultural studies 'depended on a set of mutually reinforcing conjunctions . . . that are not going to reoccur':

... changes since the 1950s have displaced the broad alliance between social democracy, adult education, and organised trade unionism from the position which it might be seen to enjoy, post-1945, as the bearer or agent of a more general historical progress. Cold War politics and economic neoliberalism have undone those hopes of social advance, while the particularity of the 'universal' subject on which that political-educational formation was centered – actually, or rather ideally, the male worker – has been increasingly clear . . . In the last two decades, academic criticism has been most productive when it has sought to represent and form alliances with people whose cultural-political identity has been centred on questions of gender, 'race'/ethnicity or sexuality never addressed in that earlier emancipatory project. Meanwhile, in a discourse increasingly inaccessible to non-specialist audiences, theoretical challenges have undermined the confident notions of subjective autonomy and cultural value which were the implicit presuppositions of critical-humanist pedagogy from Arnold through Leavis and up to Williams' *Culture and Society*.[50]

But even the point that for Williams lies at the very 'heart of Cultural Studies . . . that you cannot understand an intellectual or artistic project without also understanding its formation' (151) – and which clearly underpins Ryle's own belief that 'if cultural studies is to "understand itself as a formation" (as Steele urges that it should)' it cannot 'any longer ground that self-understanding in the original project' (39) and must instead articulate it in new terms – is open to challenge and change. For taking Williams' argument to its logical conclusion, this principle cannot be imposed onto students for fear of moving 'people away from those areas which would put the status and nature of official learning [in this case cultural studies] in question'. It, too, must be placed under suspicion lest the 'terms of the discussion' be softened.[51]

A radical interrogation of 'official learning' is an inextricable part of cultural studies, then. Despite this, in tracing 'the changes of formation that produced different definitions' of the cultural studies project since its emergence in adult education in the 1930s and 1940s, Williams is able to identify a number of instances where the 'critical possibility' inherent in cultural studies' has been largely 'incorporated and neutralized' (152, 161). These include both the institutionalization of cultural studies in the university, which he presents as having 'emasculated' the challenge it offers to pre-given knowledge by continually pulling the 'raw questions' characteristic of adult education back to something more 'manageable' through the pressures of examination and syllabus (157); and the development in the sixties of the Open University which, despite having the 'enormous advantage' of taking adult education's emphasis on 'popular access' beyond the minority sphere of adult education, nonetheless went against the ideas of adult education in that it inserted a technology 'over and above the social process of education' (157). The Open University consequently 'lacks to this day' that element of radical self-questioning that is produced by the 'process of interchange and encounter between the people offering the intellectual disciplines and those using them' (157), Williams maintains. 'This process of constant inter-change between the discipline and the students . . . was *deliberately* interrupted by the Open University' (156/7).

This last claim is particularly interesting as Williams' account of the history of cultural studies, and especially his condemnation of educational 'missionary' work and subsequent remarks on the Open University, raises a number of questions for the role of the 'organic intellectual' Stuart Hall ends 'Cultural Studies and its Theoretical Legacies' by espousing.[52] The extent to which Hall's activities at the Open University did or did not lack the sort of 'critical possibility' that was produced in the WEA for Williams requires a degree of attention to the specific details of Hall's written and institutional practices, the Open University and the institution of the university that will have to be provided elsewhere. But it is perhaps just worth making the point that the Open University should not be seen in an entirely negative light. Tony Bennett's critique of the 'myth of the margins' again provides a useful counterpoint, especially the way in which, as Bennett observes, 'Williams' comments on the differences between the Open University and earlier forms of extramural or adult education omit all mention of what is arguably the most crucial difference between them. For what was wholly new and radically progressive about the Open University in the British context was that it provided open access to degree qualifications, whereas earlier forms of university extramural or adult education did not usually or typically lead to any qualifications.' As a consequence, the Open University 'raised questions regarding the politics of credintionalism of a kind that were virtually absent from the extramural sector'.[53] Certainly the *institutionalization* of cultural studies cannot be seen in wholly negative terms. Williams himself is careful not to portray it this way, acknowledging the great gains institutionalization can bring in terms of being 'more professional, more organized, and properly resourced'.[54] And, indeed, if institutionalization is seen as creating problems for cultural studies, it is also its relation to the institution that makes cultural studies possible in the first place. As both Williams here, and Readings elsewhere, have shown, cultural studies is 'essentially linked to the University' in terms of both its 'genesis' – be it the Birmingham School or with Williams and Hoggart in Adult Education – and its 'goals'.[55] Given the theme of this chapter, however, I am more immediately concerned with another of the factors Williams identifies in 'The Future of Cultural Studies' as having led to the 'neutralization and incorporation' of cultural studies' questioning of pre-established knowledge: that which concerns cultural studies' 'quite uncritical acceptance' around the same time as the setting up of the Open University, 'of a set of theories', by which Williams mainly means 'formalism' and 'the simpler kinds (including Marxist kinds) of structuralism' (157), but which he also sees as having 'subsumed' the 'quite different work of Gramsci and Benjamin' (156–7).

At first sight Williams appears to be constructing a narrative, similar to that Stratton and Ang locate in Hall's essay, in which cultural studies is depicted as suffering a fall from some moment when it was 'purer, more authentic, more un-copted' as a result of its 'uncritical' incorporation of 'these new forms of idealist theory'. Theory here is presented as having helped to radically divert the project of cultural studies by rationalizing its bureaucratization and insti-tutionalization in the university and in this way encouraging people in the field 'not to look at their own formation' and thus not to raise difficult questions of the sort he associates with adult education (157). However, any such narrative is complicated somewhat by the fact that, as Williams insists, his emphasis on formation in this essay is itself a 'theoretical point' (151). He makes this quite clear by stressing it repeatedly in the opening two pages of 'The Future of Cultural Studies'. So, as well as helping to institutionalize cultural studies *after* its initial emergence in adult education, theory, of some kind at least (Williams does not quite say which), also lies 'at the heart of cultural studies' (151) and Williams' emphasis on 'formation' as a way of retaining that element of 'critical possibility' he sees it as being part of the job of cultural studies to provide. Theory thus appears as both villain and hero of the piece/peace: it is that which helps to neutralize cultural studies; but it is also the means by which cultural studies is able to struggle against this neutralization. Unfortunately, Williams' essay provides little by way of further assistance when it comes to understanding the complex nature of cultural studies' relationship with theory. For help with this I therefore now want to return to one of the places in the history of cultural studies where the intricacies of this relationship have been rendered most clearly visible. This is the essay by Stuart Hall with which I began – although Hall, too, in the end, tries to limit and control the challenge to 'official learning' inherent in cultural studies (a challenge which, as a result of changes in the formation and project, is indeed now associated *with* theory) lest it bring cultural studies' politics, and hence the identity of cultural studies itself, into question. For this reason this radically self-critical aspect of cultural studies can perhaps best be seen by looking at a different moment from Hall's essay: the beginning.

THE FUTURE OF CULTURAL STUDIES REVISITED

Hall begins 'Cultural Studies and its Theoretical Legacies' with a page-long introductory preamble in which he explains why, in order to think about the future of cultural studies, he (like Williams) wants to revisit its past. In doing so he makes it clear his intention is not to talk about the history of British cultural studies 'in a patriarchal way, as the keeper of the conscience of cultural studies, hoping to police you back into line with what it really was if only you knew' (277). For Hall, cultural studies:

> . . . is a discursive formation, in Foucault's sense. It has no simple origins, though some of us were present at some point when it first named itself in that way. Much of the work out of which it grew, in my own experience, was already present in the work of other people. Raymond Williams has made the same point, charting the roots of cultural studies in the early adult education movement in his essay on 'The Future of Cultural Studies'. 'The relation between a project and a formation is always decisive,' he says, because they are 'different ways of materialising . . . then of describing a common disposition of energy and direction.' Cultural studies has multiple discourses; it has a number of different histories. It is a whole set of formations; it has its own different conjunctures and moments in the past. It included many different kinds of work. I want to insist on that! It always was a set of unstable formations. It was 'centred' only in quotation marks, in a particular kind of way which I want to define in a moment. It had many trajectories; many people had and have different trajectories through it; it was constructed by a number of different methodologies and theoretical positions, all of them in contention. (278).

Cultural studies, then, does not have a single history that *can* be simply returned to. Nor does it have a fixed or stable identity that is always and everywhere the same, be it that based on an idea of the organic intellectual or otherwise.[56] Rather, cultural studies is a mix of 'founding moments, transformative challenges, and self-critical interrogations', to borrow the words of Henry Giroux.[57] It is thus constantly mobile, as changes in the different formations, methodologies and theoretical positions that go to make up cultural studies produce different and even conflicting interpretations of it. Hall emphasizes this point by drawing attention to the way in which European theory 'interrupted the already-interrupted history of its formation' (282). Indeed, he spends a large portion of the essay tracing some of the 'theoretical moments' he sees as having decentred cultural studies, forcing it to radically reconceive its identity. In doing so, he places particular emphasis on the interruptions to British cultural studies produced by feminism, by the question of race, and by the 'discovery of discursivity, of textuality', listing:

> the theoretical advances which were made by the encounters with structuralist, semiotic, and poststructuralist work: the crucial importance of

language and of the linguistic metaphor to *any* study of culture; the expansion of the notion of the text and textuality, both as a source of meaning, and as that which escapes and postpones meaning; the recognition of the heterogeneity, of the multiplicity, of meanings, of the struggle to close arbitrarily the infinite semiosis beyond meaning; the acknowledgement of textuality and cultural power, of representation itself, as a site of power and regulation; of the symbolic as a source of identity. These are enormous theoretical advances. (283)

This history has two immediate consequences as far as Hall's account of cultural studies is concerned. First, far from a simple nostalgia for the political commitment that lies at cultural studies' roots, Hall's raising of the question of the 'archive' – of what is included in the cultural studies archive, within what limits, according to what overdetermined paths – by way of a 'retrospective glance' clearly contains within it the possibility of critically 'reflecting on, *and intervening in,* the project of cultural studies itself' (277; my emphasis). This possibility occurs because cultural studies, for Hall, does not have a single history or identity, but is rather unstable, open and contested, always being challenged and changed according to the nature and specificity of the problems it addresses. The 1990 conference in Chicago on 'Cultural Studies Now and in the Future' thus provides Hall with an 'opportunity for a moment of self-reflection on cultural studies as a practice, on its institutional positioning' and on its project (277), and consequently for thinking cultural studies otherwise, for performing it differently, for re-imagining and recreating it.

Second, a contrast is established between the vision of cultural studies Hall presents at the beginning of his essay, and that which he provides at the end: between a theoretically destabilized and decentred cultural studies, in other words, which recognizes heterogeneity and multiplicity and which postpones meaning and closure and hence is open to change; and a cultural studies defined in terms of a stabilizing organic intellectual politics. These two aspects of cultural studies exist in a state of 'tension' for Hall in this essay: a 'tension between a refusal to close the field, to police it and, at the same time, a determination to stake out some positions within it and argue for them' (278). Indeed, it is precisely on these 'two fronts', the theoretical and the political, that the organic intellectual is required to operate:

On the one hand, we had to be at the forefront of intellectual theoretical work because, as Gramsci says, it is the job of the organic intellectual to know more than the traditional intellectuals do: really know, not just pretend to know, not just to have the facility of knowledge, but to know deeply and profoundly. So often knowledge for Marxism is pure recognition

– the production again of what we have always known! If you are in the game of hegemony you have to be smarter than 'them'. Hence, there are no theoretical limits from which cultural studies can turn back. But the second aspect is just as crucial: that the organic intellectual cannot absolve himself or herself from the responsibility of transmitting those ideas, that knowledge, through the intellectual function, to those who do not belong, professionally, to the intellectual class. (281)

Like Williams, then, Hall warns against uncritically accepting a set of theories, including Marxist theories. And like Williams, he, too, sees 'intellectual theoretical work' as providing a means of combating this danger. Nevertheless, Hall is extremely wary about the possibility of taking this too far. As soon as he has finished acknowledging the open, heterogeneous aspect of cultural studies, he immediately sets about trying to limit and contain its impact; the reason being, quite simply, that cultural studies' radically experimental, self-reflexive side risks rendering the field too chaotic: there is a danger in all this of theory running amok and decentring cultural studies to such an extent that it risks becoming just about anything. 'Although cultural studies as a project is open-ended, it can't be simply pluralist in that way', Hall insists. 'Yes, it is a project that is always open to that which it doesn't yet know, to that which it can't yet name. But it does have some will to connect. It does have some stake in the choices it makes' (278). So, while acknowledging that 'there are no theoretical limits from which cultural studies can turn back' (281), Hall at the same time attempts to establish a boundary line beyond which cultural studies cannot go without risk of losing its identity *as cultural studies*. And this boundary, as far as Hall is concerned, is marked by its 'politics', by cultural studies' 'political aspect'. As he says in one of this essay's most frequently cited passages:

> It does matter whether cultural studies is this or that. It can't be just any old thing which chooses to march under a particular banner. It is a serious enterprise, or project, and that is inscribed in what is sometimes called the 'political' aspect of cultural studies. Not that there's one politics already inscribed within it. But there is something *at stake* in cultural studies in a way that I think, and hope, is not exactly true of many other very important intellectual and critical practices. (278)

Although cultural studies for Hall is characterized by the tense relationship between theory and politics, then, we can see that the two sides in this relationship are not assigned equal priority. While he is perfectly happy to use the 'political aspect' of cultural studies to raise questions for its theory, he is not quite so happy about the prospect of theory challenging cultural studies' 'political aspect'. And it is this ultimate privileging of politics on Hall's part that has led to 'Cultural Studies and its Theoretical Legacies' being so often appealed to by those wishing to stress the importance of politics to cultural studies as a source of the field's continuing relevance.[58] Politics here is what marks cultural studies out as different and distinct, and which thus separates a cultural studies which limits the destabilizing and decentring effects of theory from a cultural studies which would not. It is certainly at this *political bottom line* that Hall and his followers would no doubt like the tense relationship between theory and politics to stabilize and hold firm. But what makes this essay so interesting when it comes to contemplating the relation between theory and politics in cultural studies is the sheer fragility of the border Hall attempts to draw around cultural studies' identity as a politically committed body of thought. For all Hall's efforts to keep cultural studies' theoretical aspect within manageable limits, and for all the importance that has subsequently been attached to this essay, 'Cultural Studies and its Theoretical Legacies' contains a number of openings whereby theory is able to pass through this otherwise heavily-policed frontier and place the identity of cultural studies radically in question.

His use of the expression 'I think, and hope' in the passage just quoted appears to provide one such opening: can there not be detected in this a degree of recognition on Hall's part that his attempt to locate 'something' which is 'at stake' in cultural studies, and which it has to have in order for it to *be cultural studies*, is based at least to some extent on wishful thinking? Another comes with Hall's acknowledgement, a few lines later, that the boundary line he is attempting to mark out around cultural studies by means of its politics is an 'arbitrary' one. 'I don't believe knowledge is closed', he writes, 'but I do believe that politics is impossible without what I have called "the arbitrary closure"; without what Homi Bhabha called social agency as an arbitrary closure. That is to say, I don't understand a practice which aims to make a difference in the world, which doesn't have some points of difference or distinction which it has to stake out, which really matter. It is a question of positionalities' (278).[59] Now, of course, these two aspects of cultural studies exist in a state of 'tension'. In fact it is this tension, this 'dialogic approach to theory' (278), which for Hall, later in the essay, 'defines cultural studies as a project' (284) and marks its specificity:

> . . . I want to insist that until and unless cultural studies learns to live with this tension, a tension that all textual practices must assume . . . it will have renounced its 'worldly' vocation. That is to say, unless and until one respects the necessary displacement of culture, and yet is always irritated by

its failure to reconcile itself with other questions that matter, with other questions that cannot and can never be fully covered by critical textuality in its elaborations, cultural studies as a project, an intervention, remains incomplete. If you lose hold of that tension, you can do extremely fine intellectual work, but you will have lost intellectual practice as politics. I offer this to you, not because that's what cultural studies ought to be, or because that's what the Centre managed to do well, but simply because I think that, overall, is what defines cultural studies as a project. Both in the British and the American context, cultural studies has drawn the attention itself, not just because of its sometimes dazzling internal theoretical development, but because it holds theoretical and political questions in an ever irresolvable but permanent tension. It constantly allows one to irritate, bother, and disturb the other, *without insisting on some final theoretical closure.* (284, my emphasis).

Yet included in this presumably must also be the 'arbitrary' borderline – the 'theoretical closure' – Hall himself attempts to draw around cultural studies by means of its politics. For while on the one hand Hall challenges the way in which history is used to close down and police the meaning and identity of cultural studies in 'Cultural Studies and its Theoretical Legacies', on the other hand does he, too, not strive to close down and police the identity of cultural studies by means of its 'political aspect'? Can this conception of cultural studies as being ultimately a political project be decided upon once and for all? If cultural studies does not have one fixed or stable identity that is always and everywhere the same, but is rather heterogeneous and multiplicitous and self-critical, is its politics, like its history, not also open to transformative challenge and change?

THE FUTURE IS BRIGHT, THE FUTURE IS MONSTROUS

If these questions have the effect of drawing attention to a fundamental and irreducible instability in the identity of cultural studies, at least as it is described by Hall, they are in no way intended to suggest cultural studies is absolutely unstable: certain moments of 'arbitrary closure', such as defining cultural studies as a political body of work (as Hall does in 'Cultural Studies and its Theoretical Legacies' in response to what he sees as the increasing 'textualization' of the field), or as a discipline (as Tony Bennett has advocated),[60] can and do take place. (Indeed, without some degree of stability, there would never be anything we could recognize *as* cultural studies. It is just that this stability is never absolute. Cultural studies is never absolutely stable . . . or absolutely unstable, for that matter.) But these questions *are* intended to keep open the possibility of rethinking cultural studies' politics, a possibility Hall attempts to close down at various points in 'Cultural Studies and its Theoretical Legacies', and which many of those who have since cited this essay have endeavoured to *keep* closed. When Hall ultimately privileges cultural studies' politics over its theory, he thus appears to be neglecting to take the radical self-reflexive attitude inherent in his own definition of cultural studies as far as he himself otherwise suggests he should. Hall is able to maintain this open, questioning aspect of cultural studies to a certain extent. As he emphasizes, these 'position-alities are never final, they're never absolute. They can't be translated intact from one conjuncture to another; they cannot be depended upon to remain in the same place' (278). In the discussion that followed the presentation of his paper in Chicago Hall stresses that 'the notion of a political practice where criticism is postponed until the day after the barricades precisely defines the politics I have always refused. And if you don't go that way, you go into politics of contention, of continuous argument, of continuous debate. Because what is at stake really matters' (291). Rather than risk having to rethink cultural studies and its politics, however, Hall repeatedly prefers to 'turn back' from this particular 'theoretical limit' in this essay. For clearly what 'really matters' to Hall here, is the 'political aspect' of cultural studies, its politics, its 'political project' (281), its definition *as* a 'political project' (285). Judith Butler is thus quite right when, in her new preface to the tenth anniversary edition of *Gender Trouble*, she identifies Hall as one of those in cultural studies who has been most receptive to what she labels 'cultural theory'.[61] Yet for all that he defines cultural studies, in both the British and American context, as that body of thought which holds 'theoretical and political questions in an ever irresolv-able but permanent tension', Hall tends to take on board only those aspects of theory he can recuperate and integrate within the terms of cultural studies' already existing political project. He is noticeably reluctant to take the theoret-ical aspect of cultural studies quite so far as to actually bring into question one of the fundamental premises on which cultural studies is based: that it *is* in the last instance *a political project*. Followed through to its logical conclusion, however, the consequence of the 'politics of contention, of continuous argu-ment' Hall refers to must surely be a radical interrogation of precisely the sort of politics, precisely the sort of 'political practice' (281) and 'organic intellec-tual political work' (286) he uses this essay to try to advocate and defend.

   Whereas the first trace in the history of cultural studies Hall seeks to 'deconstruct' (although I suspect he means analyse, examine or uncover more than deconstruct, as Hall's approach, in this essay at least, shows little evidence of an awareness of the specificity of the thought of Jacques Derrida with which the term 'deconstruction' is most readily associated), 'has to do with a view of

British cultural studies which often distinguishes it by the fact that, at a certain moment, it became a Marxist critical practice' (279), it would have been just as interesting and important, if not more so, to 'deconstruct' his own view of British cultural studies which distinguishes it by the fact that, at a certain moment, it became a political practice, and in this way to perhaps radically displace 'some of the inheritances of [politics] in cultural studies' (281). To paraphrase and recast Hall's own questions: What exactly does that assignation of cultural studies as a political critical theory mean? How can we think cultural studies at that moment? What moment is it we are speaking of? What does that mean for the theoretical legacies, traces and aftereffects which politics continues to have in cultural studies? (279). Indeed, for cultural studies to fail to raise the question of its politics is for cultural studies to fail to live up to its own definition of itself. Although, on the one hand, asking these questions would seem to involve reconceptualizing the notion of politics on which cultural studies is based, thus putting the very identity of cultural studies at risk, on the other the asking of such questions is very much what cultural studies is about. As Williams shows, a rethinking of politics, and with it cultural studies' own identity, to the point where it may no longer be recognizable *as cultural studies*, is inscribed at the very 'origins' of cultural studies in adult education. There, at the heart of cultural studies, we may find politics, but we also find the 'critical possibility' of keeping open the question of politics, and with it, cultural studies.

It is no doubt worth stressing, once again, that the tension this produces – between cultural studies' commitment to politics and its keeping open of the question of politics, or the need to make a decision over the question of politics and the apparent impossibility of doing so – is not an avoidance or denial of politics; it is its very condition of possibility. In a recent interview Derrida has put it this way:

> Far from opposing undecidability to decision, I would argue that there would be no decision, in the strong sense of the word, in ethics, in politics, no decision, and thus no responsibility, without the experience of some undecidability. If you don't experience some undecidability, then the decision would simply be the application of a programme, the consequence of a premise or of a matrix. So a decision has to go through some impossibility in order for it to be a decision. If we know what to do, if I knew in terms of knowledge what I have to do before the decision, then the decision would not be a decision. It would simply be the application of a rule, the consequences of a premise, and there would be no problem, there would be no decision. Ethics and politics, therefore, start with undecidability.[62]

It is precisely in the 'irresolvable but permanent tension' Hall locates *between* theory and politics, then, that the political dimension of cultural studies is opened and maintained. From this point of view, cultural studies is about doing *neither* theory *nor* politics. It is about doing both: not in a liberal fashion, where each position is equally valid; nor even in a dialectical way. These two discourses are not merely placed in a state of 'permanent tension'; their very identities are brought into question as the relationship between theory and politics pushes both beyond their traditional delimitations and forces each to rework their relations with the other through the transformation of both. This is what cultural studies is:[63] it is an experiment in playing one off against the other; an experiment which does not conform to any system of dialectical thought, which does not conform to any system at all. As Williams illustrates, there can be no pre-established programme or syllabus for such an experiment, no fixed and worked out agenda or set rules. Nor are the results of such an experiment forseeable. The future of cultural studies, if cultural studies is to have a future, cannot be predicted or predetermined – that would be just a repetition of the past. Each time, and in each context and 'singular instant', this 'tension' must take its own risks. And if this is what cultural studies is, it is also what threatens to carry cultural studies beyond itself – to the point where the identity of cultural studies becomes uncertain and is opened up to the future, the unpredictable, unforeseeable, 'monstrous' future.

CHAPTER 5

Beyond Marxism *and* Psychoanalysis

Culture is neither just the processes of the unconscious writ large nor is the unconscious simply the internalisation of cultural process through the subjective domain. . . . Psychoanalysis completely breaks that sociological notion of socialisation . . . But I cannot translate the one onto the other. I have to live with the tension of the two vocabularies, of the two unsettled objects of analysis and try to read the one through the other without falling into psychoanalytic readings of everything . . . That's what I mean by living in and with the tension. (Stuart Hall)[1]

THE SUBJECT IN QUESTION

The theoretical and political importance issues around both gender and sexuality and race and ethnicity have assumed in recent years has meant that the 'question of the subject' has been put back on the agenda for many cultural critics. For some, this has led to a turning toward psychoanalysis, in the hope that it will be able to supply their Marxist-based theories with a fully fledged theory of subjectivity. For others, such attempts to bring psychoanalysis to bear on Marxism have raised more questions than they have answered. Indeed, for others again the very idea that psychoanalysis is somehow able to add a 'theory of subjectivity to the field of historical materialism' is a mistaken one, given that, as Ernesto Laclau observes, the 'latter has been constituted, by and large, as a negation . . . of subjectivity (although certainly not of the category of the subject)'.[2] What, then, is the value of psychoanalysis for a historical materialist understanding of subjectivity? More to the point, do Marxism and psychoanalysis have competing claims to theories of the subject?

Robert Young provides an excellent starting point for addressing these questions in an essay on 'Psychoanalysis and Political Literary Theories'.[3] Part of a collection, *Psychoanalysis and Cultural Theory: Thresholds*, which arose out of a series of talks on the subject of psychoanalysis and culture held in London during the first few months of 1987 – a period when positions on this issue 'entrenched in the 1970s were becoming more fluid and self-critical', according to the volume's editor, James Donald – and situated by Donald (alongside the rest of the collection) at 'the intersections between psychoanalysis and cultural theory',[4] Young's essay begins with a description of psychoanalysis as:

> a theory of unhappy relationships [which] has itself a long history of unhappy relationships. In the first place there is the story of the tense relationships within psychoanalysis between analysts, the psychoanalytic politics that has been charted by Paul Roazen, François Roustang, Sherry Turkle and others. In the second place, psychoanalysis has a history of relationships with other disciplines. (139)

Young proceeds to trace the history of three of those relationships in the cultural sphere – psychoanalysis's relationships 'with literary criticism, with Marxism, and with feminism' (139). In doing so, he draws attention to some of the difficulties involved in any attempt on the part of Marxism and feminism to utilize psychoanalysis to produce a theory that unites and synthesizes the individual psyche with the social.[5]

The way in which this relation is usually set up is that Marxism and feminism require a theory of the subject, while psychoanalysis, in turn, needs a theory of the social. The problem with such a pairing for Young is that:

> psychoanalysis [is] already a theory of the articulation of the subject with the social: if desire, for instance, is the desire of the Other, this means that desire is a social phenomenon. Furthermore, as the concept of desire itself suggests, psychoanalytic theory amounts to the argument that the structure of the relation of the psyche to the social is one of incommensurability – which does not mean that they do not interact, only that they do so unhappily. When social analysis has tried to link itself with psychoanalysis, it seems often not to have noticed this aspect of psychoanalytic theory, with the result that those marriages between forms of social explanation and psychoanalysis, far from being able to exploit psychoanalytic theory, merely repeat the narrative of incompatibility that it theorizes. (140/141)

Moreover, Marxist theories in particular have, as Young observes:

> always tended to restrict [their] use of psychoanalysis to the occasional importation of one or two concepts in order to construct a model; [they] have] never allowed it to affect the terms of [their] own theory substantially.

Psychoanalysis always remains marginal . . . [they have] rarely attempted to rethink the Cartesian inside/outside dichotomy on which this division is based and which psychoanalysis challenges. A reworking of that dualism would also have to include a rethinking of the exclusive claims of the forms of rational logic on which it is predicated. (149)

The 'lesson of psychoanalysis' is that the psychic and the social have to be 'lived simultaneously as two irreconcilable positions' (142). And Young privileges psychoanalysis for 'producing a theory of that incompatibility', rather than getting 'caught up in acting out the conflict between the psychic and the social', as Marxism and feminism tend to do (142). Or rather, as Marxism and socialist feminism tend to do – for while alliances between Marxism and feminism 'have tended to be predicated on the exclusion of psychoanalysis' (150), other forms of feminism, Young insists, have found psychoanalysis 'critical for [their] redefinitions, critiques and explorations of questions of sexuality and identity' (153).

Feminism, then (and especially what Young refers to variously as 'Derridean feminism' or 'deconstructive feminism'), like psychoanalysis – indeed precisely because of the very closeness of its relationship to psychoanalysis – contains at least the possibility of theorizing the psyche's 'incommensurable' relation to the social. By contrast, those theories associated with Marxism (including Marxist feminism) are presented as admitting few such possibilities – in no small part because psychoanalysis has been far less important to Marxism, serving merely as 'a worry at its margins' (153). But can psychoanalysis *really* be prioritized over Marxist theories of culture on the basis that the 'living through of this incompatibility between the individual and the social is the subject . . . of psychoanalysis', whereas this incompatibility is not the subject of Marxism (142)? Even if it is not achieved by means of a close relationship with psychoanalysis, does Marxism offer so few opportunities for theorizing the individual's 'incompatibility' with the social? What is more, is this placing of Marxism in what appears to all intents and purposes to be an oppositional relationship with psychoanalysis not a little curious, given the vigour with which Young, both here and elsewhere, has defended the emphasis placed by both psychoanalysis and deconstruction on the instability of such polarities?[6] Is Young's positioning of Marxism as the subordinate term in this relationship in particular not somewhat at odds with his insistence in his earlier essay on 'The Politics of "The Politics of Literary Theory"', that 'as deconstruction has shown, there is no text so politically determined that a clever reading cannot show how it simultaneously undermines its own strategy, thus allowing the text to be claimed for an opposing point of view'.[7]

Certainly there may be strategic reasons for situating psychoanalysis in a hierarchical relationship to Marxism. Marxism and psychoanalysis may have competing claims to theories of the subject, but it is Marxism that has tended to dominate the realm of cultural theory. Is privileging psychoanalysis over and in opposition to Marxism therefore a strategic move on Young's part, designed to participate in the dislodging and overturning of Marxist discourse from its traditional position of theoretical dominance? (As feminism has never been quite so powerful, it is presumably less of a threat.) Even if it is acknowledged that, in arguing against the institutional validation of Marxist theories of the subject, the emphasis Young places on psychoanalysis may have a certain theoretical effectiveness, a number of questions remain. For while Marxism might cast a large shadow over the sphere of cultural analysis,[8] its degree of influence in the public arena, in Europe at least, has declined rapidly in the face of the new dominant consensus which, following the collapse of the Soviet Union, regards Marxism, more often that not, as a rather uninteresting discourse that has long since been outmoded. Seen from this point of view, does Young's subordination of Marxism to psychoanalysis in 'Psychoanalysis and Political Literary Theories', while offering a challenge to Marxism's 'success' within the realm of cultural theory, not at the same time risk participating in the anti-Marxist discourse that is currently holding sway in the capitalist economies of the West?

Ironically, it is precisely the prevailing common sense tendency to dismiss Marxism as a discourse relevant only to a superseded age, that prompted a recent 'deconstructive' intervention into the texts of Marx by Jacques Derrida. Prior to *Specters of Marx*,[9] the Marxist text had constituted merely a series of 'lacunae' in Derrida's work, 'explicitly calculated to mark the sites of a theoretical elaboration . . . *still to come*'.[10] But the consensus around the death of Marxism and the triumph of capitalism's free-market economy has become so unbearably dominant since the late 1980s that, for Derrida at least, there is an urgent need to reawaken the spirit of Marx's critique of capitalism via a 'radical critique' of Marx's critique. The 'radical critique' Derrida invokes in *Specters of Marx* is not to be confused with the previous sort of dogmatic Marxism with which Marxism is often associated. Indeed, it was the wish to reject this dominant, oversimplified interpretation of Marxism that for a long time made producing a 'transformational' reading of Marxism difficult for Derrida. Instead, he takes his:

> inspiration from a certain spirit of Marxism [that] . . . has always made of Marxism in principle and first of all a *radical* critique, namely a procedure ready to undertake its self-critique. This critique *wants itself* to be in principle and explicitly open to its own transformation, re-evaluation, self-interpretation. (88)

So if one problem with Young's subordination of Marxism to psychoanalysis in 'Psychoanalysis and Political Literary Theories' concerns doubts about the strategic effectiveness of such a manoeuvre, another relates to the way in which Young's presentation of Marxism tends to underestimate the extent to which, as deconstruction implicitly, and Derrida explicitly, suggest, Marxism contains within itself the possibility of its own self-critique, its own 'transformation, re-evaluation, self-interpretation'. Given sufficient time and space, it would be possible to demonstrate how Derrida's turning to the ghosts in Marx's writing – not only the ghost of Marx, but the function of the ghost in Marx's writing – and his following through of this thread in *Specters of Marx* to produce a re-reading of Marxism which is neither simply for Marxism, nor simply against it, enables a theory of the 'incommensurable' relation of the subject to the social to be located within the Marxist text itself. For the moment, such an analysis seems superfluous, given that Young himself, in an essay on 'The Dialectics of Cultural Criticism' published only five years after 'Psychoanalysis and Political Literary Theories', insists that the 'incompatibility of the inside and the outside' psychoanalysis theorizes is also the subject of a 'particularly acute and productive' Marxist analysis.[11]

THE PARADOXES OF CULTURAL CRITICISM

In 'The Dialectics of Cultural Criticism' Young describes how the dilemmas and paradoxes of the 'inside/outside dichotomy' have found themselves 'end-lessly perpetuated': from Burke, Coleridge and Arnold's embodiment of the concepts of culture in cultural institutions; through the attempt to shift the proper subject of critical attention outside such institutions and onto history, in the case of New Historicism, and culture, in that of Cultural Materialism; to Fredric Jameson's 'celebrated use of the Bonaventure Hotel as a metaphor of the post-modern condition' (16) in which the intellectual is trapped on the inside of the institution, unable to get out. Indeed, Young observes that:

> the very project of cultural criticism involves an impossible contradiction in which the critic places him or herself simultaneously inside and outside the culture. Here we find the basis for the interminable dialectic between inside and outside so characteristic of critical thinking. In general, individuals are inclined to endorse either one side or the other . . . The result is that the options remain entirely within the culture's own terms, and thus either repeat it uncritically . . or take up a transcendent position outside it and dismiss it in its entirety with the critic implicitly claiming that he or she

possesses the true knowledge (or the true culture) which the culture itself lacks. (18)[12]

An answer to the 'quandary of the choice between' these two positions, Young argues, can be found in a 'short but difficult' (18) early essay by the Marxist cultural critic Theodore W. Adorno entitled 'Cultural Criticism and Society'.[13] According to Young:

> [t]he deficiencies readily apparent in both methods led Adorno to propose that the practice of criticism must sustain an antinomy between them, a critical dissonant doubling which parallels the fissure within the individual work of art or in culture itself. He argues that cultural criticism must operate through an incompatible logic of transcendent and immanent critique, even if that removes the finality associated with either and substitutes unresolved contradiction. Dialectical criticism must sustain a duality, which means a continuous mobility between contesting positions. (21)

The point, then, for the Adorno of 'Cultural Criticism and Society' (in marked contrast to the emphasis on reproducing this interminable dialectic usually identifiable and identified in the work of the co-author of 'The Culture Industry')[14] is 'not to choose between the two at all but to practice both at the same time dialectically' (18): 'The dialectical critique of culture must both participate in culture and not participate. Only then does [the cultural critic] do justice to his object and to himself'.[15]

For Young, Adorno's analysis thus indicates the 'need to utilize the more complex antinomies that deploy in a productive way the paradoxical, impossible position of the cultural critic in society' (23).[16] But what interests me is not so much the possibilities Adorno's essay contains for 'coming to terms' with the paradoxical doubleness of the critics' situation both 'inside' and 'outside' culture at once, but rather the consequences of Young's reading of this essay for his own earlier representation of Marxism in 'Psychoanalysis and Political Literary Theories'. What Young's account of Adorno's Marxist cultural criticism seems to suggest is that, although psychoanalysis may, indeed, be itself a theory of the individual's incommensurable relation to the social, it is not the only discourse capable of theorizing this relation. Marxism also appears to contain the possibility of producing a theory of the incompatibility of the subject with the social. Like feminism, it too is apparently capable of that 'different kind of thinking and different kind of logic [that is] necessary to think them both together at the same time'.[17] The question, then, as Young observes, is 'to what extent such thinking would still be Marxist, or even perhaps feminist' (152)? Or psychoanalytic, I might add? For surely a reworking of the inside/outside dichotomy on which Marxism bases its relationship to psychoanalysis calls for a rethinking, not just of Marxism's relation to psycho-analysis, or even of the identity of Marxism, but of the very institution of psychoanalysis itself.

SUBJECT BOUNDARIES

Simply following one attempt on the part of psychoanalysis to theorize the relation between the subject and the social is enough to suggest that the challenge psychoanalysis represents to the 'Cartesian inside/outside dichotomy' has implications even more profound than those identified by Young. One way in which psychoanalysis has sought to address the issue of the individual's relation to the outside world is by means of its examination of that mode of object relationship Sandor Ferenczi termed 'introjection'. A complete history of psychoanalysis's account of 'introjection' – which can be traced through the work of Sigmund and Anna Freud, Melanie Klein, and, more recently, that of Nicolas Abraham and Maria Torok, and Jacques Derrida – is unnecessary at this point. Suffice it to say that, for psychoanalysis, the identity of the subject is based around its ability to distinguish itself from those objects that lie outside it. Taking up Ferenczi's term for use in his own work, Freud perceives the relation between subject (ego) and object (external world) as having its origin in the link between this opposition and the pleasure principle: 'In so far as the objects which are presented to it are sources of pleasure, [the ego] takes them into itself, "introjects" them (to use Ferenczi's 1909 term); and, on the other hand, it expels whatever within itself becomes a cause of unpleasure (the mechanism of projection)'.[18] This antagonism between introjection and projec-tion is first expressed, for Freud, in the language of the 'oldest' instinctual impulses – the oral – through the contrast between digesting and expelling. Here the ego's ability to judge has its basis in the desire to 'introject into itself everything that is good and to eject from itself everything that is bad'.[19] '[T]he judgement is: "I should like to eat this", or "I should like to spit it out"; and, put more generally: "I should like to take this into myself and to keep that out"'.[20] In this way, by constantly testing and measuring itself against external objects, the ego is able to determine the boundary-limits of its identity.

Psychoanalysis, and in particular Freud, thus utilizes the antagonism between introjection and projection to provide an answer to the question of the subject's relation to the social. What remains unexplained is the nature of this process's role in doing so. As Laplanche and Pontalis point out in *The Language of Psychoanalysis*, the question that still needs to be answered is does the operation of introjection and projection '*presuppose*' a distinction between ego and object (inside and outside), or does it actually '*constitute*' it?[21] Laplanche and Pontalis present Anna Freud as having taken the first view. For her ' "... we might suppose that projection and introjection were methods which depend on the differentiation of the ego from the outside world" '.[22] By contrast, the 'Kleinian school ... has brought to the fore the dialectic of the introjection/projection of "good" and "bad" objects, and ... treats this dialectic as the actual basis of discrimination between inside and outside' (355). Despite their respective differences, however, both versions of the process of introjection and projection take for granted the idea that such a distinction between 'inside and outside' *can* be achieved. And, indeed, to use the opposition between introjection and projection as a means of explaining the subject's relationship to the social *is* in many ways to prejudge the issue. After all, it is the ego's relation to the outside world that is *supposed* to be in question here. Does employing the antagonism between introjection and projection to either *articulate* the boundary which separates the ego off from the outside world, or account for this boundary's *constitution*, not therefore suggest that this question has to a certain extent already been answered? From this perspective, the contrast between introjection and projection appears to obscure, rather than explain, the nature of the subject's relationship to the social. And all the more so given that it is the boundary between the ego and the object that is used to actually establish the antithesis between introjection and projection; and which, moreover, provides a means of distinguishing between these two concepts. The problem of the ego's relation to external objects is not resolved by the antagonism between introjection and projection, then, for the simple reason that introjection and projection are themselves entirely dependent on this relation for their identities. In order to answer the question of the ego's relation to the outside world, the concepts of introjection and projection must themselves be put in question. We need to ask what exactly is meant by 'introjection' and 'projection'?

A return to Ferenczi soon reveals that answering *this* question is by no means a simple task. In his essay on 'Introjection and Transference' Ferenczi employs the term 'introjection' to refer to a process of enlargement of the ego.[23] According to Ferenczi, it is 'a kind of diluting process, by means of which [the neurotic subject] tries to mitigate the poignancy of free-floating, unsatisfied, and unsatisfiable, unconscious wish-impulses' (40). This process he places in 'diametrical contrast' to projection.

> Whereas the paranoiac expels from his ego the impulses that have become unpleasant, the neurotic helps himself by taking into the ego as large as possible a part of the outer world, making it the object of unconscious

phantasies . . . One might give to this process, in contrast to projection, the name of *Introjection*. (40)

Ferenczi thus uses the distinction between the inside and the outside of the ego to both define introjection and projection, and to distinguish between them. Introjection takes external objects and their inherent qualities into the inside, while projection reverses this process, expelling objects from the inside to the outside. But it is the very dividing line between the ego and the external world on which this distinction depends that Ferenczi's analysis of the concepts of introjection and projection also seems to bring into question and blur.

Immediately after establishing the above contrast between introjection and projection, Ferenczi observes that '[t]he neurotic is constantly seeking for objects with whom he can identify himself, to whom he can transfer feelings, whom he can thus draw into his circle of interest, i.e. introject' (40/41). Ferenczi's neurotic, then, wants to bring 'inside' only that part of the external world with which he can identify. But does this very identification of the neurotic with these external objects not put the absolute exteriority of these objects in question? Are these objects straightforwardly outside? Is it a part of the outside world that the neurotic wishes to introject, or is it merely a part of himself;[24] a part of himself, moreover, which has to be projected outside onto the external world *before* it can be introjected inside?[25]

The boundary between the ego and the external world is further complicated by Ferenczi's account of projection. 'We see the paranoiac on a similar search for objects who might be suitable for the projection of "sexual hunger" that is creating unpleasant feeling', he writes in 'Introjection and Transference' (41). The first part of each process is thus 'similar', according to Ferenczi: both the paranoiac and the neurotic are looking for objects onto which they can transfer their feelings. The difference between introjection and projection appears to rest with the final destination of those feelings. Whereas those of the neurotic are drawn back 'into his circle of interest, i.e. introject[ed]', those of the paranoiac are attached to an external object and left there. As a result, 'the psychoneurotic suffers from a widening, the paranoiac from a shrinking of his ego' (41). But given that a question mark has already been placed against the apparent externality of the objects introjected by the neurotic, should the externality of the objects onto which the paranoiac projects those impulses that have become a 'burden' (40) not also come under suspicion?

Freud's account of the origin of projection in 'Beyond the Pleasure Principle' suggests that the answer to this question is an affirmative one.[26] Speculating on the relationship between consciousness and mental process, Freud presents a picture of a living organism that is susceptible to two types of stimulation: those excitations which emanate from the external world and which would kill the organism if it were not 'provided with a protective shield' against such stimuli (298); and those excitations the organism receives from within and against which there is no such shield. Lacking the protective barrier which safeguards it from external stimuli, Freud describes how, in order to defend itself from 'any internal excitations which produce too great an increase of unpleasure', the 'living vesicle' resorts to projecting them outside itself: 'there is a tendency to treat them as though they were acting, not from the inside, but from the outside, so that it may be possible to bring the shield against stimuli into operation as a means of defence against them. This is the origin of *projection*', Freud states (301). Henceforward, the unpleasurable internal excitations are perceived as stimuli emanating from, and belonging entirely to, the outside of the organism. But this outside, as Freud suggests, is not expelled to some absolute exteriority; it is forged and maintained at the heart of the inside, and is kept outside by the very living organism from which it is supposed to be separated.

At this point a question mark can be placed against the respective abilities of both introjection *and* projection to distinguish between the inside and the outside of the ego. For while they do, indeed, maintain a distinction between the inside and the outside, both of these processes also work to problematize any such distinction. For both the inside is also on the outside, while the outside is both inside and outside too. This inability to distinguish once and for all between the inside and the outside of the ego creates a problem for the respective identities of introjection and projection – based as both of these concepts are precisely on this distinction. Introjection cannot be placed in a relationship of 'diametrical contrast' to projection. On the contrary, introjection and projection are mutually interdependent, one upon the other, both inside and outside each other at the same time. And this in turn has profound implications for the way in which psychoanalysis understands the ego's relation to the outside world.

Initially, the boundary of the ego – the place where it comes into contact with the outside world – appears to have two related functions. Firstly, this boundary acts as a container or body bag for the identity of the ego. Secondly, it acts as a protective apparatus or shield, in order to defend and separate the contents of this bag from the outside. By passing objects through this boundary, either by introjection or projection, the ego maintains its relation to the external world. However, this boundary also has a third function. At the same time as maintaining a distinction between the inside and the outside of the ego, it also acts as a point of communication and exchange between the contents of this bag and the outside. Writing on the 'skin' of the ego, first in an article and later in his book *Skin Ego*, Didier Anzieu puts it as follows:

The primary function of the skin is as the sac which contains and retains inside it the goodness and fullness accumulating there through feeding, care, the bathing in words. Its second function is as the interface which marks the boundary with the outside and keeps that outside out; it is the barrier which protects against penetration by the aggression and greed emanating from others, whether people or objects. Finally, the third function – which *the skin shares with the mouth and which it performs at least as often* – is as a primary means of communicating with others . . .[27]

The boundary between subject and object is thus complex and paradoxical. It still divides the ego from the external world; but at the same time it joins them together, too. The boundary between the ego and the external world is thus not only that which helps establish and define the identity of the ego; it is also that which puts that identity at risk, by opening the ego toward others.[28]

Indeed, it is only by means of this relationship with outside others that the identity of the ego is formed. We have already seen how, for Freud, the infant's capacity to establish the limits of its identity has its basis in the ability to take some objects into itself and to keep others out. And for Ferenczi, too: 'We may suppose that to the new-born child everything perceived by the senses appears unitary, so to speak monistic. Only later does he learn to distinguish from his ego the malicious things, forming an outer world, that do not obey his will'. This is what Ferenczi calls 'the first projection process, the primordial projection'.[29] However, it is not just the way in which the ego introjects into itself everything that is good and ejects from itself everything that is bad that is of interest here. More interesting still is what this process says about the formation of the ego. For the ego does not constitute a datum point from which self-awareness is built. Rather, its existence is linked to the existence of external objects. The ego is inconceivable without primary experience of the existence of external objects. It is the existence of these external objects (the outside world), after all, which provides the ego with an awareness of its own self. The ego is thus born out of its relationship to the external world: the latter is a constituent part of the ego. The ego is formed precisely by means of this pressure from outside: it is only by defending the ego as an ego that the ego can be constructed as an ego. The boundaries which enclose the ego thus need to be crossed *before* they can be established. Ego and object are both inside and outside each other at the same time.

THE END OF ANALYSIS: HYPNOSIS

This reformulation of the 'inside/outside dichotomy' has profound implications, not just for the identity of the concepts of introjection and projection,
nor even that of the subject, but for the very identity and institution of
psychoanalysis, despite (or precisely because of) the fact that these questions
occur in, and arise out of, psychoanalysis. Before developing psychoanalysis
Freud had tried to 'cure' hysterical symptoms by means of hypnosis. The
intention was to use hypnosis to place the patient in an unconscious, sleep-like
state. An idea would then be introduced, suggesting to the patient that the
symptom or its cause should be relieved. However, in 1896 Freud abandoned
hypnosis and began to concentrate exclusively on analysing the discourse of
the hysterical patient. It was with this abandonment of hypnosis – and with it
Freud's rejection of those practices that depend on the analyst influencing the
patient in some way (advice, manipulation, suggestion, hypnosis, etc.) – that
the 'science' of psychoanalysis was established.

   The difference and identity of psychoanalysis is thus founded on the
distinction it draws between the knowledge and information emanating from
the analyst, and that which originates with the patient. Whereas the hypnotist
makes direct suggestions to the patient, the psychoanalyst concentrates simply
on listening to, and interpreting, the patient's account of his or her own life
story. Of course, it would be too simplistic to suggest that psychoanalysis is
able to maintain a distinction between the analyst and the patient. As we have
seen, it is difficult to conceive of a boundary or dividing line that is not already
a form of joining. Nor can psychoanalysis itself be said to believe in any simple
way that it has achieved such a division. It quickly became clear to Freud that
the analyst could still sometimes have an influence on the autobiographical
story told by the patient – not least through the tendency of patients to *transfer*
unconscious ideas onto the person of the analyst; that is, to play out, as
Ferenczi puts it, 'long forgotten psychological experiences' in their current
relationship with the analyst.[30] Nevertheless, working in accordance with the
idea that the 'proper', or at any rate 'ideal', psychoanalytic experience is one
where the analyst does not intervene in the patient's story, but is merely an aid
to the patient's own self-analysis, Freud aimed to maintain the distinction
between the analyst and patient, and in this way retain control over the
analysis, by means of the dissolution of the subjective elements of the analysis:
what he literally called the transference. It was through the analysis of the
transference that Freud attempted to identify what belonged to whom in
the analysis. Hence the importance he placed on analysts themselves under-
going analysis, so that they could be aware of their own involvement in the

analysis, their own transference onto the patient, a process he termed counter-transference. As Freud observes in 'Analysis Terminable and Interminable':

> Among the factors which influence the prospects of analytic treatment and add to its difficulties in the same manner as the resistances, must be reckoned not only the nature of the patient's ego, but the individuality of the analyst . . . It almost looks as if analysis were the third of those 'impossible' professions in which one can be sure beforehand of achieving unsatisfying results. The other two, which have been known much longer, are education and government. Obviously we cannot demand that the prospective analyst should be perfect before he takes up analysis, in other words that only persons of such high and rare perfection should enter the profession. But where is the poor wretch to acquire the ideal qualifications which he will need in his profession? The answer is, in analysis of himself, with which his preparation for this future activity begins.[31]

The analysis of the transference is therefore crucial to the identity of psychoanalysis. And it is the lengths psychoanalysis has gone to investigate this relation – and thus, in a sense, question its own analytical activity – that makes it so interesting. But in an extraordinary essay which returns to psychoanalysis' founding split from hypnosis, Mikkel Borch-Jacobsen has demonstrated that it is:

> . . . difficult, at least, to maintain the thesis (authorized by Freud himself) of a pure and simple break between psychoanalysis, on the one hand, and hypnosis and suggestion, on the other. Psychoanalysis no doubt did found itself on the abandonment of hypnosis – but only, it must be recognized, to see hypnosis reappear, sometimes under other names or in other forms, at the cross-roads of all questions; hence the importance of reconsidering this so-called abandonment, not so much to initiate a 'return to hypnosis' as to examine, in light of the questions Freud was asking himself in his last phase, the reasons why in his first phase he had believed, rather too quickly, that these issues were settled. In other words, what is important is to reconsider what Freud called the 'prehistory' of psychoanalysis, to return to it with the suspicion that this 'prehistory' belongs to a certain future of psychoanalysis rather than to a long-dead past.[32]

Returning to that part of the history of psychoanalysis which extends from the rejection of hypnosis to the identification of transference as a 'distinct problem', Borch-Jacobsen shows how Freud finds it 'more and more difficult, even impossible, to distinguish between the mechanics of analysis and those of hypnosis, even though hypnosis was supposed to have been discarded once and for all' (54), precisely because it is the relation between the ego and the object that produces the ego. As Borch-Jacobsen emphasizes, the 'ego forms itself or *is born*' (60) out of its relationships with the object:

> Thus there is no ego, no subject to form an idea of the object and/or of the identificatory model, since it is precisely in the singular 'event' of the appropriation . . . that the ego as such emerges . . .
>
> This first 'emotional tie' to another, which is also the unrepresentable event of my 'own' birth, can never be remembered, never be recalled to memory. This is also why it can never be 'dissolved', as Freud would have it. (60/61)

This creates problems for any notion of an irreducible distinction between hypnosis and psychoanalysis. The rigorous, 'proper', 'true' analysis is supposed to begin where hypnosis ends – but it is now through the analysis of the relation between the ego and the object, of hypnosis, the transference. However, this relation cannot be dissolved, as it is constitutive of the ego: it is precisely the relation between the ego and the object that produces the ego. Far from their being a clear difference between them, the distinction between psychoanalysis and hypnosis is blurred:

> Thus one issue – the beginning of 'true' analysis – now becomes another, distressing one: the end of analysis. The end of analysis becomes the end of analysis. Is there an end to analysis, after all? Is analysis 'terminable'? Can hypnotic transference be 'dissolved'? Or is it instead the part of analysis that cannot be analyzed, of which the patient cannot be cured . . .? (57)

This question is of vital importance to psychoanalysis, since it is upon this issue that the identity of psychoanalysis rests. Yet it is a question that psychoanalysis has never really been able to answer. 'In the end', Borch-Jacobsen asks, 'is psychoanalysis, to use François Roustang's expression, "long drawn out suggestion"?'

> There is certainly no way to decide on the basis of the facts. Indeed, can we ever determine whether an analysis is really over, whether the transference is really gone? It is more useful to ask what the transference *is* – that is, to ask . . . what *hypnosis* is – if we want to know whether the transference can truly be eliminated. This last question rapidly brings us back to the original 'enigma', that of the . . . 'emotional tie', the 'rapport *sans* rapport' with another; for it is this rapport that Freud found in the transference, and

perhaps it was simply pointless to try to dissolve it. It is constituent of the 'subject' and, as such, unrecollectable, untellable, unrepresentable – indissoluble. (57)

POST-PSYCHOANALYSIS?

The attempt in psychoanalysis to theorize the subject's relation to society by means of introjection thus points not only to that which exists 'beyond' Marxism and feminism, but 'beyond' psychoanalysis, too.[33] This is what I was referring to when I mentioned earlier that the psychoanalysis' rethinking of the 'inside/outside dichotomy' may have implications greater even than those suggested by Young in 'Psychoanalysis and Political Literary Theories'.

To bring psychoanalysis to bear on Marxism in order to provide the latter with a fully developed theory of the subject may be, as Young insists, to overlook the extent to which psychoanalysis is already a theory of the '*impossibility*' – and yet at the same time, I would stress, also the *possibility* – of the subject's relation to the social. But even so, the last word on this matter cannot be left with psychoanalysis. Not only is such a manoeuvre questionable on strategic grounds, it also risks underestimating the extent to which Marxism is capable of providing a productive theory of the subject's 'incompatible' relation to the social – as Young himself demonstrates with his analysis of Adorno's cultural criticism.

Accordingly, it might be thought that the solution is not to choose between the competing claims to theories of the subject of Marxism and psychoanalysis at all, but to utilize both at the same time. In his introductory chapter to the collection in which 'Psychoanalysis and Political Literary Theories' first appeared (entitled, significantly enough from the point of view of this book, 'Cultural Studies and Psychoanalysis'), James Donald, emphasizing that a boundary is a point of separation as well as exchange, reminds us 'of the impossibility of any easy synthesis between [psychoanalysis and cultural theory], or of any final answers to the enigmatic transactions between subject and culture, between the psychic and the social'.[34] 'Any such attempt to merge the two bodies of theory blunts [the] specific insights' of each, according to Donald, while at the same time ignoring their 'incompatibilities and contradictions'. Refusing to collapse psychoanalysis and cultural theory into each other, Donald argues that '[w]hat seems potentially more fruitful is the dialogue in which, although the two discourses remain distinct – they are always to some extent talking past each other – the questions untranslatably specific to each can provide new thinking and insights in the other' (3). But what tends to be overlooked in such a conception of the 'threshold' or boundary between

Marxism and psychoanalysis, the subject and social, is the way in which these two discourses are not merely placed in a state of unresolvable tension by the 'different kind of logic and different kind of thinking [that] would be necessary to think them both together at the same time' (to, in Donald's words, 'hang onto to (sic) both the operations of the unconscious and the opacity of the social at the same time' (8)), the very identities of Marxism and psychoanalysis are brought into question.

As Young insists in 'Psychoanalysis and Political Literary Theories', if Marxist theorists want to add psychoanalysis's ready-made theory of the subject to their thinking (and not just restrict their use of psychoanalysis to the occasional importation of 'one or two concepts'), they need to rethink the 'Cartesian inside/outside dichotomy' on which Marxism's relationship to psychoanalysis is based and which psychoanalysis challenges. The question then is to what extent such theory would still be Marxist? '[I]f Marxism did re-examine its relation to psychoanalysis', Young asks, 'would it end up in the dreaded position of being post-Marxist?' (149).[35] But the challenge psycho-analysis presents to the 'inside/outside dichotomy' has implications not just for the identity of Marxism. Psychoanalysis' 'rethinking of the exclusive claims of the forms of rational logic' on which both the 'inside/outside dichotomy' and the relation between Marxism and psychoanalysis are 'predicated' also risks going beyond itself . . . beyond psychoanalysis, as it were. Providing a theory of the relation between Marxism and psychoanalysis, the subject and the social, is therefore not a matter of somehow negotiating the 'intersections' or 'threshold' between Marxism and psychoanalysis. The question of the subject rather opens up both Marxism and psychoanalysis to the possibility of dis-covering new forms of knowledge in the margins of, and spaces between, Marxism *and* psychoanalysis; forms of knowledge Marxism and psychoanalysis can begin to understand only by rethinking their identities *as* Marxism and psychoanalysis.

CHAPTER 6

www.culturalstudies.ac.uk

CULTURAL STUDIES OF CULTURAL STUDIES

I want to begin by risking a proposition: that 'new technology' cannot be understood *apart* from the university. No doubt some may consider this rather an odd statement to make. But if, to quote Bill Gates, new information and communications technology is transforming 'our culture as dramatically as Gutenberg's press did the Middle Ages', then this technology is also having an effect on how those of us who work in universities think about and interpret this transformation.[1] By this I'm referring not so much to the consequences of information technology for the focus of academic research (studies of cyberspace and virtual reality taking their place alongside those of more established subjects), nor even its form (with scholars now being able to communicate in bits as well as atoms), as the way in which this technology is changing the very nature of university knowledge, including knowledge of new technology. What this means, in effect, is that, to paraphrase Bill Readings, to whose work I want to return shortly, the question of new technology is a question that is posed not just *in* the university but *to* the university. Indeed, given that, as Jacques Derrida points out in 'Mochlos', 'information technology which, while appearing nowadays to escape the control of the university . . . is its product and its most faithful representative', the study of this technology in many ways *is* the study of the university.[2]

But how are we to study the university? By what means? With what frameworks? Using what methods? Previously this self-questioning role was assigned in the UK to English literature and elsewhere to philosophy. An increasing awareness of the nationalistic and political nature of English literature, however, has led to literary studies being gradually replaced as a means of thinking the university by cultural studies. Yet even if it is acknowledged that one of the spaces in which issues relating to the university are today most provocatively raised is indeed cultural studies, a number of questions remain. Not least among these is that concerning the exact nature of cultural studies' interest in the university. To be sure, given that it can be defined as a politically committed analysis of culture/power relations that at the same time reflects back on itself to analyse its own relations to politics and to power, cultural studies is capable of providing a productive starting point for addressing the question of the university, and from there new technology. Yet for all its self-reflexivity, cultural studies has tended to keep its examination of the university within certain limits.

If it is some of these limits I want to draw attention to in what follows, my intention is not to suggest cultural studies should be abandoned as a means of understanding the university. Nor do I want break with the tradition of cultural studies as it has existed until now in order to found a 'new' cultural studies. Insofar as my account is critical of some of the limits cultural studies has set to its examination of the university, it must cause problems for current conceptions of cultural studies; but this does not mean I am no longer 'doing cultural studies'. On the contrary, since the specificity of cultural studies, in certain of its dominant conceptions at least, is marked by the tension between its self-consciously politically committed nature and its theoretical self-interrogation of what it means to 'do cultural studies', this kind of radical critique of cultural studies is an inextricable part of what it is to 'do cultural studies'.[3] Granted, only relatively rarely has cultural studies taken its much vaunted self-reflexivity so far as to put the fundamental principles on which it is based explicitly at risk. But what is so interesting about cultural studies, particularly when it comes to thinking about the university, is that it contains both the possibility and the promise of doing so. By using this aspect of cultural studies against itself, as it were, to expose the exclusions on which cultural studies is dependent for its identity, I want to insist that it is possible to shift cultural studies beyond the limits it has set to its own thinking on the question of the university.

THERE IS NOTHING OUTSIDE THE UNIVERSITY

Ironically, this tendency on the part of cultural studies to limit its exploration of the university stems from what is undoubtedly one of the most notable features of cultural studies' relationship with the academic institution: the way in which its interrogation of the principles and procedures of the traditional disciplines has led cultural studies to resist placing limits around its own identity. The argument here is that, having accused the established disciplines of a repressive division of the field of knowledge, it would be somewhat hypocritical for cultural studies to then occupy itself with policing its own borders. So cultural studies presents itself as a counter- or anti-discipline instead, the fluid boundaries and changing contents of which function to unnerve other disciplines in the arts, humanities and social sciences, while simultaneously working against cultural studies' own reduction to a set of fixed or closed disciplinary methods.

Of course, this very lack of 'fixity' means it is too simplistic to describe cultural studies in this way: as if, despite all cultural, national and temporal differences, cultural studies is self-identical in its very openness. Just as there is no unified 'university', so there is no one such thing as cultural studies. Cultural studies, as its name suggests, cannot be thought of in the singular. Nevertheless, this model of cultural studies as a 'counter-' or 'anti-discipline' continues to dominate the field. Hence Richard Johnson's insistence, in what has become one of the most frequently cited definitions of cultural studies, that:

> A codification of methods or knowledges (instituting them, for example, in formal curricula or in courses on 'methodology') runs against some main features of cultural studies as a tradition: its openness and theoretical versatility, its reflexive even self-conscious mood, and, especially, the importance of critique. I mean critique in the fullest sense: not criticism merely, nor even polemic, but procedures by which other traditions are approached both for what they may yield and for what they inhibit. Critique involves stealing away the more useful elements and rejecting the rest. From this point of view cultural studies is a process, a kind of alchemy for producing useful knowledge; codify it and you may halt its reactions.[4]

It is not just the contradictory nature of this kind of presentation of cultural studies that is so striking: the way in which the refusal to claim a disciplinary status for itself is used (and cited) as a means of marking off the difference, and hence the identity, of cultural studies from other disciplines. Also worth noting is the fear of institutionalization which has so often accompanied cultural studies' anti-disciplinary emphasis; a fear clearly evident in Johnson's concerns regarding 'formal curricula' and 'courses on "methodology"'. The worry here is that the modern university's disciplinary rationale will restrict the very openness and lack of fixity that is seen as being one of cultural studies' most important characteristics. Yet as Ted Striphas observes in an issue of the journal *Cultural Studies* entirely given over to 'the institutionalization of cultural studies', arguments of this kind are based on a 'conflation of institutionalization and disciplinization' to the point where the university is reduced to 'an empty bearer of disciplinary logic'.[5] As such they display little appreciation of cultural studies' ambivalent relation to the university: the way in which, from its beginnings in the extra-mural and adult education teaching for the Universities of Oxford, Hull and Leeds of Williams, Hoggart and Thompson respectively, moving through the institution of the Centre for Contemporary Cultural Studies in the University of Birmingham, to its current and ever more visible place on university curricula, at international conferences, and in refereed journals, cultural studies has been critical of, and yet at the same time inherently bound up with, the university. Nor do such arguments take much account of the way in which, as Striphas suggests, and as the history of cultural studies in the UK, the US and elsewhere would appear to confirm, 'given the prospect, even the inevitability of institutionalization, danger, and perhaps more importantly, *possibility* exist alongside one another' (453). Instead, the university tends to be seen as a 'totalizing disciplinary regime' (461) with the institutionalization of cultural studies being viewed as equivalent to its complete assimilation.

For Alan O'Shea, writing in the same issue of *Cultural Studies*, this kind of presentation of the university as a monolithic totality has often led to the ideal 'cultural studies practitioner' being depicted as a romantic 'outsider'.[6] After all, if the university really is so powerful then opposition can only come from 'outside'. But even among those who have not adopted quite such a totalizing view of institutionalization there has been a sense that for cultural studies to concern itself with the operation of the university is for it to be too tied up with the very system it is trying to oppose. From this point of view, cultural studies has to forge relations with social movements and forces belonging to the 'real world' of historical materiality that lies 'outside' the university if it is to have the political impact it seeks. What is overlooked by such arguments is the way in which any attempt to move outside the institution is already an institutional move, the notion that there is an outside to the institution being itself an institutional idea 'as old as the institution itself'.[7] Indeed, despite (or perhaps more accurately, precisely because of) the emphasis that is placed in cultural studies on the importance of examining the concrete, practical realities of everyday experience, few of the critics who have made such claims have gone to the trouble of actually analysing the concrete practical realities of their own everyday situation – which more often than not involves the contemporary university. 'For all the vigorous debate' that has taken place within cultural studies over the question of institutionalization, 'little attention has been paid to its own institutional practices';[8] or its own 'existing institutionalizations', for that matter.[9] Instead, the politico-institutional forces which have gone to determine much of the work that has been done in cultural studies have tended to remain unexamined, and have thus been left to shape and control a cultural studies which has often proceeded to act, in this respect at least, in a blind and less than conscious fashion. Witness the number of cultural studies texts that have been written lately claiming that the writing of cultural studies texts is not enough. By refusing to concern itself with the question of the text –

because this is not the point, it's the 'real world' that matters – the only way the project of engaging with the world 'outside' the text has been able to explain how it will do so is, paradoxically, by producing more text. The debate cannot develop, and has instead justified continually repeating itself by project-ing a mistaken Other in the form of 'theory' or 'textuality', the correction of which requires the constant restatement of the original position.

FROM DISCIPLINARITY . . .

But if one university 'discipline' that cultural studies practitioners have typi-cally failed to raise fundamental questions for is cultural studies, this does not mean that the latter is incapable of providing a means of 'critiquing' discipli-narity. Far from it. A critical attitude toward disciplinarity in fact lies at the heart of cultural studies. In an essay in which he reflects on the history and origins of the subject in order to gauge the directions it may take in the future, Raymond Williams reveals how cultural studies as we now know it arose precisely out of an insistence on the part of people in adult education, in the WEA (Workers Education Authority), in university extramural Extension classes, to challenge ideas of the disciplinary:

> These people were, after all, in a practical position to say 'well, if you tell me that question goes outside your discipline, then bring me someone whose discipline *will* cover it, or bloody well get outside of the discipline and answer it yourself.' It was from this entirely rebellious and untidy situation that the extraordinarily complicated and often muddled conver-gences of what became Cultural Studies occurred; precisely because people wouldn't accept those boundaries.[10]

More than any syllabus or set of defensible disciplines, it is this that constitutes what it is to do cultural studies, for Williams. And, significantly, he extends this spirit of rebellion to take in, not just the 'established' disciplines, but cultural studies 'itself'. For if it were not self-critical, if it could 'define' itself as a 'defensible' discipline, 'justify its importance, demonstrate its rigour' (158), then the meaning claimed for cultural studies would include anything but the meaning of cultural studies. Such pressures are 'precisely the opposite of those of the original project', he insists (158).[11]

For cultural studies to fail to interrogate its identity as a body of knowledge, then, is for cultural studies to fail to live up to its own idea of itself. Yet for all its emphasis on self-conscious reflexivity, this is something cultural studies, on Williams' own account, has too often forgotten to do. Instead, as Johnson

acknowledges, cultural studies has tended to steal away the most 'useful'
elements of other traditions of thought, while rejecting the rest – including in
the process those elements that might raise problems for the identity of cultural
studies. As a result, cultural studies' status and identity as a body of knowledge
has rarely been put in question by its critique of disciplinarity. Even when
cultural studies has been at its most critical of disciplinary structures, it has
often left those structures intact. And nowhere is this perhaps more apparent
than with regard to the very means by which cultural studies has sought to
resist the disciplinary logic of the university and thus keep its identity open
and unfixed: inter-disciplinarity.

. . . TO INTER-DISCIPLINARITY . . .

'It would be a mistake to see cultural studies as a new discipline, or even a
discrete constellation of disciplines', Graeme Turner writes in the latest edition
of his introduction to *British Cultural Studies*:

> Cultural studies is an inter-disciplinary field where certain concerns and
> methods have converged; the usefulness of this convergence is that it has
> enabled us to understand phenomena and relationships that were not
> accessible through the existing disciplines. It is not, however, a unified
> field . . .[12]

And without doubt inter-disciplinarity has at times been extremely useful to
the challenge cultural studies has offered to the way in which the modern
university's disciplining of knowledge limits thought to the asking of certain
questions and the study of a relatively narrow set of things. At the same time
as helping to challenge the idea of the university, however, inter-disciplinarity
also supports it. For as Meaghan Morris intimates, there can be detected in
inter-disciplinarity a desire for a 'utopian condition, a borderless academic
world';[13] a desire, in other words, to get back to the 'unity and synthesis' of
knowledge that is seen as being the case before the academic division of labour
and trend toward specialization that is characteristic of the modern university,
and which some theorists have even equated with the dynamics of modernity
itself, took place.[14] It is a dream, moreover, that lies at the heart of the
academic institution, as the word 'university', which 'names not only the
totalising goal of the university, its purpose as rationalising everything, but also
the singleness of the university, "turning everything into one"', suggests.[15]

At which point the question arises: 'Was there ever such a "unity" of
academic labour?' Now it would not be too difficult to pursue this train of

thought by producing a history of the university which revealed this idea of an originary moment of synthesis to be something of a myth. But if the idea of the university's decline from some era of national and cultural wholeness is a myth, so, too, is the idea that at the origin of the university lies a myth. As Geoffrey Bennington has shown, this kind of 'myth of the origin' – that at the origin there is a myth of the origin – is itself a myth, one that is indicative of our own desire and drive for origins.[16] Interestingly, for Bennington, the relation at the borders is a more productive way of approaching the problem of origins. Seen in the context of the university, this call to pay attention to borders and boundaries immediately raises questions concerning the identity and institution of knowledge: what it includes and excludes. It is certainly noticeable that whereas so-called 'legitimate' 'methods or knowledges', those that either fall within or can at least be ascribed to recognized disciplines (literary studies, sociology, politics, philosophy, history, communication and media studies, etc.), have been privileged and included in cultural studies' inter-disciplinary canon, those 'less legitimate' methods or knowledge (hypnosis, for example, or death) that have not been encapsulated by the 'established' disciplines have tended to be marginalized or ignored.[17] While cultural and theoretical diversity may be positively sanctioned and actively promoted by this kind of 'inter-disciplinary' project, then, it is also simultaneously restricted and restrained. In particular, a transparent norm is produced, one which says that this inter-disciplinary negotiation and translation between disciplines is welcome, so long as it stays within certain limits; limits which cultural studies has been able to locate and define without having to bring its own identity and legitimacy as a body of knowledge radically into question.[18]

. . . AND BEYOND

It is these limits that any rigorous attempt on cultural studies' part to 'critique' ideas of disciplinarity must address. The question of course is how? Clearly it is not enough to simply adopt an inter-disciplinary approach, since at the same time as the idea of inter-disciplinarity challenges the boundaries of academic disciplines, it also works to maintain them. Instead, attention needs to be turned to what cultural studies itself 'yields' and 'inhibits'. But how are we to set about producing such a *cultural studies of cultural studies*? And perhaps more importantly, what institutional forms might such a rethought cultural studies – one which does not simply exclude those forms of 'knowledge' that are not, or at least not yet, considered legitimate – actually take?

A starting point for answering these questions can be found in a text which, since its posthumous publication in 1996, has rapidly come to be regarded as almost essential to any serious discussion of the contemporary university: Bill Readings' *The University in Ruins*.[19] Readings' book has as its basis a conviction that the 'notion of culture as the legitimating idea of the modern University has reached the end of its usefulness' (5) in the world of technological capitalism, and that there is therefore 'no longer any idea of the University'. That 'idea has now lost all content' (39), Readings insists, and has been replaced by the notion of 'excellence' which has the 'singular advantage of being meaningless, or to put it more precisely, non-referential' (22). But it is not so much the central thesis of *The University in Ruins* that interests me here as an aspect of Readings' thought which, to date, has been at best somewhat glossed over, and at worst regarded rather negatively: his analysis of cultural studies.[20]

THIS IS EXCELLENT

At first sight Readings' account of the current crisis in the idea of the contemporary university is rather devastating, at least as far as cultural studies is concerned. According to Readings, the recent institutional success of cultural studies is due to the fact that, '[t]o put it in the cruellest terms . . . Cultural Studies presents a vision of culture that is appropriate for the age of excellence' (17). From this point of view, culture 'finally becomes an object of study in direct proportion to the abandonment of the attempt to provide a determining explanation of culture' (99). The refusal of cultural studies to identify itself as a discipline is thus perceived, not so much as an attempt to resist the disciplinary control of the university, as a sign of its lack of any one notion of culture *per se*. Culture 'no longer has a specific content' (17). Like 'excellence' it 'ceases to mean anything *as such*' (99). What is more, it is only when culture is 'dereferentialized' in this way that the rise of cultural studies becomes possible: the 'very fecundity and multiplicity of work in Cultural Studies is enabled by the fact that culture no longer functions as a specific referent to any one thing or set of things – which is why Cultural Studies can be so popular while refusing general theoretical definition' (17).

Readings is not rejecting cultural studies as a means of thinking the university here in favour of, say, a return to literary studies or philosophy. Since the 'global system of capitalism no longer requires a cultural content in terms of which to interpellate and manage subjects' (103), he maintains that neither the study of literature nor philosophy, those disciplines previously assigned guardianship of culture, can be used to reflect on cultural life. Instead, 'we have to accept that the existing disciplinary model of the humanities is on the road to extinction' (176) and is likely to be replaced by cultural studies, precisely because cultural studies 'does not propose culture as a regulatory ideal for research and teaching so much as recognize the inability of culture to function as such an idea any longer' (174). But if we cannot return to the idea of the University of Culture, neither are we trapped in its ruins in the University of Excellence. Rather '[w]e have to recognize that the university is a *ruined institution*', one that has lost its historical reason for being, while at the same time 'thinking what it means to dwell in those ruins without recourse to romantic nostalgia' (169). For Readings, this means turning the process of 'dereferentialization that is characteristic of the post-historical University to good advantage. That is to say, we should try to think what it may mean to have a University that has no idea' (122). And, significantly, he sees the chance to confront this dereferentialization as being precisely the 'task incumbent upon Cultural Studies' (118):

> The chance to face up to this issue arises because the endeavor of Cultural Studies is the contemporary way to speculate on the question of what it means to be *in* the University, with the added complication that, unlike German idealism, speculation itself is not already the answer to the question. Such is the situation of the posthistorical University, the University without an idea. The question remains, then, of how to understand the work that Cultural Studies does – how to conceptualize the mass of analyses as something other than fascinating symptoms of nostalgia for what the University once was. How, that is, can Cultural Studies do something other than critique culture excellently? (118)

Cultural studies thus remains extremely important to Readings, for all its close ties to the University of Excellence, precisely because it is *the* contemporary way to think about the university.

Having said that, it is important to note that it is not so much the dominant tradition of cultural studies that is of interest to him here. As far as Readings is concerned the traditional 'cry of Cultural Studies that the University must be left behind has proved a particularly fruitful way of staying in the University' (91). Instead, the question of the university must be approached from that 'difficult space – neither inside nor outside – where one is' (171). It is this refusal to simply abandon the university for the 'real' world 'outside' that makes Readings' work on the university so interesting. For unlike so much of contemporary cultural studies, Readings has clearly learnt the 'lesson that it is necessary to think the institution'. And, ironically, given the way in which cultural studies has so often castigated 'theory' for being too naively elitist, too closely bound up with the values of the university, he has learnt this lesson precisely from 'theory' – specifically, in this case, 'deconstruction'.[21]

It would have been interesting at this point to have speculated on the significance of Readings' position in a department of comparative literature to his reflections on the university; for although he acknowledges that '"English and Comparative Literature" tends to function in the United States as a catch-all term for a general humanities department, and is likely for that reason to be gradually replaced by the less weighted title "Cultural Studies"' (173), traces of the influence of literary studies on his work remain. Any such speculation would have to take into account the way in which the very impreciseness of 'literature' as a category has proved extremely attractive to a broad range of discourses which are difficult to name or classify, but which have generally been placed under a heading of 'theory', and thus to theory's interrogation of the limits of the 'literary' and, indeed, of disciplinary boundaries *per se*. A difficult task. Nevertheless, one which would have the benefit of providing a possible explanation, both for Readings' willingness to raise fundamental questions for cultural studies, and also for the way in which my own exploration of some of cultural studies' limits here found an initial home in a journal of literary and cultural theory rather than one more strictly delineated as 'cultural studies' (the very journal, in fact, in which two of the papers which eventually went to make up *The University in Ruins* first appeared).[22] Admittedly, there would be a danger of implying such analyses ought not to be considered as 'cultural studies' (whereas, of course, this sort of 'critique' of cultural studies, which draws on other modes of thought for what they may 'yield' in order to remake cultural studies, is in many ways the most cultural studies thing to do of all).[23] In suggesting that, for all its lack of 'fixity', cultural studies has tended to take on board only those aspects of theory it can accommodate without having to bring its identity radically into question, a study of this kind would also risk conveying the impression that cultural studies (in marked contrast to literary studies) has somehow been unaffected by theory. However, cultural studies cannot be set up in an oppositional relationship with literary studies in this respect, and any investigation of the relation between the two would have to take great care to chart the unevenness of their respective positions, at one time or another, in this place or that, with regard to theory, politics, the university, and each other – always supposing, of course, that cultural and literary studies can be distinguished in the first place, which is itself something of a problem. Unfortunately, such speculation is beyond the scope of the present study. Suffice it to say that, having learnt the lesson that it is necessary to think the university from theory, Readings argues that cultural studies needs to be rethought so that it is not simply institutionalized, so that it is not so blind to the institutional problematic, but can instead find a way to approach the university without

resorting to either nostalgia for a national culture or the discourse of consumerism and excellence.

In the book's penultimate chapter he thus proceeds to sketch 'how one
might dwell in the ruins of the University' without recourse to the sort of
'romantic nostalgia' we have seen cultural studies indulge in. This means
giving up the 'religious attitude towards political action, including the pious
postponement or renunciation of action', he associates with cultural studies.
The way in which this can be achieved, for Readings, the way in which the
'impulse of Cultural Studies' can be pushed 'beyond the work of mourning for
a lost idea of culture that needs political renewal' (191), is precisely by
addressing the question of disciplinarity: by '[w]orking out . . . how thoughts
stand beside other thoughts' (191). Instead of a new inter-disciplinary space
that will once and for all reunify the university, he thus proposes a 'shifting
disciplinary structure that holds open the question of whether and how
thoughts fit together' (191):

> For example, the argument has to be made to administrators that resources
> liberated by the opening up of disciplinary space, be it under the rubric of
> the humanities or Cultural Studies, should be channeled into supporting
> short-term collaborative projects of both teaching and research (to speak in
> familiar terms) which would be disbanded after a certain period, whatever
> their success . . .
>
> What I am calling for, then, is not a generalized interdisciplinary space
> but a certain rhythm of disciplinary attachment and detachment, which is
> designed so as not to let the question of disciplinarity disappear, sink into
> routine. Rather, disciplinary structures would be forced to answer to the
> name of Thought, to imagine what kinds of thinking they make possible,
> and what kinds of thinking they exclude. It is perhaps a lesson of structur-
> alism that, when faced with a disciplinary project, a crucial way of situating
> that project is by considering what it is *not*, what it excludes. Thus a
> concentration in European philosophy, for example, would be obliged – by
> the nature of the interruptive pattern that I propose – to address both non-
> European philosophy and European non-philosophy. (176)

Readings is careful to point out that he is not attempting to provide a 'general
model' for '*the* University of the Future' with this, merely suggestions 'in the
interest of attempting to find possibilities that work in the service of Thought
in the current . . . bourgeois economic revolution in the University' (178).
And, to be sure, translating the particularities of his work on the university
into a rigorous consideration of the politics of the institution in the UK, for

example, would be no small matter, located as much of *The University of Ruins* is in the 'specific local circumstances' (178) of the North American university system, where the 'German model . . . that Humbolt instituted at the University of Berlin' (7) Readings addresses was much more influential. Nonetheless, for all the difficult issues it raises, Readings' idea for keeping open the question of disciplinarity by means of this 'shifting disciplinary structure' holds a number of attractions for me. Not least among these is the opportunity it presents for remaking cultural studies so that it does not explicitly exclude those non-legitimate forms of 'knowledge' that cultural studies can perhaps understand only by rethinking its identity *as* cultural studies.

This kind of working without 'alibis' Readings refers to as an 'institutional pragmatism' which, following Samuel Weber, he defines as working 'from the "inside" of the various disciplines, in order to demonstrate concretely, in each case, how the exclusion of limits from the field organizes the practice it makes possible'.[24] Nevertheless, the question remains: 'What institutional forms might such a reconceptualized cultural studies actually take?' Readings provides little indication in *The University in Ruins* as to how this question might be answered. Although he emphasizes that any such organizational structure would have to turn to forms of knowledge which are not already recognized as legitimate, the most he provides by way of illustration is the example of how a 'concentration in European philosophy . . . would be obliged . . . to address both non-European philosophy and European non-philosophy' (176). But this could mean 'non-philosophy' in the sense of history or physics surely? Nor does the organization of *The University in Ruins* itself offer much of a clue. Despite what Readings says about how disciplinarity can be installed as a *'permanent question'* (177), he himself appears to pay little attention to 'excluded' forms of knowledge. Indeed, is its '(inter)disciplinary' form not one of the reasons behind the institutional success of Readings' book?[25] Admittedly *The University in Ruins* provides a persuasive and even agenda-setting account of the way in which the contemporary Western university is being taken over by corporatism, a process with which a lot of academics are only too familiar. But does it not do so in ways that are relatively easy for the University of Excellence to appropriate?[26] Where, for example, are the references to the kind of non-disciplinary 'methods and knowledges' that would have kept open the question of the legitimacy and authority of Readings' own text? If we follow his own advice for 'situating' a 'disciplinary project', however, and consider what his book *'is not*, what it excludes', we discover in an endnote a reference to 'Caught in the Net', a short electronic article he published two years earlier.[27] Here Readings provides 'one simple example' of the kind of institutional pragmatism he describes in *The University of Ruins*: the 'way in which the Internet threatens to delegitimize the structure of scholarly publishing' (255, n.3).

THE UNIVERSITY IN BITS

In many ways the advent of academic electronic publishing merely continues the process of corporatization traced by *The University in Ruins*. 'We have to recognize that the university as an institution is becoming more and more corporate', Readings writes in 'Caught in the Net', 'that information is not primarily referential (information about something outside the university); instead, information is a unit of value within the system and serves to procure advancement within the university'. So in a situation where, as Meaghan Morris remarks in her contribution to *The Institutionalization of Cultural Studies*, 'the Oxbridge-derived model of what it meant to be a scholar ... has definitively gone. Being brilliant but lazy, or learned but light in publications' is just not an option for most academics any more, the development of academic journals on the Internet is seen by many as simply providing more opportunities to publish and thus further their careers.[28] Yet for all the dominance Readings assigns to the 'market-model' there are still things to be done. Just as in *The University in Ruins*, where 'the process of dereferentializa-tion is one that opens up new spaces and breaks down existing structures of defence against Thought, even as it seeks to submit Thought to the exclusive rule of exchange-value' (178), so, too, in 'Caught in the Net', although the 'economic rationale is overwhelming', there remains the possibility that 'aca-demics will be capable of turning the shift to their advantage'.

Readings identifies two main ways in which electronic publishing threatens to break down existing structures of defence against thought, forcing academ-ics, as he puts it in *The University in Ruins*, to rethink the 'categories that have governed intellectual life for over two hundred years' (169). The first concerns evaluation. 'Normally, those who review essays for inclusion in scholarly journals know what they are supposed to do. Their function is to take exciting, innovative, and challenging work by younger scholars and find reasons to reject it.' In this way the boundaries of the discipline can be maintained, as established academics get to decide what counts as a proper contribution to the field and what does not. However, as Readings points out:

in the electronic world, it is harder to find reasons to refuse publication. With no limits on space, one cannot recommend those sweeping cuts that will subsequently allow one to find the revised version insufficiently devel-oped. The speed of publication means that a younger scholars (sic) can add the footnotes referring to that obscure but definitive essay by Professor Dryasdust and still get the essay published before they are refused tenure and driven out of the profession.

Nor can such decisions be made on the basis of what a publisher can successfully market or sell, since electronic academic publishing is to a certain extent independent of this economy.[29] New information and communications technology thus makes it far harder to exclude work that challenges the boundaries of established disciplines. As a result, a 'new set of criteria for the handling of scholarly research' will need to be worked out, Readings claims, requiring us to hold open 'the grounds upon which publication can be refused', and with it the question of disciplinarity legitimacy.

The second challenge that Readings identifies the new technology as raising for academic publishing concerns 'the question of what publication means' for scholarly production. To date, scholarly '[a]rticles are published and contribute to the sum of human wisdom, and they also obtain symbolic capital for their authors based on the place and frequency of their production'. So far, electronic journals have not presented much of a challenge to this system. But Readings is able to envisage a future scenario where:

> new modes in the evaluation of reception (and the consequent gaining of scholarly legitimacy) will arise. Electronic technology makes it possible to calculate with far greater accuracy and speed the number of times a given article is consulted. The spectre arises of the intellectual star of the 21st Century with a box in the corner of her or his computer screen counting the number of times their articles have been accessed today . . . more technically-minded research assistants could [even] be deputed to write software that would repeatedly access given articles in order to ensure that end of year bonus.

This 'threat' becomes even more apparent when the possibilities this technology presents for multi-authored, interactively created and computer-generated texts are considered. How is the symbolic capital of such texts to be measured? On what basis can they be 'assessed'? And who is to receive the research points? '[T]he impact of such technology upon the academic community may not prove simply prosthetic', Readings writes. 'It may undermine, or at least restructure our understanding of the nature of academic publication, of what counts as a real scholarly article', forcing us, in the words of the editors of one electronic journal, to rethink 'what we mean by both "publishing" and "journal"'.[30]

Faced with the challenges to 'Thought' brought on by the changes in higher education in Britain, the US and elsewhere, 'Caught in the Net' shows how electronic publishing provides a means of 'dwelling in the ruins' that creates an opportunity for making an institutionally pragmatic 'tactical use of the space of the University' (18). As such, it anticipates the kind of resistance

Readings' work on the university can expect to meet from some quarters: I can imagine one or two people in the social sciences or even cultural studies, for that matter, arguing that a concern with 'deconstructing' the university is all very well, but when it comes down to it, isn't it all a bit too theoretical and textual, and doesn't work like this really need to be grounded more in concrete examples? Having said that, it is not my intention to privilege *Surfaces*, the e-journal Readings co-edited and in which 'Caught in the Net' was first published (or *Culture Machine*, the e-journal I co-edit),[31] as a *practical* example of the theory Readings develops in *The University in Ruins*: that would be to maintain precisely the sort of oppositional relationship between theory and practice, 'textuality' and politics, I am concerned to think through here. Nor should any of this be taken as suggesting that instances of keeping the question of disciplinarity open are confined solely to the sphere of 'new technology'. One important example of this kind of approach to the organization of knowledge is provided by the *Collège International de Philosophie* in France,[32] which has itself been a major influence on a number of related attempts in the UK.[33] Again, there is not the time or space to go into a detailed analysis of the specificities of each of the particular responses to the question of disciplinarity mentioned here. Still, it is perhaps significant that these examples are research-orientated, and as such bear witness to Michel de Certeau's comment, made some thirty years ago now, that 'admissions policies suddenly appear to be the price of research':

> the pluridisciplinary garden, pruned in the virgin forest of the university, makes manifest a redoubtable *contradiction between research and massification*, as if the former were possible only thanks to the establishment of an elite among the students, through a strategy of hyperselection. Inversely, wherever it is accepted (in other universities), massification seems to bring about a return to authoritarian formulas and to lecture courses, and to involve disciplines whose resolutely more 'classical' form and content consign students to silence.[34]

Seen in this context one of the things that makes new technology so interesting is that it promises to bring the question of disciplinarity into the very heart of undergraduate teaching. This last point finds confirmation in an article which appeared in the British press in March 1999, giving details of a warning from Sir Howard Newby, vice-chancellor of Southampton University and at the time of writing president of the Committee of Vice-Chancellors and Principals (which recently conformed to the spirit of the times by rebranding itself with the far more corporate sounding moniker of Universities UK), concerning the danger facing British universities from the way in which their American counterparts are using new information and communication technologies to rapidly corner the global market in higher education research, with teaching not being far behind. According to this article, large research universities in the States are 'linking up with "knowledge providers" such as Disney and Time Warner' to 'create teaching materials for distance learning and to supply the necessary technology to deliver them'. 'In future . . . why should a mature part-time student sign up for an MBA at a mediocre British institution when . . . he or she could do an MBA from Harvard or MIT over the Internet?' The situation envisaged here is one in which universities form federal consortiums with universities in other countries and continents and in which 'economics students . . . study at one centre with a strong existing economic reputation, engineers at another', with distance learning material being produced to 'serve students externally and within the group'. In this system, universities become increasingly specialized as they concentrate on their 'best subjects', dropping their worst, and so 'benefiting from division of labour and economies of scale' which in turn creates more resources to develop courseware for distance learning.[35] But while I can see any number of university managers being attracted to the economics of Sir Howard's vision, I don't think we need to prepare for the Routledge global university of cultural studies just yet. For, in Readings' words, the 'increased quantity, speed and distribution' electronic technology brings 'will not simply prosthetically improve existing practices', allowing some universities to reach more people throughout the world with their increasingly specialized brands of academic 'excellence'; 'it promises to significantly alter the basis on which the system functions'.

WHAT IF HOGGART HAD HAD E-MAIL?'

Although Readings is concerned mainly with the effect of new information and communications technology on the publication of scholarly research in 'Caught in the Net', his argument has consequences for the whole of the academic institution:

> This possibility has to do with the legitimation function of scholarly publication, and the crisis that electronic publication is going to produce in the academic community's mode of legitimation. Walter Benjamin reminds us that the mode of reproduction does not simply affect the distribution of art works but also their nature; one might add that textual production cannot be understood aside from its mode of legitimation . . . the mode of legitimation affects the nature of the texts produced . . .

What this means is that, as Jacques Derrida insists in *Archive Fever*, new technologies not only change the process of analysing, communicating, exchanging, classifying, stocking and conserving knowledge, they change the very nature of that knowledge. Derrida gives as an example psychoanalysis, speculating on the:

> geo-techno-logical shocks which would have made the landscape of the psychoanalytic archive unrecognizable for the past century if, to limit myself to these indications, Freud, his contemporaries, collaborators and immediate disciples, instead of writing thousands of letters by hand, had had access to MCI or AT&T telephonic credit cards, portable tape recorders, computers, printers, faxes, televisions, teleconferences, and above all E-mail.[36]

But Derrida has recently reminded us that when it comes to the question of new technology 'we are under no obligation to confine ourselves to psychoanalytic hypothesis'.[37] And, indeed, on transferring Derrida's 'retrospective science fiction' into the realm of cultural studies it soon becomes clear that the potential consequences of new technology are, if anything, even greater for cultural studies than they are for psychoanalysis. Psychoanalysis, after all, is the 'talking cure'. As Derrida puts it: 'we cannot say that the whole of psychoanalysis and its theoretical models depend on paper, or even on paper as a figure of speech. The analytic scene and situation seem to exclude by definition any recording on an external support . . . the *theoretical* dependence of psychoanalytic knowledge on this medium is neither certain nor homogenous' (9). Cultural studies, by comparison, is extremely reliant on the printed paper form. Hence the way in which the origins of cultural studies are generally traced (whether rightly or wrongly) to the publication of three books – *The Uses of Literacy*, *The Making of the English Working Class* and *Culture and Society* – the earliest of which, Hoggart's *The Uses of Literacy*, is concerned precisely with the importance of paper, it being primarily paper, after all, that brought mass literary and literate culture to the working class. But cultural studies depends on paper for more than just its means of recording, communication and subject matter. Given that what Hoggart was trying to do both in this book and later with the founding of the Centre for Contemporary Cultural Studies at Birmingham was to 'translate' the 'methods of literary criticism, very often Leavisite methods, close analysis, listening to a text, feeling a text and its texture' to the 'study of popular culture', cultural studies clearly relies on paper for even its theoretical method.[38]

The point here is not simply that, had new technology been around at the time, Hoggart would have had to write a different book, one which took the effects of virtual reality, cyberfeminism, the Internet, net politics, surveillance, electronic commerce, digital architecture, etc., into account alongside the other areas of cultural studies inquiry he examined in *The Uses of Literacy*. Nor that new technology would have provided Hoggart with a cheaper, faster and more efficient means of analysing, communicating and transmitting cultural studies. Nor even that this technology, had it been available, would have changed the form in which cultural studies first found expression: that the ideas which eventually went to make up *The Uses of Literacy* might have found alternative expression in e-mails and Newsgroups, on Websites and bulletin boards, instead of as essays for organs such as *The Use of English*, *Tribune* and *Essays in Criticism*. What this means is that, to recast Derrida's words, cultural studies would not have been what it was when Hoggart wrote *The Uses of Literacy* if new technology had existed then; and from the moment this technology became possible, cultural studies could in the future no longer be what Hoggart and so many other practitioners of cultural studies thought it was going to be.[39]

Let me conclude with a few brief comments concerning the relationship between cultural studies, the university and new technology. The first thing I want to draw attention to is the way in which, as the examples of both psychoanalysis and cultural studies demonstrate, new information and communications technology forces us to keep open the question of disciplinarity, turning our attention back onto the disciplinary categories and combinations which make up the modern university. In doing so, this technology provides a means of raising the questions of cultural studies – what it includes and excludes – that are needed to think the university. And this is what then enables us to think about new technology.

This last suggestion may *appear* somewhat paradoxical, but we cannot rely merely on the modern 'disciplinary' methods and frameworks of knowledge in order to think about and interpret the transformative effect new technology is having on our culture, since it is precisely these methods and frameworks that new technology requires us to rethink. Nor is an inter-disciplinary combination of pre-established disciplines sufficient to enable us to respond to the challenge this technology presents to the identity and legitimacy of university knowledge. Cultural studies practitioners cannot understand cultural studies after the invention of the Internet simply by doing more courses in HTML. The idea that there could in the future be a Routledge- or Microsoft-sponsored electronic institution specializing in 'excellent' teaching and research in cultural studies is problematic, for the simple reason that new technology changes the very nature of cultural studies, rendering it, as Derrida says of psychoanalysis, 'unrecognizable'. New technology opens up the academic institution to the possibility of discovering new objects and new forms of knowledge, not just in the gaps between already constituted disciplines, but which are 'everywhere at all times': objects and forms of knowledge which are not already 'known' or indeed 'knowable, [especially] if "knowable" means direct apprehension by the senses', but which instead require the development of new methods and frameworks and new techniques of analysis.[40] To borrow once again from Derrida's 'Mochlos', then (and in a way this chapter has been nothing more than an extended reflection on this little commented upon passage from Derrida's lecture), the relationship between the university and new information technology is only 'apparently paradoxical'. And it is in 'facing the law of this apparent paradox that an ultimate responsibility' – including, in this case, 'an ultimate responsibility' to cultural studies, to the modern university and to new technology – 'would be, if such a thing were possible, there for the taking today'.[41]

Notes

Chapter One: Some Frequently Asked Questions

1. Sections of some of the arguments contained in this chapter appeared in an earlier form in 'This is a Test', *Culture Machine*, No. 1, 1999, http://culture-machine.tees.ac.uk/Backissues/j002/Articles/test/index.htm, and 'Prospectus', *Culture Machine*, No. 2, 2000, http://culturemachine.tees.ac.uk/Backissues/j002/Articles/prospectus.htm.
2. Although I have used Derrida's name as a form of shorthand here, there is not one deconstruction. Nor is deconstruction the property of Jacques Derrida, even if it is with his writings that what is known as deconstruction is most closely identified. With reference to *Culture in Bits*, the names of Nicolas Abraham and Maria Torok, Mikkel Borch-Jacobsen, Homi K. Bhabha, Bill Readings, Geoffrey Bennington, Robert J.C. Young, J. Hillis Miller and Judith Butler, among others, could all be raised in this context alongside that of Derrida.
3. Samuel Weber, *Institution and Interpretation*, Minneapolis: University of Minnesota Press, 1987, 56.
4. Sadie Plant, *Parallax*, No. 1, 1995, p. 100.
5. Jacques Derrida, *Resistances of Psychoanalysis*, trans. Peggy Kamuf, Pascale-Anne Brault and Michael Naas, Stanford, California: Stanford University Press, 1998, pp. 54–5.
6. Bill Readings, *The University in Ruins*, Cambridge, Massachusetts and London, England: Harvard University Press, 1996, p. 91. Further page references are given in parenthesis in the body of the text. For more on Readings, see Chapter 6.
7. Readings, *ibid.*, p. 219, n.19, emphasis mine. See also Samuel Weber, 'The Future Campus: Destiny in a Virtual World', http://www.hydra.umn.edu/weber/text1.html; Samuel Weber, 'The Future of the Humanities: Experimenting', *Culture Machine*, No. 2, 2000, http://culturemachine.tees.ac.uk/Backissues/j002/Articles/art_webe.htm; Peggy Kamuf, *The Division of Literature or The University in Deconstruction*, Chicago and London: University of Chicago Press, 1997; Robert Young, 'The Idea of a Chrestomatic University', in Richard Rand (ed.), *Logomachia: The Conflict of the Faculties*, Lincoln and London: University of Nebraska, 1992, revised and reprinted in *Torn Halves: Political Conflict in Literary and Cultural Theory*, Manchester: Manchester

University Press, 1996; Simon Wortham, *Rethinking the University: Leverage and Deconstruction*, Manchester: Manchester University Press, 1999; J. Hillis Miller, 'Literary Study in the Transnational University', in J. Hillis Miller and Manuel Asensi, *Black Holes: J. Hillis Miller; or, Boustrophedonic Reading*, Stanford, California: Stanford University Press, 1999. For more on Giroux and Steele, see Chapter 4.

8. Cf. Geoffrey Bennington, 'Inter', in Martin McQuillan *et al.* (eds), *Post-Theory: New Directions in Criticism*, Edinburgh: Edinburgh University Press, 1999, p. 106; Geoffrey Bennington, *Legislations: The Politics of Deconstruction*, London: Verso, 1994, p. 4.

9. Jacques Derrida, 'The Other Heading: Memories, Responses and Responsiblities', *The Other Heading: Reflections on Today's Europe*, trans. Pascale-Anne Brault and Michael B. Naas, Bloomington and Indianapolis: Indiana University Press, 1992, p. 41. As Joanna Zylinska points out, 'for the project of cultural studies to be truly political and ethical, it has to remain open to the possibility of its pervertibility, collapse, annihilation and withering down' (Joanna Zylinska, 'An Ethical Manifesto for Cultural Studies . . . Perhaps', *Strategies: Journal of Theory, Culture and Politics*, Vol. 14, No. 2, 2001). For more on the importance of the 'perhaps', see 'Perhaps or Maybe: Jacques Derrida in Conversation with Alexander Garcia Düttmann', *Pli: Warwick Journal of Philosophy*, Vol. 6, Summer, 1997: 1–18; and Jacques Derrida, *Politics of Friendship*, trans. George Collins, London and New York: Verso, 1997.

10. Ivor Gaber, 'Timely Attack on Nonsense', *The Times Higher Education Supplement*, March 16, 2001; Fred Inglis, 'Leaden Theory in Boots of Concrete Jargon', *The Times Higher Education Supplement*, October 8, 1999.

11. Geoffrey Bennington, 'Inter', *op.cit.*, p. 105.

12. Richard Johnson, ' "Politics By Other Means"?: or, Teaching Cultural Studies in the Academy is a Political Practice', in Nannette Aldred and Martin Ryle (eds), *Teaching Culture: The Long Revolution in Cultural Studies*, Leicester: The National Organisation for Adult Learning, 1999, p. 23.

13. Bill Readings, *ibid.*, p. 100.

14. See Chapter 4.

15. Timothy Clark, *Derrida, Heidegger, Blanchot: Sources of Derrida's Notion and Practice of Literature*, Cambridge: Cambridge University Press, 1992, p. xi/xii.

16. Geoff Mulgan, 'Whinge and A Prayer', *Marxism Today*, November/December, 1998.

17. Richard Johnson, 'Politics By Other Means', *op.cit.*, p. 29. Johnson draws on Judith Butler's notion of 'performativity' to indicate the way in which transgressive performances are also possible *within* the academy: 'Performativity describes this relation of being implicated in that which one opposes, this turning of power against itself to produce alternative modalities of power, to establish a kind of political contestation that is not a *pure* opposition, a transcendence of contemporary relations of power, but a difficult labour of forging a future from resources inevitably impure' (Judith Butler, *Bodies That Matter*, London and New York: Routledge, 1993), 241; cited by Richard Johnson, *op.cit.*, p. 29). From this point of view, far from being a sign of deconstruction's apolitical theoreticism, the very 'literariness' of

many of Derrida's texts can be seen to constitute an actual performative engagement with the institution of the university. (See Stephen Jarvis, 'Belonging Without Belonging: Deconstruction, Literature and the Institution', *Culture Machine*, No. 2, 2000, http://culturemachine.tees.ac.uk/Backissues/j002/Articles/_jarvis.htm).

18. Samuel Weber, *Mass Mediauras: Form, Technics, Media*, Stanford, California: Stanford University Press, 1996, p. 201.

19. Jacques Derrida, 'Mochlos; or, The Conflict of the Faculties', trans. Richard Rand and Amy Wygant, in Richard Rand (ed.), *Logomachia: The Conflict of the Faculties*, Lincoln and London: University of Nebraska, 1992, pp. 22–3.

20. In a recent interview Derrida emphasizes how in many of his published texts he engages with questions which even those capable of identifying the political 'only with the help of prewar road signs' would recognize: questions concerning political resistance, the intellectual, Marxism, democracy, social justice, the 'International', etc. (Jacques Derrida, 'Intellectual Courage', trans. Peter Krapp, *Culture Machine*, No. 2, 2000, http://culturemachine.tees.ac.uk/Backissues/j002/Articles/art/derr.htm).

21. Jacques Derrida, 'As if I were Dead: An Interview with Jacques Derrida', in John Brannigan *et al.* (eds), *Applying: To Derrida*, London: Macmillan, 1996, pp. 218, 217.

22. Bill Readings, *op.cit.*, p. 5. Further page references are given in parenthesis in the body of the text. See also Robert Young, 'The Idea of a Chrestomatic University', *op.cit.*; and Diane Elam, 'Why Read?', *Culture Machine*, No. 2, 2000, http://culturemachine.tees.ac.uk/Backissues/j002/Articles/art_elam.htm.

23. Angela McRobbie, 'The Es and the Anti-Es: New Questions for Feminism and Cultural Studies', in Marjorie Ferguson and Peter Golding (eds), *Cultural Studies in Question*, London, Thousand Oaks, New Delhi: Sage, 1997, p. 183; reprinted in *In the Culture Society*, London and New York: Routledge, 1999. Further page references are given in parenthesis in the body of the text.

24. Ted Striphas, 'The Long March: Cultural Studies and its Institutionalization', *Cultural Studies*, Vol. 12, No. 4, 1998, p. 461.

25. Gary Hall and Simon Wortham, 'Interdisciplinarity and its Discontents', *Angelaki*, Vol. 2, No. 2, 1996.

26. See Chapters 3 and 5 respectively.

27. See Chapter 5.

28. Jacques Derrida, 'Canons and Metonymies: An Interview with Jacques Derrida', in Richard Rand (ed.), *Logomachia, op.cit.*, p. 198.

29. Jacques Derrida, *Archive Fever: A Freudian Impression*, trans. Eric Prenowitz, Chicago: University of Chicago Press, 1996; Jacques Derrida, *The Post Card: From Socrates to Freud and Beyond*, trans. Alan Bass, Chicago: University of Chicago Press, 1987.

30. J. Hillis Miller, 'The Ethics of Hypertext', *Diacritics*, Vol. 25, No. 3, 1995, pp. 32, 38; revised and reprinted in J. Hillis Miller and Manuel Asensi, *Black Holes, op.cit.*

31. Angela McRobbie, 'Introduction', in Angela McRobbie (ed.), *Back To Reality: Social Experience and Cultural Studies*, Manchester and New York: Manchester University Press, 1997, p. 2.

32. Naomi Klein, *No Logo*, London: Flamingo, 2000.

33. Angela McRobbie, *op.cit.*
34. Jacques Derrida, *Archive Fever, op.cit.*, p. 72.

Chapter Two: 'It's a Thin Line Between Love and Hate':
Why Cultural Studies is so 'Naff'

1. *The Oxford Dictionary of Modern Slang*, Oxford: Oxford University Press, 1992.
2. The phrase 'cultural dopes' is Stuart Hall's. See Stuart Hall, 'Notes on Deconstructing the Popular', in Raphael Samuel (ed.), *People's History and Socialist Theory*, London: Routledge and Kegan Paul, 1981.
3. Dick Hebdige, *Subculture: The Meaning of Style*, London: Methuen, 1979.
4. Erica Carter, 'Alice in the Consumer Wonderland', in Angela McRobbie and Mica Nava (eds), *Gender and Generation*, London: Macmillan, 1984, p. 213.
5. John Fiske, *Reading the Popular*, London: Routledge, 1989, p. 107.
6. I am restricting myself here to how popular culture has been understood within cultural studies. It has of course been understood differently elsewhere and previously. As Jim McGuigan notes, cultural studies' celebratory view of popular culture (or 'mass-popular culture', as McGuigan rather awkwardly has it) is in many ways a resolution of 'the old tension between a notion of "popular culture" derived in one version or another from Herder's "folk culture", on the one hand, and "mass culture" in the Frankfurt School sense, on the other hand' (Jim McGuigan, 'Cultural Populism Revisited', in Marjorie Ferguson and Peter Golding (eds), *Cultural Studies in Question*, London: Sage, 1997, p. 138).
7. Mica Nava, 'Consumerism and its Contradictions', *Cultural Studies*, Vol. 1, No. 2, 1987; reprinted in *Changing Cultures: Feminism, Youth and Consumerism*, London: Sage, 1992. Further page references are given in parenthesis in the body of the text.
8. See Jean-François Lyotard, *The Postmodern Condition: A Report on Knowledge*, trans. Geoffrey Bennington and Brian Massumi, Manchester: Manchester University Press, 1984.
9. Andreas Huyssen, *After the Great Divide: Modernism, Mass Culture, Postmodernism*, Bloomington: Indiana University Press, 1986. This opening up of the cultural critic's field of interest – although not confined to cultural studies – is of course one reason for the 'boom' many theorists have detected in cultural studies.
10. For a rehearsal of some of the relevant arguments on this subject, see Duncan Webster, *Looka Yonder!: The Imaginary America of Populist Culture*, London: Routledge, 1989; Jim McGuigan, *Cultural Populism*, London: Routledge, 1992; and David Harris, *From Class Struggle to the Politics of Pleasure: The Effects of Gramscianism on Cultural Studies*, London and New York: Routledge, 1992. See also Chapter 3.
11. Duncan Webster uses this term to describe Steve Beard's attitude toward academics in an article in *Arena* entitled 'Is Watching Star Trek Dangerous?'

(Spring/Summer 1990). Webster writes that '[a]s consumers, academics are fairly naff' in Beard's view (Duncan Webster, 'Pessimism, Optimism, Pleasure: The Future of Cultural Studies', *News from Nowhere*, No. 8, Autumn 1990: p. 83; reprinted in John Storey (ed.), *What is Cultural Studies? A Reader*, London: Arnold, 1996.

12. Jim Collins, *Uncommon Cultures: Popular Culture and Postmodernism*, London: Routledge, 1989, p. 20.

13. Duncan Webster, *op.cit.*, p. 96. Further page references are given in parenthesis in the body of the text.

14. For more on this aspect of 'the gift' and the related concept of 'the debt', see Jacques Derrida's 'Des Tours de Babel', trans. J. F. Graham, in *Difference in Translation*, J. F. Graham (ed.), Ithaca: Cornell University Press, 1985; *Glas*, trans. J. P. Leavey and Richard Rand, Lincoln: Nebraska University Press, 1986; 'Ulysses Gramophone: Hear Say Yes in Joyce', trans. Tina Kendall and Shari Benstock, in Derek Attridge, (ed.), *Acts of Literature*, London: Routledge, 1992; and *Given Time: 1. Counterfeit Money*, trans. Peggy Kamuf, Chicago and London: University of Chicago Press, 1992.

15. For some of the problems with this type of reading/appropriation of 'deconstruction' – which in effect reduces it to 'a mechanical exercise similar to academic thematism or formalism' – see Rodolphe Gasché, 'Deconstruction as Criticism', *Glyph*, No. 6, 1979.

16. Francis Mulhern, 'The Politics of Cultural Studies', Monthly Review, July/August, 1995, pp. 31–40; reprinted in E. M. Wood, and J. B. Foster, *In Defence of History: Marxism and the Postmodern Agenda*, New York: Monthly Review Press, 1998. Since part of my aim here is to argue that neither side in this running battle constitutes a stable or homogeneous identity, I am using terms such as 'cultural studies', 'cultural critique', 'traditional criticism', 'elitism', 'cultural populism' strictly in their improper senses. Taking this as read, I will henceforth attempt to dispense with the scarequotes around these terms as much as clarity allows. Jim McGuigan provides one definition of 'elitism' and 'cultural populism' in *Cultural Populism*, *op.cit.*

17. Dick Hebdige, 'The Bottom Line on Planet One', *Hiding in the Light On Images and Things*, London: Routledge, 1988. It is from this essay that the first part of my title derives. In 'The Bottom Line on Planet One', Hebdige imagines a 'galaxy containing two quite different worlds'. Planet One he associates with language, with the search for truth and justice, with depth and commitment, and with critics like John Berger and journals such as *Ten.8*. Planet Two he associates with images, with blankness and flatness, with the 'People of the Post (post structuralism and post modernism)' and with those pleasure-seeking consumers who are the ideal readers of the style magazine *The Face*. Hebdige then proceeds to imagine a war between these two worlds, a war in which he comes down firmly on the side of Planet One. Although he admits that Planet Two may have its merits, hearing the voice of Chrissie Hynde singing 'It's a bitter [sic] line between love and hate' serves to remind Hebdige that 'words like "love" and "hate" and "faith" and "history" . . . the depth words drawn up like ghosts from a different dimension will always come back in the eleventh hour to haunt the Second World' (*ibid.*, pp. 175–6). Hebdige thus concludes that: 'Whatever Baudrillard or The Tatler or Saatchi

and Saatchi, and Swatch have to say about it, I shall go on reminding myself that this earth is round not flat, that there will never be an end to judgement, that the ghosts will go on gathering at the bitter line which separates truth from lies, justice from injustice, Chile, Biafra and all the other avoidable disasters from all of us, whose order is built upon their chaos' (*ibid.*, p. 176).

18. See Jacques Derrida, '. . . That Dangerous Supplement . . .', *Of Grammatology*, trans. Gaytri Chakravorty Spivak, London: Johns Hopkins University Press, 1976; Jacques Derrida, 'Différance', *Speech and Phenomena and Others Essays on Husserl's Theory of Signs*, trans. David Allison, Evanston, Northwestern University Press, 1973; Jacques Derrida, 'Difference', *Margins of Philosophy*, trans. Alan Bass, Chicago: University of Chicago Press, 1982.

19. For more on cultural studies' struggle to establish itself as a body of work in its own right while simultaneously refusing to claim a fixed disciplinary identity for itself, see Chapter 6.

20. See Jacques Derrida's argument concerning what he calls 'theoretical jetties', from which this part of my analysis of the relation between these two bodies of work is derived (Jacques Derrida, 'Some Statements and Truisms about Neologisms, Newisms, Postisms, Parasitisms, and other Small Seismisms', trans. Anne Tomiche in David Carroll (ed.), *The States of 'Theory': History, Art and Critical Discourse*, New York: Columbia University Press, 1990, pp. 65–6). Along with the general opening up of the cultural critic's field of interest referred to earlier (n.9), the desire to understand and explain other theories may be one reason for cultural studies' continuing development of a multidisciplinary or interdisciplinary approach by means of the incorporation of literature, history, philosophy, sociology, Marxism, feminism and deconstruction, to name but a few. For more on the way in which cultural studies' multidisciplinarity and interdisciplinarity works to incorporate all other theories into a greater whole, see Chapter 6. For a discussion of some of the problems of the universalizing and colonizing tendencies in cultural studies, see Benita Parry, 'The Contradictions of Cultural Studies', *Transition*, No. 53, 1991; Ann Gray and Jim McGuigan's introduction to their *Studying Culture: An Introductory Reader*, London: Edward Arnold, 1993; and also the 'Dismantling "Freemantle"' edition of *Cultural Studies*, Vol. 6, No. 3, 1992. According to Ien Ang, this edition of *Cultural Studies*, like the conference from which it arose, was a response to 'the largest international cultural studies gathering so far, the "Cultural Studies: Now and the Future" conference, held at the University of Illinois, USA in 1990', and the threat this was seen to embody of providing a definitive (and largely American) account of what cultural studies actually is, which would exclude the more marginal perspectives of those working in places such as Australia, Taiwan or Holland (Ien Ang, 'Dismantling Cultural Studies', *ibid.*, pp. 312–3). Despite 'overt refusals . . . to come up with fixed or unified theoretical positions and agendas', Grossberg *et al.*'s book of the 'Cultural Studies: Now and the Future' conference (Lawrence Grossberg, Cary Nelson and Paula Treichler (eds), *Cultural Studies*, New York: Routledge, 1992) 'runs the risk', in Ang's words, 'of being read as an attempt at totalizing definitiveness, a politics of closure resulting in a hegemonic demarcation of what "cultural studies" is' (*op.cit.*, p. 313) – and this despite this text's self-awareness of this risk (see Ted Striphas, 'Banality, Book Publishing and the

Everyday Life of Cultural Studies', *Culture Machine*, No. 2, 2000, http://
culturemachine.tees.ac.uk/Backissues/j002/Articles/art_strip.htm). Indeed, Ang
sees both the conference and the book as being 'motivated at least in part by
an understandable desire to put "cultural studies" emphatically on the US
academic agenda' (Ien Ang, *op.cit.*, p. 313); in short to establish something
called 'cultural studies' as a distinct and identifiable body of work in its own
right.

21. See Andrew Ross, *No Respect: Intellectuals and Popular Culture*, London:
    Routledge, 1989; John Frow, *Cultural Studies and Cultural Value*, Oxford:
    Clarendon Press, 1995.
22. See Homi K. Bhabha, 'DissemiNation', in Homi K. Bhabha (ed.), *The Location
    of Culture*, London: Routledge, 1994, p. 301. Bhabha locates the 'significance
    of this narrative splitting of the subject of identification . . . in Lévi-Strauss's
    description of the ethnographic act (Claude Lévi-Strauss, *Introduction to the
    Work of Marcel Mauss*, trans. Felicity Baker, London: Routledge, 1987). This
    demands that the observer be part of the observation: that, in the process of
    identifying the field of knowledge, he split himself into subject and object. The
    ethnographic act is thus constituted ' "by dint of the subject's capacity for
    indefinite self-objectification . . . for projecting outside itself ever-diminishing
    fragments of itself" '.
23. Theodore Adorno and Max Horkheimer, 'The Culture Industry: Enlighten-
    ment as Mass Deception', *Dialectic of Enlightenment*, trans. John Cumming,
    London: Verso, 1979.
24. Mica Nava, 'Consumerism Reconsidered: Buying and Power', *Changing Cul-
    tures: Feminism, Youth and Consumerism*, *op.cit.*, p. 186.
25. Umberto Eco, 'Apocalyptic and Integrated Intellectuals: Mass Communi-
    cations and Theories of Mass Culture', *Apocalypse Postponed*, London: BFI,
    1994, pp. 25–6.
26. For more on projection and identification, see Chapter 5.
27. For Francis Mulhern, for example, cultural studies '. . . faithfully repeats the
    basic patterns of kulturkritik. It does indeed negate kulturkritik, but only as a
    mirror-image reverses its original, preserving the form intact. Here if anywhere
    lies the source of the paradoxes that make up the life of the interventionist
    discipline called cultural studies' (Francis Mulhern, 'The Politics of Cultural
    Studies', *op.cit.*, p. 37).
28. This relation is further complicated by the way in which both of these
    approaches are labelled 'cultural studies'. The term 'cultural studies' thus has
    at least two interconnected meanings. It refers to the populist, celebratory
    approach which attempts to undermine the externality between the intellectual
    and popular culture. But it also refers to that field or body of work which has
    as its object of study 'culture'. This latter sense of the term encompasses both
    'cultural populism' and the more traditional approach of 'cultural critique and
    critical distance'. The identity of cultural studies is therefore complex and
    contradictory, part of a highly conflictual and ambivalent power struggle. As
    Chapters 4 and 6 of this book make clear, there is no one such thing as cultural
    studies. And these two meanings of the term 'cultural studies', in particular,
    continually intertwine.
29. Meaghan Morris, 'Things to do with Shopping Centres', in Susan Sheridan

(ed.), *Grafts: Feminist Cultural Criticism*, London: Verso, 1988. Page references are given in parenthesis in the body of the text.

30. Iain Chambers, *Popular Culture: The Metropolitan Experience*, London: Methuen, 1986, p. 13.

31. Meaghan Morris, 'Banality in Cultural Studies', *Block*, No. 14, 1988, p. 20. Further page references are given in parenthesis in the body of the text.

32. See Kuan-Hsing Chen, 'Post-Marxism: Between/Beyond Critical Postmodernism and Cultural Studies', *Media, Culture and Society*, No. 13, 1991; republished in David Morley and Kuan-Hsing Chen (eds), *Stuart Hall: Critical Dialogues in Cultural Studies*, London and New York: Routledge, 1996. Chen adopts a strategy of 'cut'n'mix' in an attempt to move beyond 'the limits of both postmodernism and cultural studies' (36).

33. Patrice Petro, 'Modernity and Mass Culture in Weimar: Contours of a Discourse on Sexuality in Early Theories of Perception and Representation', *New German Critique*, No. 40, Winter, 1987; cited in Meaghan Morris, 'Banality in Cultural Studies', *op.cit.*, p. 22.

34. Walter Benjamin, 'The Work of Art in the Age of Mechanical Reproduction', in Hannah Arendt (ed.), *Illuminations*, trans. Harry Zohn, London: Fontana, 1973; cited by Iain Chambers, *op.cit.*

35. Iain Chambers, *Popular Culture*, *op.cit.*, p. 12.

36. The term 'himbo' refers to a male 'bimbo', a 'bimbo' being 'a woman who is both sexy and stupid' (Alan Richter, *Dictionary of Sexual Slang: Words, Phrases, and Idioms from AC/DC to Zig-Zig*, New York: John Wiley and Sons, 1993).

37. Elaine Showalter, 'Critical Cross-Dressing: Male Feminists and the Woman of the Year', in Alice Jardine and Paul Smith (eds), *Men in Feminism* (New York: Methuen, 1987); cited in Meaghan Morris, 'Banality in Cultural Studies', *op.cit.*, p. 22.

38. This aspect of Morris's argument is further complicated by her extended revision of 'Banality in Cultural Studies', in Patricia Mellencamp (ed.), *Logics of Television: Essays in Cultural Criticism*, London: BFI, 1990.

39. Duncan Webster, 'Pessimism, Optimism, Pleasure', *op.cit.*, p. 94. This is not to say Webster is without criticism of Morris's essay. He challenges both her lack of history, and the left-Leavisite associations of a word like 'discrimination'.

40. These are references to a two-part 1990 Channel Four programme, which responded to the broadcast of Bernard Henri-Lévy's *Spirit of Freedom* television series in France by comparing the role of intellectuals in France to Britain. However, Drabble and Hall can be placed in that 'long British tradition of "ethnographic" observation', particularly of the working class, Patrick Bratlinger identifies as 'stretching back' at least as far as 'Henry Mayhew's *London Labour and the London Labour Poor*, the "industrial novels" of Dickens, Disraeli and Elizabeth Gaskell, and Engels' *The Condition of the Working Class in England in 1844*'. As Bratlinger points out: 'the act of social observation in this tradition ordinarily extended across class lines in a patronizing direction: a bourgeois or sometimes aristocratic writer would "travel into the poor man's country" and report what he or she saw, just as an explorer or anthropologist would report on, say, travels into "darkest Africa"' (Patrick Bratlinger, *Crusoe's*

Footprints: Cultural Studies in Britain and America, London: Routledge, 1990, p. 45).

41. See Dick Hebdige, 'The Impossible Object: Towards a Sociology of the Sublime', *New Formations*, No. 1, Spring, 1987, p. 55.

42. This is of course a point about their respective structural relations to popular culture, and not about their views of what popular culture (or 'mass culture', as it should be in the case of the Frankfurt School) actually is.

43. Theodore Adorno, 'Letters to Walter Benjamin', *Aesthetics and Politics*, London: New Left Books, 1977, p. 129; cited by Meaghan Morris, 'Things to do with Shopping Centres', *op.cit.*, p. 196.

44. *op.cit.*, p. 196. This link is made across Morris's work by the way in which both the sociology of consumerism she describes in her 'Shopping Centres' essay and now cultural studies (at least as it is practised by Fiske) are described as having an ethnographic approach. It is a similarity that links all three approaches – that of Chambers and Fiske, as well as the traditional stance of 'critical distance'.

45. The reference to the feminine here is significant. As Robert Young notes: 'The difficulties which arise from this structure are familiar from the debates within feminism, where "woman" seems to be offered an alternative of either being the "other" as constituted by man, that is, conforming to the stereotypes of patriarchy, or, if she is to avoid this, of being an absolute "other" outside knowledge, necessarily confined to inarticulate expressions of mysticism or *jouissance*. The only way to side-step these alternatives seems to be to reject the other altogether and become the same, that is, equal to men – but then with no difference from them' (Robert Young, *White Mythologies: Writing History and the West*, London: Routledge, 1990, p. 6). 'Exactly the same double bind is encountered in any theorization of racial difference', according to Young. And, I would add, of popular culture. Hence the way in which popular culture is generally described. Take the first of these examples: the popular as different from the intellectual. Here the popular is described in one of two ways: either conservatively or radically. In the conservative version, the popular is seen as being constituted by the stereotypes of intellectual elitism. From this point of view, it is 'naturally' different from the intellectual. In the radical version, the argument is that the popular must be allowed to be different to prevent it from being pulled back under the auspices of the totalized, patriarchal, contemplative gaze. This version of the popular runs all the way from seeing it in terms of resistance and subversion, to a form of socialist essentialism which maintains that if 'the people' get pleasure from popular culture, then it must have some socialist features. Despite their differences, however, both of these versions of popular culture (conservative and radical) are largely the same. In both, the popular is described in much the same terms: The alternative to describing the popular as different from the intellectual is, as we have seen, to describe it as the same. Here the popular is seen merely in terms of the other side of the stereotype. It is regarded as the intellectual's other; as different, as other, and yet as nevertheless the same. The popular is thus described in much the same terms as the intellectual. Both are seen to offer resistance and subversion in much the same way.

46. Much the same applies to those critics who seek to avoid the problems which

would obviously trouble any analysis having its basis in a claim to 'reality', by giving their analysis the status merely of a discursive 'representation' of the 'other'; that what they are depicting is merely an 'image'. The term 'representation'/'image' functions here in the same way as 'reality' did previously. It acts simply as a substitute or alibi for 'reality', while occupying exactly the same place and function in the analysis. My thanks to Geoffrey Bennington for this point.

47. For Stuart Hall, for example, in the Channel Four programme to which I referred earlier (n.40), Brixton is contrasted to the ICA: whereas the latter is full of intellectuals, the former is not. What this suggests is not simply that Hall hasn't been to Brixton lately, although he certainly didn't arrive there in this particular programme. Or, to be precise, he didn't actually get out of the taxi that drove him to Brixton from the ICA. He didn't even stop the car: he just drove up and down Railton Road a few times. This of course could be put down to the fact that, as one person put it when I mentioned the programme to them, 'he was too scared he was going to get the shit kicked out of him'. However, the windows of the taxi also seemed to act as a barrier between the two 'worlds'; a barrier which, while transparent enough to allow the intellectual to see what is happening on the other side, was nevertheless rigid enough to prevent any confusion as to their respective identities. It is thus not simply that Hall hasn't been invited to any recent dinner parties in SW9, then; the implication is rather that it is actually impossible for Hall to arrive in Brixton. For the latter represents his fantasy of what the popular – or at least the non-intellectual – looks like. Consequently, Hall will never be able to go to Brixton, since as soon as he arrives there, this place will become non-popular, thus making his arrival one of infinite deferral. Brixton will always be somewhere else, for Hall; somewhere where he, as an intellectual, is not.

Chapter Three: 'Something Else Besides':
The Third Way of Angela McRobbie

1. Tony Blair, *The Third Way*, London: The Fabian Society, 1998.
2. As David Morley notes, drawing on Stuart Hall's argument in 'The Hinterland of Science', *Working Papers in Cultural Studies*, No. 10, 1977, 'cultural studies stands not against sociology *per se*, but rather against one particular, long dominant positivist tradition within it . . . Hall himself has always argued that a crucial part of what was going on in Birmingham in the 1970s was the "posing of sociological questions against sociology"' (David Morley, 'So-Called Cultural Studies: Dead Ends and Reinvented Wheels', *Cultural Studies*, Vol. 12, No. 4, 1998, p. 479, quoting Stuart Hall from 'Cultural Studies and the Centre', in Stuart Hall *et al.* (eds), *Culture, Media, Language*, London: Hutchinson, 1980, p. 21).
3. Lawrence Grossberg, 'Cultural Studies and Political Economy: Is Anyone Else Bored With This Debate?', *Critical Studies in Mass Communications*, Vol. 12, No. 1, 1995, p. 74; revised and reprinted as Lawrence Grossberg, 'Introduc-

tion: "Birmingham" in America?', *Bringing It All Back Home: Essays on Cultural Studies*, Durham and London: Duke University Press, 1997, p. 7.

4. See, for example, David Harris, *From Class Struggle to the Politics of Pleasure: The Effects of Gramscianism on Cultural Studies*, London: Routledge, 1992; Jim McGuigan, *Cultural Populism*, London: Routledge, 1992; Jim McGuigan, 'Cultural Populism Revisited', in Marjorie Ferguson and Peter Golding (eds), *Cultural Studies in Question*, London: Sage, 1997; Simon Frith and Jon Savage, 'Pearls and Swine: The Intellectuals and the Mass Media', *New Left Review*, No. 198, 1992; Francis Mulhern, 'The Politics of Cultural Studies', *Monthly Review*, July–August, 1995; republished in E. M. Wood, and J. B. Foster, *In Defence of History: Marxism and the Postmodern Agenda*, New York: Monthly Review Press, 1998; Francis Mulhern, *Culture/Metaculture*, London and New York: Routledge, 2000; Nicholas Garnham, 'Political Economy and Cultural Studies: Reconciliation or Divorce?', *Critical Studies in Mass Communications*, Vol. 12, No. 1, 1995; reprinted as 'Political Economy and the Practice of Cultural Studies', in Marjorie Ferguson and Peter Golding (eds), *Cultural Studies in Question*, London: Sage, 1997; Marjorie Ferguson and Peter Golding (eds), *Cultural Studies in Question*, London: Sage, 1997; David Miller and Greg Philo, *Cultural Compliance: Dead Ends of Media/Cultural Studies and Social Science*, Glasgow Media Group, Glasgow University, London: Longman, 1998; revised and republished as 'Cultural Compliance: Media/Cultural Studies and Social Science', in Greg Philo and David Miller (eds), *Market Killing: What the Free Market Does and What Social Scientists Can Do About It*, London: Longman, 2001.

5. See, for example, Lawrence Grossberg, 'Cultural Studies and Political Economy: Is Anyone Else Bored With This Debate?', *op.cit.*; Richard Johnson, 'Reinventing Cultural Studies', in Elizabeth Long (ed.), *From Sociology to Cultural Studies*, Oxford: Blackwells, 1997; Richard Johnson, '"Politics by Other Means"? Or, Teaching Cultural Studies in the Academy is a Political Practice', in Nannette Aldred and Martin Ryle (eds), *Teaching Culture: The Long Revolution in Cultural Studies*, Leicester: National Institute of Adult Continuing Education, 1999; David Morley, 'So-Called Cultural Studies', *op.cit.*; Angela McRobbie, *In the Culture Society*, London: Routledge, 1999; Lola Young, 'Why Cultural Studies?', *parallax* 11, Vol. 5, No. 2, 1999.

6. Lawrence Grossberg, 'Cultural Studies and Political Economy: Is Anyone Else Bored With This Debate?', *op.cit.*

7. See Lawrence Grossberg, *ibid.*; Nicholas Garnham, 'Political Economy and Cultural Studies: Reconciliation or Divorce?', *op.cit.*

8. Robert Young, 'The Idea of a Chrestomatic University', in Richard Rand (ed.), *Logomachia: The Conflict of the Faculties*, Lincoln and London: University of Nebraska, 1992, p. 121; revised and reprinted in *Torn Halves: Political Conflict in Literary and Cultural Theory*, Manchester: Manchester University Press, 1996, p. 216.

9. Robert J. C. Young, 'Capitalism and Theory', *Torn Halves*, *ibid.*, p. 4. Further page references are given in parenthesis in the body of the text.

10. Lawrence Grossberg, 'Cultural Studies and Political Economy: Is Anyone Else Bored With This Debate?', *op.cit.*, p. 75.

11. Angela McRobbie, 'Looking Back at *New Times* and its Critics', in David

Morley and Kuan-Hsing Chen (eds), *Stuart Hall: Critical Dialogues in Cultural Studies*, London: Routledge, 1996, p. 255; revised and reprinted in *In the Culture Society*, London: Routledge, 1999.

12. David Morley, 'So-Called Cultural Studies', *op.cit.*, p. 491. Morley is here referring to an argument made by Ann Gray in 'Audience and Reception Research in Retrospect: The Trouble with Audiences', in Perti Alasuutari (ed.), *The Inscribed Audience*, London: Sage, 1999.

13. David Morley, 'Cultural Studies and Common Sense: Unresolved Questions', in Paul Gilroy, Lawrence Grossberg and Angela McRobbie (eds), *Without Guarantees: In Honour of Stuart Hall*, London: Verso, 2000, p. 249; see also David Morley, 'So-Called Cultural Studies', *op.cit.*, p. 488; and David Morley, 'Theoretical Orthodoxies: Textualism, Constructivism and the "New Ethnography" in Cultural Studies', in Marjorie Ferguson and Peter Golding (eds), *Cultural Studies in Question*, *op.cit.*, p. 121

14. See Lola Young, 'Why Cultural Studies?', *op.cit.*, pp. 5–7. See also Lawrence Grossberg, 'Cultural Studies and Political Economy: Is Anyone Else Bored With This Debate?', *op.cit.*, p. 74; Lawrence Grossberg, 'Introduction: "Birmingham" in America?', *op.cit.*, pp. 7, 9; Tony Bennett, *Culture: A Reformer's Science*, London, Thousand Oaks, New Delhi: Sage, 1998, p. 19; John Storey, 'Cultural Studies: An Introduction', in John Storey (ed.), *What is Cultural Studies?*, London and New York, Arnold, 1996, p. 7.

15. Ernesto Laclau, 'Psychoanalysis and Marxism', *New Reflections on the Revolution of Our Time*, London: Verso, 1990, p. 93. As Robert Young makes clear in 'Psychoanalysis and Political Literary Theories', Marxism and psychoanalysis 'provide mutually exclusive causal explanations – that is, economics and class versus sexuality and the unconscious' (Robert Young, 'Psychoanalysis and Political Literary Theories', in James Donald (ed.), *Psychoanalysis and Cultural Theory: Thresholds*, London: Macmillan, 1991, p. 144; revised and reprinted as 'The Dangerous Liaisons of Psychoanalysis', in Robert J. C. Young, *Torn Halves*, *op.cit.*). For more on this difficult relation, see Chapter 5.

16. Angela McRobbie, 'Afterword: In Defence of Cultural Studies', *In the Culture Society*, *op.cit.*, p. 93.

17. Lawrence Grossberg, 'Cultural Studies and Political Economy: Is Anyone Else Bored With This Debate?', *op.cit.*, p. 74. See also Lawrence Grossberg, 'Introduction: "Birmingham" in America?', *op.cit.*, p. 7.

18. Angela McRobbie, *In the Culture Society*, *op.cit.* McRobbie's own book on the 'micro-economies' of the fashion industry, *British Fashion Design: Rag Trade or Image Industry*, London and New York: Routledge, 1998, could also be mentioned here. However I have preferred to focus on McRobbie's essays as this is where her thinking on this subject has perhaps been most influentially laid out.

19. Angela McRobbie, 'All the World's a Stage, Screen or Magazine: When Culture is the Logic of Late Capitalism', *Media, Culture and Society*, Vol. 18, 1996, p. 337; reprinted in *In the Culture Society, op.cit.* Further page references are given in parenthesis in the body of the text.

20. Simon Frith and Jon Savage, 'Pearls and Swine', *op.cit.*, pp. 113, 107; cited by Angela McRobbie, *ibid.*

21. Angela McRobbie, '*More!*: New Sexualities in Girls' and Women's Magazines',

in James Curran, David Morley and Valerie Walkerdine (eds), *Cultural Studies and Communications*, London: Arnold, 1996, p. 178; revised and reprinted in A. McRobbie (ed.), *Back to Reality?: Social Experience and Cultural Studies*, Manchester: Manchester University Press, 1997; and in Angela McRobbie, *In the Culture Society*, *op.cit.* Further page references are given in parenthesis in the body of the text. The passages quoted are taken from the original version of this essay, and are not included in the subsequently revised and reprinted versions.

22. Angela McRobbie, 'All the World's a Stage, Screen or Magazine', *op.cit.*, p. 336.
23. Angela McRobbie, 'Introduction', *In the Culture Society*, *op.cit.*, p. x.
24. Meaghan Morris, 'Banality in Cultural Studies', *Block*, No. 14, 1988. See also Lawrence Grossberg, 'Cultural Studies and Political Economy: Is Anyone Else Bored With This Debate?', *op.cit.*, p. 74.
25. Angela McRobbie, 'Looking Back at *New Times* and its Critics', *op.cit.*, p. 244. This quotation is taken from the opening section of the original version of this essay which is not included in the version reprinted in *In the Culture Society*.
26. Angela McRobbie, 'All the World's a Stage, Screen or Magazine', *op.cit.*, p. 337. Further page references are given in parenthesis in the body of the text.
27. Angela McRobbie, 'Bridging the Gap: Feminism, Fashion and Consumption', *In the Culture Society*, *op.cit.*, pp. 40–1; originally published in *Feminist Review*, No. 55, Spring, 1997. Further page references are given in parenthesis in the body of the text.
28. Angela McRobbie, 'All the World's a Stage, Screen or Magazine', *op.cit.*, p. 338.
29. Angela McRobbie, 'Bridging the Gap', *op.cit.*, pp. 34, 40. Further page references are given in parenthesis in the body of the text.
30. Angela McRobbie, 'Afterword: In Defence of Cultural Studies', *op.cit.* Page references are given in parenthesis in the body of the text.
31. Angela McRobbie, 'Feminism and the Third Way', *Feminist Review*, No. 64, Spring, 2000.
32. Nicholas Garnham, 'Political Economy and Cultural Studies', *op.cit.* The idea of 'reconciliation' of course implies that at some point in the past cultural studies and political economy were 'married'. For a problematization of this idea, see Lawrence Grossberg, 'Cultural Studies and Political Economy: Is Anyone Else Bored With This Debate?', *op.cit.*
33. Lawrence Grossberg, *ibid.*, p. 77.
34. Judith Butler, 'Merely Cultural', *New Left Review*, No. 227, 1998.
35. Lawrence Grossberg, 'Introduction: "Birmingham" in America?', *op.cit.*, p. 391, n.6.
36. See, for example, John Storey's positioning of McRobbie's work as an example of neo-Gramscian hegemony theory in his 'Cultural Studies: An Introduction', *op.cit.*, p. 9.
37. Robert J.C. Young, 'Capitalism and Theory', *op.cit.*, p. 8.
38. Angela McRobbie, 'Feminism and the Third Way', *op.cit.*, p. 97. Further page references are given in parenthesis in the body of the text.
39. Angela McRobbie, 'All the World's a Stage, Screen or Magazine', *op.cit.*, p. 335.

40. Angela McRobbie (ed.), *Back to Reality? Social Experience and Cultural Studies*, Manchester: Manchester University Press, 1997.

41. Angela McRobbie, 'The Es and the anti-Es: New Questions for Feminism and Cultural Studies', in Marjorie Ferguson and Peter Golding (eds), *Cultural Studies in Question, op.cit.*; reprinted in *In the Culture Society, op.cit.* Further page references are given in parenthesis in the body of the text.

42. Spivak outlines her 'strategic essentialism' in, among other places, her interview with Ellen Rooney in *Outside in the Teaching Machine* (Gayatri Chakravorty Spivak, 'In a Word: Interview', *Outside in the Teaching Machine*, London and New York: Routledge, 1993). However, she also identifies certain concerns with 'strategic essentialism' both here and in a later interview with Peter Osborne, not least that 'the strategic use of essentialism was bound to become a simple convenience for identitarians' (Gayatri Chakravorty Spivak, 'Setting to Work (Transnational Cultural Studies)', in Peter Osborne (ed.), *A Critical Sense: Interviews with Intellectuals*, London and New York: Routledge, 1996, p. 165).

43. Timothy Clark, Review of Robert J. C. Young's *Torn Halves*, *The Oxford Literary Review*, Vol. 18, Nos 1–2, 1996, p. 240.

44. Robert J.C. Young, 'The Dialectics of Cultural Criticism', in Gary Hall and Simon Wortham (eds), *Authorizing Culture, Angelaki*, Vol. 2, No. 2, 1996, pp. 23, 22; reprinted in *Torn Halves, op.cit.* For more on this, see Chapter 4.

45. Robert Young, 'The Politics of "The Politics of Literary Theory"', *The Oxford Literary Review*, Vol. 10, Nos 1–2, 1998, p. 146; revised and reprinted in *Torn Halves, op.cit.*, quoting Samuel Weber, *The Legend of Freud*, Minneapolis: Minnesota University Press, 1982, p. 33.

46. See Chapter 5.

47. Jacques Derrida, 'As if I were Dead: An Interview with Jacques Derrida', in John Brannigan *et al.* (eds), *Applying: To Derrida*, London: Macmillan, 1996, p. 218. As Geoffrey Bennington puts it: 'Derrida's work consists essentially in bringing out the textual resources that question the "official" version. These resources are demonstrably put forward, however discreetly, by the texts being read, and are not imported by Derrida, whose place in this process is thereby rendered problematical: it is not that Derrida (actively) deconstructs anything at all, but rather that he shows *metaphysics in deconstruction*. This is not the expression of a preference, but a bolder claim, namely that the deconstructive operation of apparent oppositions is the only possible "ground" upon which metaphysics could ever claim to identify itself in the first place' (Geoffrey Bennington, *Interrupting Derrida*, London: Routledge, 2000, p. 11).

48. For more on the relation between theory and politics, see Chapter 4; for more on theory and 'responsibility', see Chapter 1.

49. Isaac Julien and Mark Nash, 'Dialogues with Stuart Hall', in David Morley and Kuan-Hsing Chen (eds), *Stuart Hall, op.cit.*, pp. 477–8.

50. Homi K. Bhabha, 'The Commitment to Theory', *The Location of Culture*, London and New York: Routledge, 1994, p. 22; originally published in *New Formations*, No. 5, Summer, 1988. Further page references are given in parenthesis in the body of the text.

51. Angela McRobbie, 'The Es and the anti-Es', *op.cit.*, p. 182.

52. Judith Butler, *Gender Trouble: Feminism and the Subversion of Identity*, New York and London: Routledge, 1999, p. ix.

53. See Chapter 1.
54. Jacques Derrida, 'As if I were Dead', *op.cit.*, pp. 217–18. Further page references are given in parenthesis in the body of the text.

Chapter Four: The (Monstrous) Future of Cultural Studies

1. Jacques Derrida, 'Passages – from Traumatism to Promise', trans. Peggy Kamuf, in Elizabeth Weber (ed.), *Points . . . Interviews, 1974–1994*, Stanford, California: Stanford University Press, 1995, pp. 386–7.
2. Gerald Graff, Janice Radway, Gita Rajan and Robert Con Davis, 'A Dialogue on Institutionalizing Cultural Studies', in Isaiah Smithson and Nancy Ruff (eds), *English Studies/Cultural Studies: Institutionalizing Dissent*, Champaign, Illinois: University of Illinois Press, 1994, p. 28.
3. Cary Nelson, Paula A. Treichler and Lawrence Grossberg, 'Cultural Studies: An Introduction', in Lawrence Grossberg, Cary Nelson and Paula Treichler (eds), *Cultural Studies*, London and New York: Routledge, 1992, p. 5.
4. See, for an example, Chapters 2 and 3.
5. Geoffrey Bennington, 'Inter', in Martin McQuillan, Graeme MacDonald, Robin Purves and Stephen Thomson (eds), *Post-Theory: New Directions in Criticism*, Edinburgh: Edinburgh University Press, 1999, p. 106. Further page references are given in parenthesis in the body of the text.
6. For a further example see the various summary analyses of cultural studies scattered throughout Robert J. C. Young's *Torn Halves*, Manchester: Manchester University Press, 1996 – although Young's references to the work of Stuart Hall are often an exception (see, for example, *ibid.*, p. 141). In fact it is from Hall's work, among other places, specifically his 'The Local and the Global' (Stuart Hall, 'The Local and the Global: Globalization and Ethnicity', in Anthony D. King (ed.), *Culture, Globalization and the New World System*, London: Macmillan, 1991; cited by Young, *ibid.*, p. 8), that Young has taken his account of capitalism's radical logic of incompatibility (see Chapter 3). This of course immediately creates problems for any notion that cultural studies can somehow be rejected or renounced in favour of deconstruction, as cultural studies is clearly already at the heart of Young's deconstructive theory. Peggy Kamuf's analysis of Raymond Williams' *Television: Technology and Cultural Form* ('Derrida on Television', in John Brannigan *et al.* (eds), *Applying: To Derrida*, London: Macmillan, 1996), and Gayatri Spivak's recent 'argument for a deconstructive cultural studies' ('Deconstruction and Cultural Studies: Arguments for a Deconstructive Cultural Studies', in Nicholas Royle (ed.), *Deconstructions: A User's Guide*, Basingstoke: Palgrave, 2000), are two further exceptions to this treatment of cultural studies by theory.
7. Stuart Hall, 'Cultural Studies and its Theoretical Legacies', in Lawrence Grossberg *et al.* (eds), *Cultural Studies*, *op.cit*. Further page references are given in parenthesis in the body of the text.
8. Jon Stratton and Ien Ang, 'On the impossibility of a global cultural studies: "British" cultural studies in an "international" frame', in David Morley and

Kuan-Hsing Chen (eds), *Stuart Hall: Critical Dialogues in Cultural Studies*, London: Routledge, 1996, p. 373. Further page references are given in parenthesis in the body of the text.

9. Tony Bennett, *Culture: A Reformer's Science*, London, Thousand Oaks, New Delhi: Sage, 1998, p. 49. Further page references are given in parenthesis in the body of the text.

10. Nor is this idea that 'theory' somehow neglects or denies politics restricted to those who are in the main critical of poststructuralist theory. Witness the debate within American literary criticism and theory between those who are called, and at times even call themselves, 'poststructuralists', over whether to follow Derrida '*into* the text, or Foucault *in and out*', to quote Edward Said (E. W. Said, 'The Problem of Textuality: Two Exemplary Positions', *The World, the Text, and the Critic*, Cambridge, Massachusetts: Harvard University Press, 1983, p. 183). As Jonathan Culler observed in his 1988 book *Framing the Sign*, the 'situation is frequently presented in the following terms: Derrida says 'il n'y a pas de hors texte' [there is no outside-the-text] and Foucault is said to reply 'there is so! – there's history, there's power'. From this perspective, 'Foucault is seen as providing a call to a model for historical and political criticism that would relate texts to historically-defined forces' (Jonathan Culler, 'The Call to History', *Framing the Sign: Criticism and its Institutions*, Oxford: Blackwell, 1988, p. 62). This model is then contrasted favourably with what is seen as the disabling textualism of Derrida and his followers at Yale. But as Bill Readings emphasized in a critique of Said's reading of Derrida and deconstruction in *The World, the Text, and the Critic* (a reading on which Hall appears to draw in 'Cultural Studies and its Theoretical Legacies', with his emphasis on cultural studies' ' "worldly" vocation', on 'the "worldliness" of cultural studies, to borrow a term from Edward Said' (*op.cit.*, pp. 284, 278)), to set Derrida and Foucault up in terms of an emphasis on language and textuality versus history, politics and power is to rely on a rather '*undeconstructed notion of textuality*' (Bill Readings, 'The Deconstruction of Politics', in Martin McQuillan (ed.), *Deconstruction: A Reader*, Edinburgh: Edinburgh University Press, 2000, p. 391.

11. Fredric Jameson, 'On "Cultural Studies"' in Jessica Munns and Gita Rajan (eds), *A Cultural Studies Reader: History, Theory, Practice*, London and New York: Longman, 1995, p. 614; first published in *Social Text*, 34, Vol. 11, No. 1, 1993.

12. Stuart Hall, *op.cit.*, p. 281.

13. Fredric Jameson, *op.cit.*, p. 621.

14. Stuart Hall, *op.cit.*, p. 281. Further page references are given in parenthesis in the body of the text. Indeed, so deeply ingrained is this idea that even those cultural studies practitioners who have raised problems for this aspect of Hall's thought have tended to offer only variations on this theme as an alternative. Tony Bennett, for example, in *Culture: A Reformer's Science*, presents Hall's notion that cultural studies 'might furnish a stratum of intellectuals who will prepare the way for an emerging historical movement to which that stratum will then attach itself in a moment of organicity', as growing ever more improbable by the day (*op.cit.*, p. 32). Yet for all that he is critical of Hall's thinking in this respect, Bennett's own response to the problem – that the

relationship between cultural studies and the idea of the organic intellectual be reformulated in terms of the 'development of forms of work – of cultural analysis and pedagogy – that could contribute to the development of the political and policy agendas associated with the work of organic intellectuals so defined' (33) – continues to operate very much within the terms of Hall's own juxtaposition of theory and politics. Witness his proposal of a 'pragmatics for cultural studies': a 'revisionary program' in which cultural studies is 'to be developed in closer association with the policy concerns of government and industry as a means of developing a more prosaic concept of practice, one that will sustain actual and productive connections with the field of the practicable' (17). Rather than analysing the complexity of the relation between theory and political practice, Bennett, on his own admission, simply adopts what he regards as 'an appropriately more limited usage' of this relation (33).

15. See Robert Young, *White Mythologies: Writing, History and the West*, London and New York, Routledge, 1990, pp. 22–3; and also 'The Politics of "The Politics of Literary Theory"', *The Oxford Literary Review*, Vol. 10, Nos 1–2, 1988; revised and reprinted in *Torn Halves*, *op.cit.* It is of course from the latter that my sub-heading for this section derives.

16. See n.10.

17. Rodolphe Gasché, 'Deconstruction as Criticism', *Glyph*, No. 6, 1979.

18. Stuart Hall, 'Cultural Composition: Stuart Hall on Ethnicity and the Discursive Turn', *Journal of Composition Theory*, Vol. 18, No. 2, 1998, p. 184.

19. Geoffrey Bennington, 'Deconstruction is Not What You Think', in Andrea Papadakis, Catherine Cooke and Andrew Benjamin (eds), *Deconstruction Omnibus Volume*, London: Academy Editions, 1989, p. 84.

20. Jacques Derrida, 'But, beyond . . . (Open Letter to Anne McClintock and Rob Nixon)', trans. Peggy Kamuf', *Critical Inquiry*, Vol. 13, No. 1, 1986, pp. 167–8. The text Derrida is responding to here is Anne McClintock and Rob Nixon's 'No Names Apart: The Separation of Word and History in Derrida's "Le Denier Mot du Racisme"', which appeared in the same issue of *Critical Inquiry*.

21. See, for example, Bill Readings, 'The Deconstruction of Politics', *op.cit.* (see also n.10); and Robert Young, 'The Politics of "The Politics of Literary Theory"', *op.cit.*

22. See Richard Johnson, '"Politics By Other Means"?: Or, Teaching Cultural Studies in the Academy is a Political Practice', in Nannette Aldred and Martin Ryle (eds), *Teaching Culture: The Long Revolution in Cultural Studies*, Leicester: The National Organisation for Adult Learning, 1999, p. 30.

23. As Jameson indicates, Hall is not alone among practitioners of cultural studies in thinking this way. Nor can the relation between British and American cultural studies be set up in terms of a simple 'politics versus textuality' opposition, as the quotes from Radway, Nelson *et al.* with which this chapter opened show.

24. Robert Young, 'The Politics of "The Politics of Literary Theory"', *op.cit.*, p. 145.

25. Angela McRobbie, 'Post-Marxism and Cultural Studies: A Post-script', in Lawrence Grossberg *et al.*, (eds), *Cultural Studies*, *op.cit.*, p. 719. Further page references are given in parenthesis in the body of the text.

26. Homi K. Bhabha, 'The Commitment to Theory', *The Location of Culture*, London: Routledge, 1990. See also Chapter 3.

27. See the account of the debate between cultural studies and political economy, and indeed McRobbie's own work, provided in Chapter 3.

28. Jacques Derrida, 'Politics and Friendship: A Discussion with Jacques Derrida', Centre for Modern French Thought, University of Sussex, 1 December, 1997, http://www.sussex.ac.uk/Units/frenchthought/derrida.htm.

29. Jacques Derrida, 'Intellectual Courage', trans. Peter Krapp, *Culture Machine*, No. 2, 2000, http://culturemachine.tees.ac.uk/Backissues/j002/Articles/art_derr.htm. Derrida is not opposing algorithmic actions and choices (those which involve the application of a rule) to those which contain an element of undecidability with this. To borrow a phrase from *On Cosmopolitanism and Forgiveness*, '[i]t is between these two poles, *irreconcilable but indissociable*, that decisions and responsibilities are to be taken', for Derrida. Nor is he arguing that when it comes to making a just or responsible decision it is 'necessary *not to know*'. A little later in the same text Derrida emphasizes that 'it is necessary to know the most and the best possible, but between the widest, most refined, the most necessary knowledge, and the responsible decision, an abyss remains, and must remain' (Jacques Derrida, *On Cosmopolitanism and Forgiveness*, trans. Mark Dooley and Michael Hughes, London and New York: Routledge, 2001, pp. 45, 54). What this means for political action and decision making has been nicely summed up by Simon Critchley and Richard Kearney: 'On the one hand, pragmatic political or legal action has to be related to a moment of unconditionality or infinite responsibility if it is not going to be reduced to the prudential demands of the moment. Political action has to be based on a moment of universality that exceeds the pragmatic demands of the specific context. But, on the other hand, such unconditionality cannot, must not, Derrida insists, be permitted to programme political action, where decisions would be algorithmically deduced from incontestable ethical precepts. Just political action requires active respect for both poles of this tension' (Simon Critchley and Richard Kearney, 'Preface' to Jacques Derrida, *On Cosmopolitanism and Forgiveness*, *op.cit.*, p. xii). For more on the politics of deconstruction, see Geoffrey Bennington, *Legislations: The Politics of Deconstruction*, London: Verso, 1994; Geoffrey Bennington, *Interrupting Derrida*, London and New York: Routledge, 2000; Richard Beardsworth, *Derrida and the Political*, London and New York: Routledge, 1996; Simon Critchley, *Ethics, Politics, Subjectivity*, London and New York, Verso, 1999.

30. Paul Ricoeur, *Hermeneutics and the Human Sciences: Essays on Language, Action and Interpretation*, Cambridge: Cambridge University Press, 1981, p. 99; cited in Johan Fornäs, 'Life After Death of the Text: Mediational Cultural Studies', *Culture Machine*, No. 1, 1999, http://culturemachine.tees.ac.uk/Backissues/j002/Articles/art_forn.htm.

31. Raymond Williams (1986), 'The Future of Cultural Studies', in Tony Pinkney (ed.), *The Politics of Modernism: Against the New Conformists*, London: Verso, 1989. Further page references are given in parenthesis in the body of the text.

32. See Henry A. Giroux, *Disturbing Pleasures*, New York and London: Routledge, 1994, pp. 130, 191, n.11. As Alan O'Shea notes, if anything this has been even more the case in Britain (Alan O'Shea, 'Education For What? The

Politics of Pedagogy in Cultural Studies', in Nannette Aldred and Martin Ryle (eds), *Teaching Culture: The Long Revolution in Cultural Studies, op. cit.*, pp. 167–8).

33. See Bill Readings, *The University in Ruins*, Cambridge, Massachusetts and London, England: Harvard University Press, 1996; and, for an account of these developments in a specifically British context, Alan O'Shea, 'A Special Relationship? Cultural Studies, Academia and Pedagogy', *Cultural Studies*, Vol. 12, No. 4, 1998; and Jim McGuigan, 'Whither Cultural Studies?', in Nannette Aldred and Martin Ryle (eds), *Teaching Culture: The Long Revolution in Cultural Studies, op. cit.*

34. Cary Nelson, 'Always Already Cultural Studies: Academic Conferences and a Manifesto', in John Storey (ed.), *What is Cultural Studies? A Reader*, London and New York: Arnold, 1996, p. 278; first published in *The Journal of the Midwest Modern Language Association*, Vol. 24, 1991.

35. Those who have argued for the latter include Tony Bennett and Ted Striphas. See Tony Bennett, *Culture: A Reformer's Science, op. cit.*; Ted Striphas, 'The Long March: Cultural Studies and its Institutionalization', *Cultural Studies*, Vol. 12, No. 4, 1998; Ted Striphas, 'Banality, Book Publishing, and the Everyday Life of Cultural Studies', *Culture Machine*, No. 2, 2000, http://culturemachine.tees.ac.uk/Backissues/j002/Articles/art_strip.htm.

36. See, for example, Henry Giroux, *Disturbing Pleasures, op. cit.*; Lawrence Grossberg, 'Bringing it all Back Home: Pedagogy and Cultural Studies', *Bringing it all Back Home: Essays on Cultural Studies*, Durham and London: Duke University Press, 1997; Alan O'Shea, 'A Special Relationship?', *op. cit.*; Tom Steele, *The Emergence of Cultural Studies 1945–65: Cultural Politics, Adult Education and the English Question*, London: Lawrence & Wishart, 1997; Tom Steele, 'Marginal Occupations: Adult Education, Cultural Studies and Social Renewal', in Nannette Aldred and Martin Ryle (eds), *Teaching Culture, op. cit.*

37. See, for example, Francis Mulhern, 'The Politics of Cultural Studies', *Monthly Review*, July–August, 1995; republished in E. M. Wood, and J. B. Foster, *In Defence of History: Marxism and the Postmodern Agenda*, New York: Monthly Review Press, 1998.

38. Tony Bennett, *Culture: A Reformer's Science, op. cit.*, p. 223. Further page references are given in parenthesis in the body of the text.

39. Raymond Williams, 'The Future of Cultural Studies', *op. cit.*, p. 154. For more on the importance of paper to cultural studies, see Chapter 6.

40. Tom Steele, *The Emergence of Cultural Studies 1945–65, op. cit.*, p. 7; Tom Steele, 'Marginal Occupations, *op. cit.*, p. 11.

41. Raymond Williams (1961), 'An Open Letter to WEA Tutors', in John McIlroy and Sallie Westwood (eds), *Border Country: Raymond Williams in Adult Education*, Leicester: National Institute of Adult Continuing Education, 1993, pp. 223, 224.

42. Raymond Williams (1983), 'Adult Education and Social Change', in John McIlroy and Sallie Westwood (eds), *Border Country, op. cit.* Further page references are given in parenthesis in the body of the text.

43. Tony Bennett, for example, is wary of any attempt to celebrate the radical marginality of adult education on the grounds that the WEA 'typically had few connections with the industrial or political sectors of the working class' (*op. cit.*,

p. 48). '[T]he view of the extra-mural department as a space on the margins of the academy capable of nourishing cultural studies in providing a direct and unmediated contact with "the dirty outside world" of working class experience will not withstand scrutiny', he argues (*op.cit.*, p. 48). Williams, however, associates this kind of approach more with the 'Plebs' League' (*op.cit.*, p. 260) and 'a consciously socialist affiliated workers' education which eventually produced the National Council of Labour Colleges' (Raymond Williams, 'Adult Education', *Politics and Letters: Interviews with New Left Review*, London: New Left Books, 1979, p. 79); whereas the origins of cultural studies, for Williams, lie more with adult education, and particularly the WEA, with its *mass*- rather than *class*-based approach and closer ties to the universities. Either way it is important not to generalize. The WEA differed greatly within itself, especially in terms of the attitude and relationship to working class education and the universities of each WEA district, different WEA classes having markedly different make-ups of students. For an introductory account of some of the differences between these two sets of organizations and their respective approaches to adult education, see Steele (1997).

44. See my 'Asking the Question: What is an Intellectual?', *Parallax*, No. 2, February 1996, and 'Answering the Question: What is an Intellectual?', *Surfaces*, Vol. VI, 1996, http://pum12.pum.umontreal.ca/revues/surfaces/vol6/hall.html.

45. Tom Steele, *The Emergence of Cultural Studies 1945–65*, *op.cit.*, pp. 187–8.

46. For a distinction 'between the future and what is to come', see 'Perhaps or Maybe: Jacques Derrida in Conversation with Alexander Garcia Düttmann', *Pli: Warwick Journal of Philosophy*, Vol. 6, Summer, 1997, p. 2.

47. Ironically enough, nowhere is this more apparent than in that part of 'The Future of Cultural Studies' which is often cited as having the most immediate relevance to practical politics and policy: that where Williams turns his attention to the situation facing cultural studies at the time of writing (1986). If in the period in which cultural studies first developed pressures of money and work were the main obstacles which prevented young people from getting an education, the main threat is now seen as coming from the way in which the Thatcher government's emphasis on vocationalism has resulted in the teaching of the majority of the sixteen to eighteen age group being taken out of the hands of 'the old damaging educators'. The emphasis in this latter period is thus on people gaining 'work experience within the forms of the economy to which they must adapt', with the economy in effect writing the educational syllabus with no input 'from people like us', people in cultural studies. Tellingly, what such training lacks most of all, according to Williams, is not political commitment, or a left politics, but an element of 'human and social knowledge and critical possibility' he regards it as being the task of cultural studies to provide. Indeed, Williams concludes 'The Future of Cultural Studies' by arguing forcefully that cultural studies must put forward 'persuasive, reasoned and practical' proposals to local authorities and government for a new formation of cultural studies; one which is capable of responding to this changed situation and keeping this 'dimension of human and social knowledge and critical possibility which again and again has been one of the elements of our project' alive (161). Once again, then, there is in Williams' account of

cultural studies an emphasis, not just on practical politics (or on 'human and social knowledge', for that matter), but also on a certain radical questioning. What is more, the former appears to be subordinate to the latter: it is politics, after all, that has to be employed here in the service of keeping, among other things, the 'critical possibility' inherent in cultural studies alive, and not the other way round. As we have already seen was the case in his adult education teaching, Williams' account of cultural studies thus clearly contains the possibility of bringing its politics into question, should this be needed in order to keep its 'critical' element alive.

48. I could perhaps have said more about the 'promise' of cultural studies at this point, developing Williams' argument by relating it to Derrida's notion of the 'promise'. But I have already *promised* in my 'introduction' that I would not ignore the specificity of cultural studies by doing too much of this sort of thing. So, instead, I will just refer the reader interested in the 'promise of cultural studies' to Joanna Zylinska's discussion of this idea in 'An Ethical Manifesto for Cultural Studies ... Perhaps', *Strategies: Journal of Theory, Culture and Politics*, Vol. 14, No. 2, 2001.

49. See Tony Bennett, *op.cit.*, p. 239, n.2.

50. Martin Ryle, ' "Relevant Provision": The Usefulness of Cultural Studies', in Nannette Aldred and Martin Ryle (eds), *Teaching Culture: The Long Revolution in Cultural Studies*, *op.cit.*, pp. 41, 39–40. Further page references are given in parenthesis in the body of the text.

51. Raymond Williams, *Adult Education and Social Change*, *op.cit.*, p. 259.

52. As David Morley and Kuan-Hsing Chen indicate in their introduction to *Stuart Hall: Critical Dialogues in Cultural Studies*, *op.cit.*, it was partly a desire to continue to live out the contradictions of the organic intellectual that motivated Hall to eventually move in 1979 from the Centre for Contemporary Cultural Studies at Birmingham to the Open University (*op.cit.*, p. 20).

53. Tony Bennett, *op.cit.*, pp. 221–2.

54. Raymond Williams, 'The Future of Cultural Studies', *op.cit.*, p. 158.

55. Readings, for instance, focused on cultural studies when analysing the university: 'not because it is more important than Women's Studies, African-American Studies or Lesbian and Gay Studies, but because it is the most essentially academic of these various trans-disciplinary movements. By this I mean that the denunciation of the University as an institution within Cultural Studies is a problem not merely *for* the University but *of* the University . . . ; it is a response to the repressed *of* the University itself. To put it another way, the lesbian and gay, African-American, and feminist movements are different in that neither their genesis nor their goals are essentially linked to the University' (*The University in Ruins*, *op.cit.*, p. 91).

56. That this is indeed the case becomes even more apparent as soon as cultural studies' international formations are taken into account. It is usually its early developments in Britain that are emphasized: Adult Education, the establishment of the Birmingham Centre, the development of the Open University; Bennett adding to this list the SEFT (the Society for Education in Film and Television), while Carolyn Steedman emphasizes the way in which many of the 'formative and distinguishing characteristics of cultural studies were in fact prefigured in the changing norms and practices of English teaching within

secondary schools' (Caroline Steedman, 'Culture, cultural studies and the historians', in Lawrence Grossberg *et al.* (eds), *Cultural Studies, op.cit.*; cited by Tony Bennett, *op.cit.*, pp. 49–50). But there is also the important role played by the former polytechnics (including Portsmouth, Middlesex and Central London) and art schools, the history of which has so far been somewhat neglected by the various accounts of the origins of cultural studies. (My thanks to Ben Knights for this point.) Other traditions of cultural studies, in Canada, Australia, the Netherlands, Taiwan, Singapore, Japan, etc., have different sources of origin, which again serve to further 'decentre' any notion of a 'centre' for cultural studies (see Tony Bennett, *op.cit.*, p. 26; also Jon Stratton and Ien Ang, *op.cit.*). Interestingly, the WEA, or at least a version of it, appears in some of these histories, too. John Frow and Meaghan Morris, for example, report that their 'first encounter with a "culture and society" approach in the late 1960s came not from reading Raymond Williams but from attending WEA summer schools on film run at Newport Beach in Sydney by John Flaus' (John Frow and Meaghan Morris, 'Introduction', *Australian Cultural Studies: A Reader*, Sydney: Allen and Unwin, 1993, p. xxvi).

57. Henry A. Giroux, *Disturbing Pleasures, op.cit.*, p. 128.
58. See Lola Young, 'Why Cultural Studies?, *Parallax* 11, Vol. 5, No. 2, 1999, who also cites the above passage, for a recent example; as well as Henry A. Giroux, *op.cit.*; David Morley, 'Textual Orthodoxies: Textualism, Constructivism and the "New Ethnography" in Cultural Studies', in Marjorie Ferguson and Peter Golding (eds), *Cultural Studies in Question, op.cit.*; and Sean Nixon, 'Intervening in Popular Culture: Cultural Politics and the Art of Translation', in Paul Gilroy, Lawrence Grossberg and Angela McRobbie (eds), *Without Guarantees: In Honour of Stuart Hall*, London: Verso, 2000. As well as a response to others that might accuse cultural studies of lacking a politics, is the constant repetition of such statements evidence of a certain insecurity and anxiety on cultural studies' part that its politics is not perhaps quite as assured as it would like?
59. The reference to Bhabha's contribution to the Chicago conference in this passage is interesting. Hall uses Bhabha here to support his belief in the importance of politics to cultural studies. But in his essay Bhabha (who himself takes the term from Hall's own 1988 book *The Hard Road to Renewal*, London: Verso, 1988) sees in this 'arbitrary closure', not just 'that object of contemporary, postmodern political desire' he associates with Hall, but also a 'cultural space for opening up *new* forms of agency and identification' (Bhabha, *op.cit.*, pp. 58–9). Although claims to politics can be made for Bhabha here, then, they are arbitrary precisely to the extent that the meaning of politics *is not* fixed in advance but is open to question and change.
60. Tony Bennett, 'Cultural Studies: A Reluctant Discipline', *Cultural Studies*, Vol. 12, No. 4, 1998.
61. Judith Butler, *Gender Trouble: Feminism and the Subversion of Identity*, New York and London: Routledge, 1999, p. ix.
62. Jacques Derrida, 'Hospitality, Justice and Responsibility: A Dialogue with Jacques Derrida', in Richard Kearney and Mark Dooley (eds), *Questioning Ethics: Contemporary Debates in Philosophy*, London and New York: Routledge, 1999, p. 66.

63. 'Is' here is not being used to assert a fixed identity for, or definitive *being* of, cultural studies. It is not another attempt at closure, albeit one based on cultural studies' openness. Rather it is an acknowledgement of a certain openness and instability of cultural studies. And although doing so inevitably involves drawing on the language of metaphysics, this language does not *have* to be repeated passively: 'This is where we are with respect to a whole variety of concepts. We can't do without them, but we don't mean them in the old way so we have to use them, as Derrida suggests, "under erasure" . . . That's what deconstruction means to me; that's what I understand Derrida to be saying: we have no other language but the language of the old metaphysics, the language in which philosophy has been conducted, and it no longer works; but we are not yet in some other language, and we may never be' (Stuart Hall, 'Cultural Composition', *op.cit.*, pp. 188–9).

Chapter Five: Beyond Marxism and Psychoanalysis

1. Stuart Hall, 'Cultural Studies and its Theoretical Legacies', in Lawrence Grossberg, Cary Nelson and Paula Treichler (eds), *Cultural Studies*, New York and London: Routledge, 1992, p. 291.
2. Ernesto Laclau, 'Psychoanalysis and Marxism', *New Reflections on the Revolution of Our Time*, London: Verso, 1990, p. 93.
3. Robert Young, 'Psychoanalysis and Political Literary Theories', in James Donald (ed.), *Psychoanalysis and Cultural Theory: Thresholds*, London: Macmillan, 1991; revised and reprinted as 'The Dangerous Liaisons of Psychoanalysis', in Robert J. C. Young, *Torn Halves: Political Conflict in Literary and Cultural Theory*, Manchester: Manchester University Press, 1996. Further page references are given in parenthesis in the body of the text.
4. James Donald, 'Preface', in James Donald (ed.), *Psychoanalysis and Cultural Theory*, *op.cit.*, p. vii.
5. Young notes that '[i]n so far as it implies bringing a body of knowledge, psychoanalysis, to bear on a body of unselfconscious experience, literature', psychoanalytic criticism no longer exists. The reason for this is that Lacan's emphasis on the role of language in psychoanalysis has meant that the 'knowledge of psychoanalysis is at least partly grounded in literature', and therefore cannot at the same time provide a 'grounding for literature' (143).
6. See, for example, 'The Same Difference', *Screen*, Vol. 28, No. 3, 1987, where, referring to the dualisms through which the politics of sexual difference are often thought, Young concludes that 'the trick . . . is not to get caught within the binary terms of an either/or choice' (91). While such a strategy 'remains unthinkable according to the normal procedures of logic', Young invokes Derrida's reading of Freud in 'Différance' (Jacques Derrida, 'Différance', *Speech and Phenomena and Others Essays on Husserl's Theory of Signs*, trans. David Allison, Evanston: Northwestern University Press, 1973; Jacques Derrida, 'Difference', *Margins of Philosophy*, trans. Alan Bass, Chicago: University of Chicago Press, 1982) to demonstrate that 'it is precisely the moves of such

procedures that deconstruction, and indeed psychoanalysis, trace' (*op.cit.*, p. 90).

7. Robert Young, 'The Politics of "The Politics of Literary Theory"', *The Oxford Literary Review* Vol. 10, Nos 1–2, 1988, p. 133; revised and reprinted in *Torn Halves: Political Conflict in Literary and Cultural Theory*, Manchester: Manchester University Press, 1996.

8. As Campbell and Harbord observe in their introduction to the volume in which this chapter first appeared, a cultural studies which has Marxism as its 'explicit foundation' is the 'ascending star in international [academic] circles and institutions' (Jan Campbell and Janet Harbord (eds), *Psycho-Politics and Cultural Desires*, London and Pennsylvania: UCL Press, 1998 pp. 4, 2).

9. Jacques Derrida, *Specters of Marx: The State of the Debt, the Work of Mourning, and the New International*, trans. Peggy Kamuf, London: Routledge, 1994. Page references are given in parenthesis in the body of the text.

10. Jacques Derrida, 'Positions: Interview with Jean-Louis Houdebine and Guy Scarpetta', *Positions*, trans. Alan Bass, Chicago: University of Chicago Press, 1981, p. 62.

11. Robert J. C. Young, 'The Dialectics of Cultural Criticism', in Gary Hall and Simon Wortham (eds), *Authorizing Culture, Angelaki*, Vol. 2, No. 2, 1996, pp. 12, 17; reprinted in *Torn Halves, op.cit.* Further page references are given in parenthesis in the body of the text.

12. For an analysis of this tendency in critical attitudes toward popular culture, and thus of some of the irreducible paradoxes that produce cultural studies, see Chapter 2.

13. Theodor W. Adorno, 'Cultural Criticism and Society', *Prisms*, trans. Samuel and Shierry Weber, Cambridge, Massachusetts: MIT Press, 1981.

14. See Chapter 2 for a reading which locates, albeit very briefly, some of the impossible contradictions Young ascribes here to cultural criticism in Theodor W. Adorno and Max Horkheimer's celebrated essay 'The Culture Industry: Enlightenment as Mass Deception', *Dialectic of Enlightenment*, trans. John Cumming, London: Verso, 1979.

15. Theodor W. Adorno, *Negative Dialectics*, trans. E. B. Ashton, London: Routledge & Kegan Paul, 1973, p. 12; Theodor W. Adorno, 'Cultural Criticism and Society' *op.cit.*, p. 33; cited in Young, 'The Dialectics of Cultural Criticism', *op.cit.*, p. 21.

16. See Chapter 6 for an account of some of the possible forms this might take.

17. Robert Young, 'Psychoanalysis and Political Literary Theories', *op.cit.*, pp. 151–2.

18. Sigmund Freud (1915), 'Instincts and their Vicissitudes', *Pelican Freud Library*, Vol. 11, Harmondsworth: Penguin, 1984, p. 133.

19. Sigmund Freud (1925), 'Negation', *Pelican Freud Library*, Vol. 11, Harmondsworth: Penguin, 1984, p. 439.

20. *Ibid.*

21. Jean Laplanche, and J.-B. Pontalis, *The Language of Psychoanalysis*, London: Hogarth, 1973, p. 353. Further page references are given in parenthesis in the body of the text.

22. Anna Freud quoted in Laplanche and Pontalis, *The Language of Psychoanalysis*, *ibid.*, p. 353.

23. Sandor Ferenczi, 'Introjection and Transference', *Contributions to Psycho-analysis*, trans. Ernest Jones, London: Stanley Phillips, 1909. Page references are given in parenthesis in the body of the text.

24. Hence also the distinction Abraham and Torok are able to establish between incorporation and introjection. For Abraham and Torok, incorporation is 'to refuse to take within oneself *the part of oneself contained in what has been lost . . . in short, it is to refuse its introjection*' (Nicolas Abraham and Maria Torok, 'Introjection – Incorporation: *Mourning and Melancholia*', in S. Lebovici, and D. Widlöcher (eds), *Psychoanalysis in France*, New York: International University Press, 1980, p. 5, my emphasis).

25. An obvious objection can be raised against this notion of introjection as somehow already involving projection. As we have seen, for Freud, the opposition between introjection and projection is closely related to that between pleasure and unpleasure. Introjection is the process whereby the ego takes inside itself those objects which are a source of pleasure, while projection enables the ego to expel that part of itself that has become a source of unpleasure. How, then, can the ego's identification with these external objects be ambivalently inhabited by projection, if it is only the unpleasurable that is projected? One answer to this question can be found in Jacques Lacan's account of how the moment when a child recognizes its own image in the mirror is crucial for the construction of the ego (Jacques Lacan, 'The mirror stage as formative of the function of the I as revealed in psychoanalytic experience', *Écrits*, trans. Alan Sheridan, London: Tavistock, 1977). As Laura Mulvey so succinctly puts it in her highly influential analysis of 'Visual Pleasure in Narrative Cinema': 'The mirror phase occurs at a time when children's physical ambitions outstrip their motor capacity, with the result that their recognition of themselves is joyous in that they imagine their mirror image to be more complete, more perfect than they experience in their own body. Recognition is thus overlaid with misrecognition: the image recognised is conceived as the reflected body of the self, but its misrecognition as superior projects this body outside itself as an ideal ego, the alienated subject which, reintrojected as an ego ideal, prepares the way for identification with others in the future' (Laura Mulvey, 'Visual Pleasure and Narrative Cinema', *Screen*, Vol. 16, No. 3, 1975, pp. 9–10).

26. Sigmund Freud (1920), 'Beyond the Pleasure Principle', *Pelican Freud Library*, Vol. 11, Harmondsworth: Penguin, 1984. Page references are given in parenthesis in the body of the text.

27. Didier Anzieu, *Skin Ego*, London and New Haven: Yale University Press, 1989, p. 40, my emphasis; see also Didier Anzieu, 'Skin Ego', in S. Lebovici, and D. Widlöcher (eds), *Psychoanalysis in France*, *op.cit.*

28. As Anzieu suggests, the ego's boundary limits take on a similar form to the mouth. Like the mouth (which is also a point of digesting/taking in), this boundary is not just a system of edges that divides inside from outside; it is also and equally a blurring of edges.

In view of this, the location 'precisely in the mouth' (Abraham and Torok, *Mourning and Melancholia*, *op.cit.*, p. 6) of both Freud's boundary between introjection and projection, and Abraham and Torok's boundary between introjection and incorporation, takes on an added significance. We have already seen how this is expressed for Freud 'in the language of the oldest – the oral – instinctual impulses'. And for Abraham and Torok, too: 'It is because the mouth cannot articulate certain words, cannot utter certain phrases . . . that in fantasy one will take into the mouth the unspeakable, the thing itself. The empty mouth, calling in vain to be filled with introjective words, again becomes the mouth greedy for food over speech: unable to obtain nourishment from words exchanged with others, it will take within itself, in fantasy, all or part of a person, the only depository for that which is nameless. When introjection proves impossible, then the mouth's . . . *words* do not succeed in filling up the subject's emptiness, so he fills it instead with an imaginary *thing*' (*op.cit.*, p. 6). Although it is outside the scope of the present essay, it would be interesting to examine the consequences of this reading of the relation between the ego and the outside world for the rigorous distinction that is traced between introjection and incorporation by Abraham and Torok (*op.cit.*); and also for their related notion of the 'crypt' (Nicolas Abraham and Maria Torok, *The Wolf Man's Magic Word: A Cryptonymy*, trans. Nicholas Rand, Minneapolis: University of Minnesota Press, 1986). For one such analysis of the 'problematic border between incorporation and introjection', and of what he refers to in *Specters of Marx* as the 'effective but limited pertinence of this conceptual opposition' (Derrida, *op.cit.*, p. 178, n.3), see Derrida's 'Fors' (Jacques Derrida, 'Fors: The Anglish Words of Nicholas Abraham and Maria Torok', trans. Barbara Johnson, in Nicolas Abraham and Maria Torok, *The Wolf Man's Magic Word: A Cryptonymy, op.cit.*)

29. Sandor Ferenczi, *op.cit.*, p. 41.
30. Sandor Ferenczi, *op.cit.*, p. 31. Significantly, transference lies at the origin of introjection, for Ferenczi. 'The first loving and hating is a transference of auto-erotic pleasant and unpleasant feelings on to the objects that evoke those feelings. The first "object-love" and the first "object-hate" are, so to speak, the primordial transferences, the roots of every future introjection' (*op.cit.*, p. 42).
31. Sigmund Freud (1937), 'Analysis Terminable and Interminable', *The Standard Edition of the Complete Psychological Works of Sigmund Freud*, Vol. XXIII, London: Hogarth Press, pp. 247–8.
32. Mikkel Borch-Jacobsen, 'Hypnosis in Psychoanalysis', trans. Angela Brewer and X. P. Callahan, in *The Emotional Tie: Psychoanalysis, Mimesis and Affect*, Stanford, California: Stanford University Press, 1993, pp. 43–4. Further page references are given in parenthesis in the body of the text.
33. I am here following Homi K. Bhabha's use of the term 'beyond' in 'The Postcolonial and the Postmodern: The Question of Agency'. The phrase 'beyond theory' is employed by Bhabha in this essay to suggest 'that beyond theory you do not simply encounter its opposition, theory/practice, but an "outside" that places the articulation of the two – theory and practice, language and politics – in a productive relation similar to Derrida's notion of supplementarity'. See Homi K. Bhabha, 'The Postcolonial and the Postmodern: The Question of Agency', *The Location of Culture*, London: Routledge, 1994, p. 179.
34. James Donald, 'On the Threshold: Psychoanalysis and Cultural Studies', in James Donald (ed.), *Psychoanalysis and Cultural Theory, op.cit.*, p. 8. Further page references are given in parenthesis in the body of the text.
35. As Young indicates, the challenge psychoanalysis presents to the 'Cartesian

inside/outside dichotomy' and the 'exclusive claims of the forms of rational logic on which it is predicated' (Robert Young, 'Psychoanalysis and Political Literary Theories', op.cit., p. 149) also has implications for conceptions of politics based on traditional notions of agency and identity. At the end of 'Psychoanalysis and Political Literary Theories', Young acknowledges that for some Marxist feminists, by 'deconstructing' the identity of the subject, psycho-analysis has undermined those coherent notions of agency and self that are needed if women are to organize themselves politically around their identities as 'women'. But the problem with the call for a return to the old, totally unified and unproblematic notion of the subject, Young suggests, is that it presupposes, among other things, 'a kind of imperialism of identity, so that we are only allowed one, and our politics then has to have a single meaning too'. 'The point about the challenge of psychoanalysis', Young concludes, 'is that it questions all that' (155). But for Jan Campbell and Janet Harbord, Young's privileging of psychoanalysis: 'leaves unresolved the criticism leveled from gay identity politics, postcolonialism, and feminism; that psychoanalysis decentres the subject, but it does so in "the name of the father", producing accounts of sexuality, femininity and "racial" identity that are either pathologized, excluded or given as a purely relational category' (Jan Campbell and Janet Harbord (eds), *Psycho-Politics and Cultural Desires*, London: UCL Press, 1998, pp. 12–13). And yet I would argue in turn that psychoanalysis's *rethinking* of the subject does not disavow the possibility of political organization and change. What it does suggest is that the relation between the subject and the social needs to be rethought so as not to exclude other forms of identity and agency operating 'beyond' the patriarchal, rational and Cartesian inside/outside models. This would apply not just to Marxist feminist notions of political agency, but to the forms of gay identity politics and theories of postcolonialism and 'racial' identity Campbell and Harbord refer to. Once again, the problem would then be to what extent such thinking would still be 'political'? What is it to be political? Is the political a genre, or, as Lyotard suggests in *The Differend*, a name for the heterogeneity of regimes and incommensurability of genres which resists any such totalization (Jean-François Lyotard, *The Differend: Phrases in Dispute*, trans. Georges Van Den Abbeele, Manchester: Manchester University Press, 1988, p. 138, n.190)?

Chapter Six: www.culturalstudies.ac.uk

1. Bill Gates, *The Road Ahead*, London and New York: Viking, 1995, p. 9.
2. Jacques Derrida, 'Mochlos; or, The Conflict of the Faculties', trans. Richard Rand and Amy Wygant, in Richard Rand (ed.), *Logomachia: The Conflict of the Faculties*, Lincoln and London: University of Nebraska Press, 1992, pp. 18.
3. See Chapter 4.
4. Richard Johnson, 'What is Cultural Studies Anyway?', *Social Text*, No. 16, 1986/7, p. 38.

5. Ted Striphas, 'The Long March: Cultural Studies and Its Institutionalization', *The Institutionalization of Cultural Studies*, Vol. 12, No. 4, 1998, p. 461. Further page references are given in parenthesis in the body of the text.

6. Alan O'Shea, 'A Special Relationship? Cultural Studies, Academia and Pedagogy', *The Institutionalization of Cultural Studies*, *Cultural Studies*, Vol. 12, No. 4, 1998, p. 513.

7. Robert J. C. Young, 'The Dialectics of Cultural Criticism', in Gary Hall and Simon Wortham (eds), *Authorizing Culture, Angelaki*, Vol. 2, No. 2, 1996, p. 10; reprinted in Robert J. C. Young, *Torn Halves: Political Conflict in Literary and Cultural Theory*, Manchester: Manchester University Press, 1996.

8. Alan O'Shea, *op.cit.*, p. 513.

9. Ted Striphas, *op.cit.*, p. 453. The recent edition of *Cultural Studies* on *The Institutionalization of Cultural Studies*, in which the work of Striphas and O'Shea referred to here appears, can be seen as one attempt on the part of cultural studies practitioners to address this state of affairs.

10. Raymond Williams, (1986) 'The Future of Cultural Studies', in Tony Pinkney (ed.), *The Politics of Modernism: Against the New Conformists*, London: Verso, 1989, p. 157. Further page references are given in parenthesis in the body of the text.

11. See Chapter 4.

12. Graeme Turner, *British Cultural Studies: An Introduction*, 2nd edition, London and New York: Routledge, 1996, p. 11.

13. Meaghan Morris, 'A Question of Cultural Studies', in Angela McRobbie (ed.), *Back to Reality? Social Experience and Cultural Studies*, Manchester and New York: Manchester University Press, 1997, p. 46.

14. For Julie Thompson Klein, 'all interdisciplinary activities are rooted in the ideas of unity and synthesis, evoking a common epistemology of convergence' (Julie Thompson Klein, *Interdisciplinarity*, Detroit: Wayne State University Press, 1990, p. 11); cited in Bill Readings, *The University in Ruins*, Cambridge, Massachusetts and London, England: Harvard University Press, 1996, p. 201, n.23. For a different analysis of interdisciplinarity, see Simon Wortham, *Rethinking the University: Leverage and Deconstruction*, Manchester: Manchester University Press, 1999, Chapters 5 and 6.

15. J. Hillis Miller, 'The University in Dissensus', *The Oxford Literary Review*, Vol. 17, 1995, p. 136; reprinted in J. Hillis Miller and Manuel Asensi, *Black Holes: J. Hillis Miller; or, Boustrophedonic Reading*, Stanford: Stanford University Press, 1999.

16. Geoffrey Bennington, 'Postal Politics and the Institution of the Nation', in Homi K. Bhabha (ed.), *Nation and Narration*, London: Routledge, 1990, p. 121.

17. For more on hypnosis see Chapter 5. For more on death, see Derrida's *Aporias* where death is perceived as a figure 'flashing like a sort of indicator-light (a light at a border) . . . between cultures, countries, languages, but also between the areas of knowledge and disciplines' (Jacques Derrida, *Aporias: Dying – Awaiting (one another at) the 'limits of truth'*, trans. Thomas Dutoit, Stanford University Press, California, 1993, pp. 23–4) cited in Simon Wortham, *Rethinking the University: Leverage and Deconstruction*, Manchester: Manchester University Press, 1999, p. 154).

18. Gary Hall and Simon Wortham, 'Interdisciplinarity and its Discontents', *Authorizing Culture, Angelaki*, Vol. 2, No. 2, 1996.

19. Bill Readings, *The University in Ruins*, Cambridge, Massachusetts and London, England: Harvard University Press, 1996. Page references are given in paraenthesis in the body of the text.

20. For more on the central thesis of *The University in Ruins* see Samuel Weber, 'The Future Campus: Destiny in a Virtual World', http://www.hydra.umn.edu/weber/text1.html; Fred Botting, 'Culture and Excellence', *Cultural Values*, Vol. 1, No. 2, 1997, pp. 139–58; Dominic LaCapra, 'The University in Ruins?', *Critical Inquiry*, Vol. 25, No. 4, Autumn, 1998; Simon Wortham, *Rethinking the University: Leverage and Deconstruction, op.cit.*; Timothy Clark, 'Literary Values: Institutional Force', *Culture Machine*, No. 1, 1999, http://culturemachine.tees.ac.uk/Backissues/j001/Articles/art_clar.htm; Nicholas Royle, 'Yes, Yes, the University in Ruins' and Dominic LaCapra, 'Yes, Yes, Yes Yes . . . Well Maybe', *Critical Inquiry*, Vol. 26, No. 1, 1999.

21. Readings, *op.cit.*, p. 219, n.19.

22. This chapter first appeared in the *Technologies of the Sign* issue of *The Oxford Literary Review*, Vol. 21, Nos 1–2, 1999.

23. See Chapter 4.

24. Readings, *op.cit.*, p. 129. Readings is here adapting Samuel Weber's term 'deconstructive pragmatics' from his book *Institution and Interpretation*, Minneapolis: University of Minnesota Press, 1989. For Weber, a 'deconstructive pragmatics' would 'work from the "inside" of the various disciplines, in order to demonstrate concretely, in each case, how the exclusion of limits from the field organizes the practice it makes possible' (*ibid.*, p. 32; cited by Readings, *op.cit.*, p. 225, n.8).

25. Witness the number of journal 'special' issues that have been given over to discussions of Readings' work on the university, including both *The Oxford Literary Review*'s edition on *The University in Ruins*, *OLR*, Vol. 17, 1995, and also *The University of Toronto Quarterly*'s special issue on Readings' book, Fall (October), 1997.

26. This is not a criticism of Readings. As the editors of *The Oxford Literary Review* suggest in their introduction to their *The University in Ruins* special edition, '[t]o try out ways of negotiating or alleviating this [kind of] structural or institutionalised double-mindedness may be the best way forward for rethinking the university – in inventive kinds of institutional reform, in experimental ventures in teaching and research, in the exploration of new modes of publishing and new modes of intellectual accreditation' (Timothy Clark and Nicholas Royle, 'Editorial Audit', *The Oxford Literary Review*, Vol. 17, 1995, p. 12).

27. Bill Readings, 'Caught in the Net: Notes from the Electronic Underground', *Surfaces*, Vol. 4, 1994, p. 104, http://tornade.ere.umontreal.ca/guedon/Surfaces/vol4/readings.html.

28. Meaghan Morris, 'Publishing Perils and How to Survive Them: A Guide for Graduate Students', *The Institutionalization of Cultural Studies, Cultural Studies*, Vol. 12, No. 4, 1998, p. 499.

29. See, for example, Stevan Harnad, 'For Whom the Gate Tolls? How and Why to Free the Refereed Research Literature Online Through Author/Institution

Self-Archiving, Now', http://www.cogsci.soton.ac.uk/~harnad/Tp/resolution. htm.

30. *Seulemonde Online Journal*, Tampa/Florida, 1994, www.cas.usf.edu/journal/ bennington/gbennington.htm.

31. The *Culture Machine* electronic journal can be found at: http:// culturemachine.tees.ac.uk.

32. See the account of the *Collège International de Philosophie* provided by Jacques Derrida in 'Sendoffs', trans. Thomas Pepper, *Yale French Studies*, No. 77, 1990.

33. These include (and I'm restricting myself here to those with which I am most familiar) the *Frontiers* series of seminars, which ran at the University of Sussex from October 1989 to June 1992, under the auspices of the *Collège International de Philosophie* and the directorship of Geoffrey Bennington (see *Frontiers*, *The Oxford Literary Review*, Vol. 14, 1992); and *Foreign Body*, which was set up at the University of Stirling in February 1993, and which itself has (or at least had) a related electronic presence at www.hydra.umn.edu/fobo/ (see Nicholas Royle, 'Foreign Body: "The deconstruction of a pedagogical institution and all that it implies"', *After Derrida*, Manchester: Manchester University Press, 1995, pp. 143–58). Indeed, the journal in which this chapter first appeared, *The Oxford Literary Review*, may itself be an example of keeping open the question of disciplinarity.

34. Michel de Certeau, 'Universities versus Popular Culture', in Luce Giard (ed.), *Culture in the Plural*, trans. Tom Conley, London: Minneapolis: University of Minnesota Press, 1997, p. 44.

35. Peter Kingston, 'Britain Has to Push the Pace', *Guardian Higher Education Supplement*, March 30, 1999, p. ii–iii.

36. Jacques Derrida, *Archive Fever: A Freudian Impression*, trans. Eric Prenowitz, Chicago: University of Chicago Press, 1996, p. 16. Interestingly, the 'most important and obvious' reason Derrida gives for privileging e-mail here concerns not the 'major role' letter writing has played in the history of psychoanalysis, but rather the effect of e-mail on 'property rights, publishing and reproduction rights' (*ibid.*, p. 17).

37. Jacques Derrida, 'Paper or Myself, You Know . . . (New Speculations on a Luxury of the Poor)', trans. Keith Reader, *Paragraph*, Vol. 21, No. 1, 1998, p. 12. Further page references are given in parenthesis in the body of the text.

38. Richard Hoggart, 'An Interview with Richard Hoggart: Studying Culture: Reflections and Assessments', *The Uses of Literacy*, London: Penguin, 1992, p. 391.

39. See Jacques Derrida, *Archive Fever*, *op.cit.*, p. 17.

40. J. Hillis Miller, 'The Ethics of Hypertext', *Diacritics*, Vol. 25, No. 3, 1995, p. 31; reprinted in J. Hillis Miller and Manuel Asensi, *Black Holes: J. Hillis Miller; or, Boustrophedonic Reading*, *op.cit.*

41. Jacques Derrida, 'Mochlos', *op.cit.*, pp. 18–19.

Index